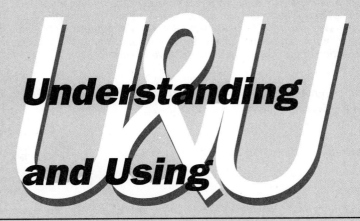

Understanding and Using

Microsoft® Word

for Windows™ 6.0

Emily Ketcham
Hankamer School of Business
Baylor University

WEST PUBLISHING COMPANY
Minneapolis/St. Paul • New York
Los Angeles • San Francisco

WEST'S COMMITMENT TO THE ENVIRONMENT

In 1906, West Publishing Company began recycling materials left over from the production of books. This began a tradition of efficient and responsible use of resources. Today, up to 95 percent of our legal books and 70 percent of our college and school texts are printed on recycled, acid-free stock. West also recycles nearly 22 million pounds of scrap paper annually—the equivalent of 181,717 trees. Since the 1960s, West has devised ways to capture and recycle waste inks, solvents, oils, and vapors created in the printing process. We also recycle plastics of all kinds, wood, glass, corrugated cardboard, and batteries, and have eliminated the use of Styrofoam book packaging. We at West are proud of the longevity and the scope of our commitment to the environment.

Production, Prepress, Printing and Binding by West Publishing Company

Project Management by Labrecque Publishing Services

 Text is Printed on 10% Post Consumer Recycled Paper

MS-DOS®, Microsoft Access®,PowerPoint®,Microsoft®, and Windows™ are registered trademarks of Microsoft Corporation.
Macintosh and TrueType are trademarks of Apple Computer, Inc.
Arial and Times New Roman are registered trademarks of The Monotype Corporation PLC.
Avery is a registered trademark of Avery Denison Corporation.
Helvetica and Palatino are registered trademarks of Linotype AG and its subsidiaries.
Hewlett-Packard and Laserjet are registered trademarks of Hewlett-Packard Company.
PC Paintbrush is a registered trademark of ZSoft Corporation.
TIFF is a trademark of Aldus Corporation.
Screens are reprinted with the permission of Microsoft Corporation.
All rights reserved. Reprinted by permission.

Library of Congress Cataloging-in-Publication Data

Ketcham, Emily.
    Understanding and using Microsoft Word for Windows 6.0 / Emily
Ketcham.
        p.   cm. — (The Microcomputing series)
    Includes index.
    ISBN 0-314-03978-3
    1. Microsoft Word for Windows   2. Word processing. I. Title.
II. Series.
Z52.5.M523K48 1994
652.5'536–dc20
                                                    94-8271
                                                       CIP

Contents

Advanced Word Processing Techniques

The use of computers in the world today has become ubiquitous. As a result, modern society's expectations have raised standards for documents to levels that were unattainable just five years ago. The advent of the graphical user interface has taken the production of documents from the realm of professional printers and placed it in the hands of microcomputer users everywhere. With a Macintosh or a personal computer running Windows on the desktop and with a laser printer nearby, an individual can create sophisticated documents—letters, reports, and newsletters—using a variety of typefaces and including pictures, charts, and graphs. No longer does a business letter neatly typewritten convey professionalism by itself.

With this in mind, this textbook has three main goals: to introduce students to the use of computers in creating documents; to instruct them not only in *how* to use the word processor, but *why*; and to give them practical, real-world examples and exercises. This book is appropriate for new users of computers, as it begins with step-by-step instructions in the most basic procedures. The user builds a base of knowledge and skills in simple word processing, and gradually proceeds to more advanced techniques and processes.

Content Highlights

Each unit contains key features that enhance learning:

LEARNING OBJECTIVES list the skills and knowledge contained in the unit.

IMPORTANT COMMANDS list the Microsoft Word 6.0 menu commands used in the procedures covered.

GUIDED ACTIVITIES give step-by-step instructions in performing word processing tasks. Often, the guided activities give the student several ways to accomplish the same task to develop flexibility and experience, rather than using a rigid, cookbook approach.

SCREEN PICTURES presented throughout the units offer a frame of reference to the student reading the material for the first time or reviewing it away from the computer. The screens place the various commands, buttons, and dialog boxes in the proper context.

EXERCISES offer additional opportunities for hands-on practice of the skills and knowledge gained in each unit. Open-ended applications require the student to apply the procedures learned to custom material. In many cases, the exercises involve writing about concepts while using word processing techniques. Writing and word processing are interrelated: one hardly exists without the other. Involving writing in the exercise gives the student practice in composing at the keyboard, editing words and therefore thoughts, and giving the ideas color or emphasis with various formats.

REVIEW QUESTIONS focus the student's attention on important concepts and reinforce knowledge of word processing procedures. The answers are given in Appendix B.

KEY TERMS are listed to allow the student to review and self-test.

DOCUMENTATION RESEARCH opens the door to more advanced features contained in Word 6.0 but not covered in detail within the unit. Answers to the questions may be found in the Word *User's Guide* or the on-line help screens.

Sprinkled throughout the text are useful tips on word processing concepts and specific Word 6.0 techniques. The **QUICK REFERENCE** gathers all the buttons and shortcut keys at the back of the book where students can easily refer to them.

Acknowledgments

Many individuals contributed much to the creation of this textbook. My grateful appreciation is offered to the following individuals:

- G. W. Willis, chairman of the Information Systems Department, and Dean Richard C. Scott of the Hankamer School of Business, Baylor University

- Editor Nancy Hill-Whilton of West Publishing Company, who gave me everything I needed both to start and to finish

- Larry Lozuk, who pioneered *Understanding and Using Word* textbooks and established the tone and structure

- Mark Woodworth, copyeditor, and Lisa Auer, who performed the accuracy check, both of whom made excellent suggestions to enhance the exactness and clarity of the material

- My colleagues who reviewed the manuscript at various stages, directing both content and style: Karla Adamson, Community College of Aurora; Susan Balestra, Northeast Community College; Lisa L. Friedrichsen, Johnson County Community College; Lillian Lenhoff, Hillsborough Community College; Katye Mindhardt, Cincinnati Technical College; and Mark Purcell of LaSalle University

- The production crew (Lisa Auer, Curt Philips, Patti Douglass, and Mark Rhynsburger) who created an attractive and readable book out of my words and pictures

- My husband, Don, my support

- My mother, Mabel Meibuhr, who always told me I could do anything

Emily Ketcham

Publisher's Note

This book is part of THE MICROCOMPUTING SERIES. This popular series provides the most comprehensive list of books dealing with microcomputer applications software. We have expanded the number of software topics and provided a flexible set of instructional materials for all courses. This unique series includes five different types of books.

1. *West's Microcomputing Custom Editions* give instructors the power to create a spiral-bound microcomputer applications book especially for their course. Instructors can select the applications they want to teach and the amount of material they want to cover for each application—essentials or intermediate length. The following titles are available for the 1994 Microcomputing Series custom editions program:

Understanding and Using QBasic	*Lotus 1-2-3 Release 2.01*
Understanding Information Systems	*Lotus 1-2-3 Release 2.2*
Understanding Networks	*Lotus 1-2-3 Release 2.3*
DOS (3.x) and System	*Lotus 1-2-3 Release 2.4*
DOS 5 and System	*Lotus 1-2-3 Release 3*
DOS 6.x and System	*Lotus 1-2-3 for Windows Release 4*
Windows 3.0	*Microsoft Excel 3*
Windows 3.1	*Microsoft Excel 4*
WordPerfect 5.0	*Quattro Pro 4*
WordPerfect 5.1	*Quattro Pro 5.0 for DOS*
WordPerfect 6.0	*Quattro Pro 5.0 for Windows*
WordPerfect for Windows (Release 5.1 and 5.2)	*dBASE III Plus*
	dBASE IV Version 1.0/1.1/1.5
WordPerfect 6.0 for Windows	*dBASE IV Version 2.0*
Microsoft Word for Windows Version 1.1	*Paradox 3.5*
Microsoft Word for Windows Version 2.0	*Paradox 4.5 for Windows*
Microsoft Word for Windows 6.0	*Microsoft Access*
PageMaker 4	
PageMaker 5.0	

For more information about *West's Microcomputing Custom Editions*, please contact your local West Representative, or call West Publishing Company at 508-388-6685.

2. General concepts books for teaching basic hardware and software philosophy and applications are available separately or in combination with hands-on applications. These books provide students with a general overview of computer fundamentals including history, social issues, and a synopsis of software and hardware applications. These books include *Understanding Information Systems*, by Steven C. Ross.

3. A series of hands-on laboratory tutorials (*Understanding and Using*) are software specific and cover a wide range of individual packages. These tutorials, written at an introductory level, combine tutorials with complete reference guides. A complete list of series titles can be found on the following pages.

4. Several larger volumes combining DOS with three application software packages are available in different combinations. These texts are titled *Understanding and Using Application Software*. They condense components of the individual lab manuals and add conceptual coverage for courses that require both software tutorials and microcomputer concepts in a single volume.

5. A series of advanced-level, hands-on lab manuals provide students with a strong project/systems orientation. These include *Understanding and Using Lotus 1-2-3: Advanced Techniques Releases 2.2 and 2.3*, by Judith C. Simon.

THE MICROCOMPUTING SERIES has been successful in providing you with a full range of applications books to suit your individual needs. We remain committed to excellence in offering the widest variety of current software packages. In addition, we are committed to producing microcomputing texts that provide you both the coverage you desire and also the level and format most appropriate for your students. The Acquisitions Editor of the series is Nancy Hill-Whilton of West Educational Publishing; the Consulting Editor is Steve Ross of Western Washington University. We are always planning for the future in this series. Please send us your comments and suggestions:

Nancy Hill-Whilton
West Educational Publishing
Hamilton Gateway Building
5 Market Square
Amesbury, MA 01913

Steve Ross
Associate Professor/MIS
College of Business and Economics
Western Washington University
Bellingham, Washington 98225
Electronic Mail: STEVEROSS@WWU.EDU

We now offer these books in THE MICROCOMPUTING SERIES:

General Concepts

Understanding Information Systems
by Steven C. Ross

Understanding Computer Information Systems
by Paul W. Ross, H. Paul Haiduk, H. Willis Means, and Robert B. Sloger

Understanding and Using the Macintosh
by Barbara Zukin Heiman and Nancy E. McGauley

Operating Systems/Environments

Understanding and Using Microsoft Windows 3.1
by Steven C. Ross and Ronald W. Maestas

Understanding and Using Microsoft Windows 3.0
by Steven C. Ross and Ronald W. Maestas

Understanding and Using MS-DOS 6.x
by Jonathan P. Bacon

Understanding and Using MS-DOS/PC DOS 5.0
by Jonathan P. Bacon

Understanding and Using MS-DOS/PC DOS 4.0
by Jonathan P. Bacon

Networks

Understanding Networks
by E. Joseph Guay

Programming

Understanding and Using QBasic
by Jonathan Barron

Word Processors

Understanding and Using WordPerfect 6.0 for Windows
by Jonathan P. Bacon

Understanding and Using WordPerfect for Windows (5.1 and 5.2)
by Jonathan P. Bacon

Understanding and Using Microsoft Word for Windows 6.0
by Emily Ketcham

Understanding and Using Microsoft Word for Windows 2.0
by Larry Lozuk and Emily M. Ketcham

Understanding and Using Microsoft Word for Windows (1.1)
by Larry Lozuk

Understanding and Using WordPerfect 6.0
by Jonathan P. Bacon and Robert G. Sindt

Understanding and Using WordPerfect 5.1
by Jonathan P. Bacon and Cody T. Copeland

Understanding and Using WordPerfect 5.0
by Patsy H. Lund

Desktop Publishing

Understanding and Using PageMaker 5.0
by John R. Nicholson

Understanding and Using PageMaker 4
by John R. Nicholson

Spreadsheet Software

Understanding and Using Quattro Pro 5.0 for Windows
by Larry D. Smith

Understanding and Using Quattro Pro 5.0 for DOS
by Steven C. Ross and Lee McLain

Understanding and Using Quattro Pro 4
by Steven C. Ross and Stephen V. Hutson

Understanding and Using Microsoft Excel 4
by Steven C. Ross and Stephen V. Hutson

Understanding and Using Microsoft Excel 3
by Steven C. Ross and Stephen V. Hutson

Understanding and Using Lotus 1-2-3 for Windows Release 4
by Steven C. Ross and Dolores Pusins

Understanding and Using Lotus 1-2-3 Release 2.01
by Steven C. Ross

Understanding and Using Lotus 1-2-3 Release 2.2
by Steven C. Ross

Understanding and Using Lotus 1-2-3 Release 2.3 and Release 2.4
by Steven C. Ross

Understanding and Using Lotus 1-2-3 Release 3
by Steven C. Ross

Understanding and Using Lotus 1-2-3: Advanced Techniques
Releases 2.2 and 2.3
by Judith C. Simon

Database Management Software

Understanding and Using Microsoft Access
by Bruce J. McLaren

Understanding and Using Paradox 4.5 for Windows
by Larry D. Smith

Understanding and Using Paradox 3.5
by Larry D. Smith

Understanding and Using dBASE III Plus, 2nd Edition
by Steven C. Ross

Understanding and Using dBASE IV Version 2.0
by Steven C. Ross

Understanding and Using dBASE IV
by Steven C. Ross

Integrated Software

Understanding and Using Microsoft Works for Windows
by Gary Bitter

Understanding and Using Microsoft Works 3.0 for the PC
by Gary Bitter

Understanding and Using Microsoft Works 3.0 for the Macintosh
by Gary Bitter

Understanding and Using ClarisWorks
by Gary Bitter

Understanding and Using Microsoft Works 2.0 on the Macintosh
by Gary Bitter

Understanding and Using Microsoft Works 2.0 on the IBM PC
by Gary Bitter

Combined Books

Essentials of Application Software, Volume 1: DOS, WordPerfect 5.0/5.1,
Lotus 1-2-3 Release 2.2, dBASE III Plus
by Steven C. Ross, Jonathan P. Bacon, and Cody T. Copeland

Understanding and Using Application Software, Volume 4: DOS, WordPerfect 5.0, Lotus 1-2-3 Release 2, dBASE IV
by Patsy H. Lund, Jonathan P. Bacon, and Steven C. Ross

Understanding and Using Application Software, Volume 5: DOS, WordPerfect 5.0/5.1, Lotus 1-2-3 Release 2.2, dBASE III Plus
by Steven C. Ross, Jonathan P. Bacon, and Cody T. Copeland

Advanced Books

Understanding and Using Lotus 1-2-3: Advanced Techniques Releases 2.2 and 2.3
by Judith C. Simon

About the Author

Emily Ketcham earned a B.A. degree from Taylor University and an M.B.A. degree from Baylor University. She is a lecturer in Information Systems for the Hankamer School of Business at Baylor. Her responsibilities include teaching classes in advanced and introductory microcomputer applications and in managerial communications. Because Baylor's business school is quick to advance to the latest version of Windows software, Mrs. Ketcham, as course coordinator, is the first to learn new applications and explain the features both to her colleagues and to students. She also advises students interested in Information Systems courses and careers.

Mrs. Ketcham previously served as the information coordinator for the business school's Casey Computer Center, supporting faculty and staff in the use of microcomputers and application software. For many years she has participated in beta testing Microsoft applications and upgrades.

I Fundamental Word Processing Techniques

■ **PART ONE** This is the first of three parts in this text. To use Word for Windows, it is essential that you master the material in this part. The skills you learn in the Introduction will also allow you to use several other Windows applications at a beginner's level. Once these are mastered, you will learn to enter text in a new document, edit text in an existing document, save documents to files on disk, and open files stored on disk. You will learn to use the spell checker to ensure spelling accuracy in documents and the thesaurus to replace repeated or awkward words. The final unit in Part One covers the way you select a printer in Windows applications, set up the printer, and print your document. When you complete this section, you will be able to produce useful documents, print them, and save them on a disk for future use.

Which Version Are You Using?

At this writing, Word 6.0 is the current version of Word for Windows. In this book, all references to "Word"and "Word for Windows" relate to Microsoft Word for Windows 6.0. All references to "Windows" relate to Microsoft Windows 3.1. If you are using Word for Windows 1.1 or 2.0 (there are no versions numbered 3, 4, or 5), or Windows 3.0, consider upgrading to the latest version of each. Microsoft and many computer stores offer very reasonable upgrade prices for both software packages.

Introduction to Windows

Before you can comfortably use Word for Windows, it is important that you understand some of the advantages that Windows provides to all applications. A distinct advantage of the Windows environment is that, whatever the application, some commands will always be located in the same place and will always work the same way. This *common user interface* reduces the amount of time required to learn a new software package.

In addition, Windows allows you to run several applications at the same time. You may be using a spreadsheet to calculate values, a drawing package to create a picture, and Word for Windows to type and edit text. Depending on how you set up the Windows environment, the applications can be viewed one at a time or simultaneously. The Windows environment allows you to copy numbers, text, and pictures from one application to another with ease.

This introduction gives an overview of several parts of Windows with which you should be familiar before using Word for Windows. It is very important to master the procedures discussed here before continuing, for they will speed your progress not only through Word for Windows but also through every Windows application. Without these features, you will not be able to take full advantage of all that the Windows environment offers you.

Learning Objectives

At the completion of the introduction you should know

1. what a window is,

2. what common parts all windows have,

3. how to manipulate a window,

4. how to start a Windows application,

5. how to move among several Windows applications,

6. how to copy information from one Windows application to another.

Important Commands

Edit/Copy

Edit/Paste

File/Exit

Graphical Versus Text Environment

Before Windows became popular in the last few years, all *applications* (that is, computer programs or software such as a word processor or game) created for IBM-compatible computers were written under *Disk Operating System (DOS)*, a text-based operating system. DOS has been used by all generations of IBM-compatible computers. However, DOS applications were limited in that they only displayed on the screen a certain size and shape of set characters (such as those represented on the keyboard). DOS is capable of producing and displaying graphics if additional components and programs are added to the computer. Graphics were added to some DOS programs in a limited fashion, but the large majority of applications displayed only text on the screen most of the time.

Despite its limitations, DOS is still a requirement for IBM-compatible personal computers. A future release of Windows is expected to completely replace DOS. IBM currently markets OS/2, an operating system that takes advantage of the power of personal computers more comprehensively by allowing the user to run several applications at once. The UNIX operating system, in existence for many years, is becoming increasingly popular in the IBM-compatible computer world. All of these operating systems remove many of the technical limitations of DOS but have yet to become as widespread in the computer market.

The operating systems just discussed went through several generations, gaining popularity and power. Eventually, however, they reached a level of sophistication beyond which they could not progress. Text-based applications could only display a limited amount of information on a screen; therefore, to add commands, programmers were forced to use complex keystrokes or multiple-level menus. Both of these compromises forced users of these applications to memorize the steps necessary to perform the advanced commands. The applications were powerful but difficult to use.

The Windows *graphical user interface (GUI)* can best be described as a face-lift for DOS. Computer monitors display information the same way a magazine or newspaper displays photographs, by turning selected dots across the display surface on or off. By using a magnifying glass you can actually see on the monitor screen the dots (called *pixels*, for picture elements) that make up the images you see.

Windows removes the limitation of displaying only text characters and allows programmers to control each pixel on the screen. This permits a much wider variety of information to be displayed. The result is the creation of applications that have more advanced commands available on screen at the same time, and that do not require the user (you) to memorize as many commands or menus to operate them.

These advantages do not come free of charge. Computers can display text very quickly. Only 1,920 characters will fit on a standard-sized computer screen at a time; thus, it is easy for the computer to keep up with changes on a text-based application screen. In a graphical environment like Windows, the computer must deal with each pixel on the screen, even when only word processing text is being displayed. Current monitors contain 307,200 or 786,432 pixels, depending on the quality of the screen. Obviously, it takes much more work to keep up with hundreds of thousands of pixels than with a simple text screen. The drawback of a graphical environment, therefore, is the amount of extra time the computer will require to respond to your requests.

How much will the computing burden delay you? When working on a word processing document without any pictures, you will probably not notice a difference. As the document gets more complicated with graphics or special characters, however, you will begin to see a visible delay as the computer redraws the screen after you insert or move information. When large pictures are included, the pause may increase to several seconds. The delay is largely dependent on the type of computer being used. As computer processors get faster, this difference between a DOS application and a similar application under Windows will diminish.

The graphical environment allows a programmer to be more creative when designing the way a screen will look. Pictures (*icons*) can be created that represent a command. The toolbars that you will use in Unit 1 contain examples of these icons. Rather than selecting the Bold command from a menu or having to remember a set of keystrokes, you will be able to make a word boldface by clicking on a small icon of a bold letter on the toolbar. Graphical commands are designed to be more intuitive than menu or keystroke commands.

The graphical interface allows the programmer of a Windows application unlimited flexibility when designing a software package. To maintain some kind of standard for all programs, designers of **Windows applications** have agreed to a common user interface. This common interface guarantees that certain features will be located in the same place in all Windows programs and that commands will work the same way, as shown, for example, in Figure 0.1. If you have ever used a Windows application, when you use another for the first time you will already know how to open and save files, how to select a printer, how to print, and how to exit the package.

Using a Keyboard

This introduction and the subsequent units contain activities that require you to enter information from the keyboard. Your input must be accurate or the results will vary from what is described in the text. We have established a number of typographical conventions that will make it easier for you to know exactly which keys to press.

FIGURE 0.1

File, Edit, and Help commands on the menu are located in the same location in three applications.

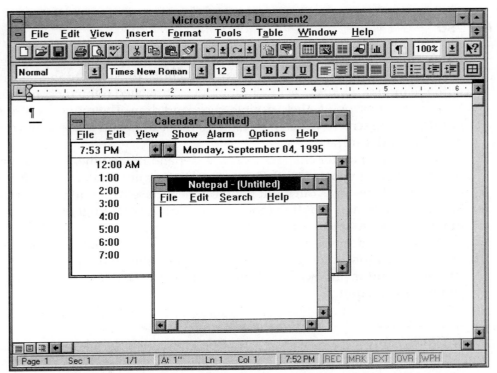

The word *Press* is used whenever you are instructed to push a single keystroke. For instance, after highlighting a command option, you will be instructed to

Press [Enter].
or
Press the [Enter] key.

This means you press the Enter or Return ([Return]) key on your keyboard once. On older personal computer (PC) keyboards, the Enter key is unlabeled except for a broken (crooked) arrow (↵). In this text, that key is always referred to with the symbol [Enter].

Three other keys ([Alt], [Ctrl], and [Shift]) are used in combination with a second key. For example, if instructed to press [Alt][Tab], you would hold down [Alt], press the [Tab] key once, and then release [Alt].

When keys are pressed one right after another, as opposed to the first key being held and the next pressed, the key notations are separated by commas. For example:

Press [Alt][H], [I]

In this case, you would press [Alt] then [H], release both, and then press [I] once.

The word *Type* is used to indicate that multiple keystrokes must be entered on the keyboard. The specific keys to be typed are shown in the following typeface:

Type Good morning, good people.

In this example, you would type "*Good morning, good people.*" (including the period).

Using a Mouse

Although most functions can be performed from the keyboard, the graphical user interface of Windows allows many functions to be easier and faster to execute with the mouse. A *mouse* is a pointing device attached to many computers. It has four procedures: point, click, double-click, and drag. The mouse controls a *mouse pointer* on the screen, which moves in a similar direction to the way you move the mouse on a flat surface.

The mouse pointer changes its shape depending on where you place it on the screen and what you *point* at. The *mouse buttons* are located along the top of the mouse. While resting your right hand on the mouse, you will use your index finger to *click* the left mouse button (and your middle or ring finger to click the right mouse button) to select commands from the menu.

Some procedures require you to click twice very quickly, or *double-click*, on the left mouse button. To *drag* an item, you position the mouse pointer over it, press the left mouse button and hold it down, then move the mouse pointer to a new location and release the button.

The Windows Environment

The Windows screen may show any combination of boxes containing applications, documents, spreadsheets, and many other items. It is from these boxes that Windows gets its name. The user sees a part of the application or document through a box, or *window*. Many windows can appear simultaneously on the screen, as illustrated in Figure 0.1, and most can be sized and moved by the user. All windows have in common certain components that you must recognize and understand to be able to manipulate them.

Components of a Window

A *title bar* appears at the top of every window. The title bar shows the name of the application and any document in the window. While more than one window can be displayed at once, you may use only one window at a time. A window you are currently using is called the *active window*. When there are several windows on the screen at once, the active window can be identified because its title bar will be a different color than that of all other title bars on the screen. In Figure 0.1, you can tell that Notepad is the active window because the title bar is darker than the others (a different color on a color monitor), and also because that window is on top of the others.

The title bar is also used to move windows from one location to another. Windows are frequently moved, like shuffling file folders in your lap, so that you can see or use an application that is behind them.

GUIDED ACTIVITY 0.1

Opening and Moving a Window

Program
Manager

1. Start Windows. If necessary, double-click on the Program Manager icon (the small picture on the screen that represents the Program Manager) to open that window.

    Depending on how your system is configured, you will probably see at least four icons at the bottom of the Program Manager window, such as Accessories, Main, Startup, and Games. These, called *program groups*, are not applications themselves. Each program group is a window that contains application icons and other program group icons. Program groups are always represented by the program group icon, with the name of the group underneath.

Accessories

2. Double-click on the Accessories program group icon.

    The Accessories window opens and displays application icons. You will use the Notepad application in this unit as an example. Any of the Windows applications could be used in the same fashion.

Notepad

3. Double-click on the Notepad icon to start that application. After the application starts, if Notepad takes up the whole screen, click on the *restore* button ⊡ in the top-right corner. This button will only appear if Notepad fills the entire screen.

    Notepad is now in a window on the screen and should appear something like Figure 0.2. The *cursor*, a flashing vertical bar in the work area, marks the point where text will appear when you type. One of the things you can do with this window is move it to another location by dragging its title bar with the mouse.

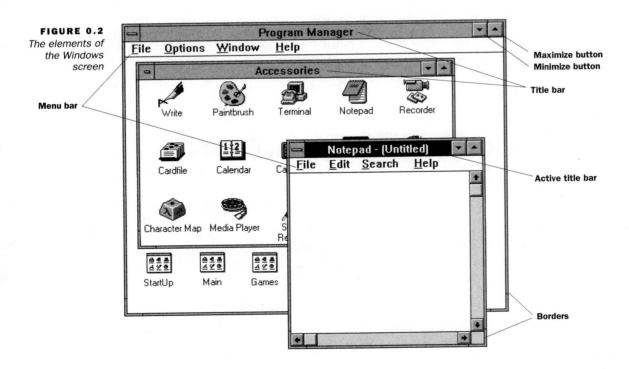

FIGURE 0.2
The elements of the Windows screen

4. Move the mouse pointer to the Notepad title bar. Hold down the mouse button and drag the window to another spot on the screen.

The size and contents of the window do not change; only its location does.

All windows have **borders** around them. The borders define the edge of a window and are used to change its size.

A window is sized by pointing the mouse at the top, bottom, left, or right border, holding down the left mouse button, and dragging the border to a new location. The size that a window needs to be is largely determined by what application is running in it and what you need to see in that application.

GUIDED ACTIVITY 0.2

Sizing a Window

1. Move the Notepad window back to the center of the screen (review the previous Guided Activity, if you need to).

 2. Position the mouse pointer over the bottom border of the Notepad window. The pointer should change shape and appear as a double-headed arrow.

3. When the mouse pointer appears as a double-headed arrow, drag the border up about one inch by holding down the left mouse button and moving the mouse up. Release the button when the line is where you want it. This step may take a few tries. Using the mouse requires practice; therefore, be patient when attempting these activities.

The bottom of the window is now about an inch higher that it was. All of the window borders can be moved in the same manner.

 4. Position the mouse pointer over the left border of the Notepad window. The mouse pointer will change shape again and appear as a horizontal double-headed arrow. Hold down the mouse button and drag the left border about one inch to the right.

The Notepad window has decreased in size. You reduced the height by moving the bottom border upward and the width by moving the left border to the right. Most windows can be sized by grabbing any border and dragging it to the new desired position. However, a few windows cannot be sized. The mouse pointer will not change shape when positioned over the border of a window that cannot be sized. (You will probably not encounter many of these windows.)

Occasionally, you will want to make a window as large as possible to see as much information as you can in one application. This happens many times when you are working with a single program and are not necessarily interested in viewing several applications at once. An application that fills the entire screen is said to be *maximized*. A maximized application cannot be moved or sized, and it has no borders.

There are also times when you will want to move an application out of the way temporarily to perform another task. A simple way to do this is to *minimize* the program. A minimized program is stored as an icon at the bottom of the screen until the user recalls it. It is still running in the computer's memory and contains your data, but is minimized to move it out of the way.

GUIDED ACTIVITY 0.3

Maximizing, Minimizing, and Restoring

1. Maximize the Notepad window by clicking on the maximize button at the top-right corner of the Notepad window.

   The Notepad now fills the entire screen. It is no longer really a window, and it has no borders. As soon as any window has been maximized, the maximize button is replaced by the restore button.

2. Restore Notepad to its former size by clicking on the restore button at the top-right corner of the screen.

   Notepad is now a window again and is restored to the same size it was before being maximized. The borders are back, and the window can now once again be sized and moved.

   Windows allows you to use several applications at the same time without having to close one and open another. As an example, assume you are using the Notepad and need to access the Calculator application to calculate a value. There is no need to exit the Notepad to start the Calculator. The Notepad can be minimized on the screen and will wait there until you finish with your other application.

3. Minimize the Notepad by clicking on the minimize button in the upper-right corner of the window.

   The Notepad becomes an icon at the bottom of the screen, and you can see all of the other windows.

   Notice that within the Accessories window, there is another icon for Notepad, as shown in Figure 0.3. That icon is used to start or open Notepad for the first time. The icon at the bottom-left corner of the screen is a Notepad that is already running, but temporarily inactive.

Calculator

4. In the Accessories program group, double-click on the Calculator icon.

   Move the mouse pointer to the border of the Calculator. The pointer does not change shape; therefore, the Calculator window cannot be sized. You may see a subtle difference in the border of the Calculator window in Figure 0.3 compared to the other, sizable windows.

5. The Calculator is a simple program used to calculate values. Click on the following buttons: 4 5 * 7 5 =

   The result of the calculation—3375—is displayed in the result window of the Calculator.

FIGURE 0.3
*Calculator and
Clock open and
Notepad
minimized*

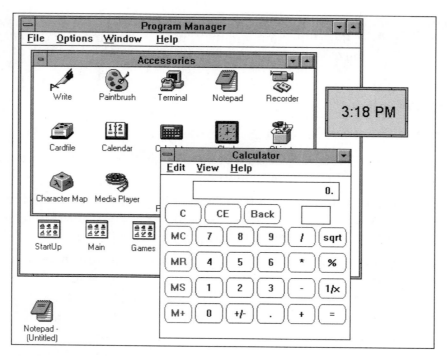

6. Double-click on the Notepad icon at the bottom-left corner of the screen. This restores the Notepad to the size it was before you minimized it.

You now have the basic skills needed to size, move, maximize, minimize, and restore applications. These skills allow you to switch quickly from one application to another within the Windows environment. Windows comes with many features that you may practice and even play with. You can learn all about Windows and using a mouse by clicking on Help on the menu bar on Program Manager. Windows provides several applications in the Main, Accessories, and Games program groups for you to explore. Two enjoyable examples are Solitaire and Minesweeper, mouse–eye coordination tutorials that give you a little break from your serious work.

Copying Data

Since you can switch between several applications running at once, it would be useful to be able to copy information from one application to another. This would allow you to calculate values in the Calculator and place the result in the Notepad. The commands required to copy and paste information are located in an area of the screen called the *menu bar*, illustrated in Figure 0.4. The menu bar is directly below the title bar and contains the names of menus available in that application. You may see the commands in each menu by clicking on the menu name.

The general steps required to copy data between applications are as follows:

1. Highlight the data to be copied in the application that contains it. To highlight, place the mouse pointer over the material and click-and-drag. Then select from the menu bar the command Edit/Copy (that is, first click Edit on the menu bar, and then click the Copy command).

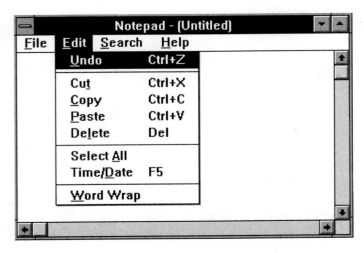

2. Select the application to which you will be copying the data by clicking on it (if it is already visible on the screen) or restoring it (if it is minimized), then select Edit/Paste (click Edit on the menu bar, and then click on the Paste command).

Data can be transferred to and from almost all Windows applications. Windows allows you to do this by means of a special program called the ***Clipboard***. Each time you select Edit/Copy from any application, the information you highlighted is moved to the Clipboard, a temporary storage area. The Clipboard keeps a copy of this information as you maximize, minimize, and restore applications. When Edit/Paste is selected, the contents of the Clipboard are copied to the location of the cursor in the active window.

GUIDED ACTIVITY 0.4

Copying Data Between Applications

1. Minimize the Notepad (review the previous Guided Activity, if necessary).

2. Click once on the Calculator to make it the active window. The result of the calculation you performed in the Calculator (3375) is still displayed. This Guided Activity will show how to copy this result to the Notepad.

   Since there is only one piece of information in the Calculator, it is unnecessary (and impossible) to highlight it. Windows assumes that the information you want to copy is in the result window of the Calculator. Other applications require you to highlight information before selecting the Copy command.

3. Click on the Edit menu, and then on the Copy command.

   From this point forward, menu commands will be displayed in the form "select Menu/Command," for "click on Menu-name and then on Command-name." For example, the previous command would be expressed as Edit/Copy.

4. Restore the Notepad by double-clicking on the icon at the bottom-left corner of the screen.

5. Select Edit/Paste.

The result of the calculation from the Calculator is now in the Notepad.

Exiting Applications

Now that you have made the calculation and copied the results to the Notepad, you may not need to use it again for a while. When you minimize an application, it is still running (although it is out of the way) and it is still taking up space in the computer's memory. To remove the application from the computer's memory, you need to exit from it. Exiting a Windows application may be done two ways. The first is to select the command File/Exit. The second is to double-click on the *Control-menu box* in the upper-left corner of each Window, shown in the left margin.

GUIDED ACTIVITY 0.5

Exiting Applications

1. Select the command File/Exit from the Notepad menu.

2. Because you have information that has not been permanently stored, a notice appears asking you whether you wish to save the changes. In this case, we are not interested in saving a permanent copy, so click on the No button. The Notepad window is immediately closed and removed from the computer's memory. It is not minimized in the lower-left part of the screen, but it is available in the Accessories window for you to open any time you wish to jot down a few notes.

3. Click anywhere on the Calculator so that it becomes the active window. You can tell that it is the active window because its title bar is a different color or shade.

4. Close the Calculator by double-clicking the Control-menu box on the upper-left corner.

5. Click on the minimize button near the top-right corner of the Accessories window to change it to a group icon at the bottom of the Program Manager window.

Customizing the Windows Environment

You can work more easily in an environment in which you feel comfortable. With this in mind, Microsoft designed Windows so that many parts of its environment can be customized by the user. You may customize the colors of different areas of the screen, the speed of the mouse and the mouse button, and even the color and pattern of the background. These features make Windows more pleasant to use by letting you tailor the program to fit your needs, rather than requiring you to adjust the way you work to fit a rigid program.

Control Panel

The Control Panel program group is used to customize the Windows environment. The Control Panel is located within the Main window; therefore, to reach it, double-click on the Main icon. If the Main icon is obscured, select Main from the

Window menu. When the Main program group window opens, you will see the Control Panel icon.

Double-click on that icon. The Control Panel window opens, displaying all the areas of Windows that can be customized by you the user, as shown in Figure 0.5.

FIGURE 0.5
Control Panel

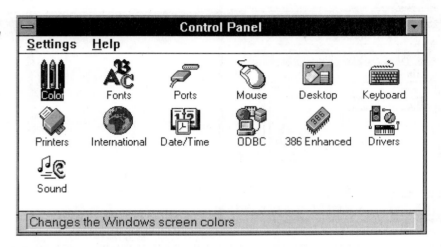

Color

Windows uses colors to differentiate the areas of its environment from each other. Active and inactive windows, title bars, borders, application workspaces, and desktop colors all give you information about every aspect of the Windows screen. Because these colors are so important, Windows allows you to change them to a combination that will be most meaningful (and pleasant) to you. This customization will make Windows easier for you to use because you, not the software, will determine what different colors mean.

To change any of the colors on the screen, double-click on the Color icon.

The Color program in the Control Panel allows you to change virtually any color on the screen. The Color program has a small sample of a Windows session in the current colors, as shown (obviously, in black-and-white) in Figure 0.6.

Windows comes with a list of standard color schemes. Press ⬇ and ⬆ to see what color schemes are available, and watch the effect each one has on the sample.

Many times a color scheme is very close to what a user wants, but may need one or two colors changed. For example, the Desktop is the color of the screen behind all the open windows and icons. If you like the Rugby color scheme but dislike the color of the desktop, you can change that color individually. Select the Rugby color scheme from the list of standard color schemes. The Rugby colors will appear in the sample window.

When you click on the *Color Palette* button, the Color window expands to include a palette of colors available to use in the color scheme, as shown in Figure 0.7. The screen element that is being changed is listed directly above the palette. The screen element whose color you want to change is selected by clicking on it in the sample window. Click on the title bar on either side of the word Active. The Screen Element box now reads Active Title Bar. You may now change the color of the

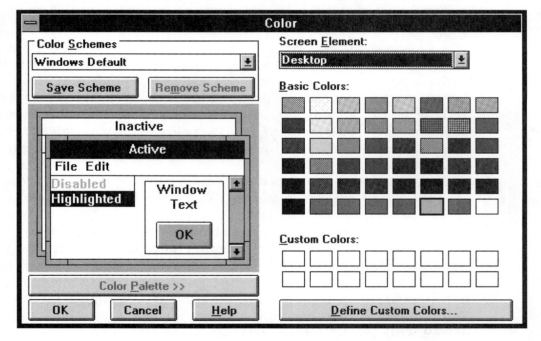

FIGURE 0.6
The Color window showing a sample of color arrangements

FIGURE 0.7
The Color window with the color palette displayed

active title bar by selecting the desired color from the palette. Click on the gray area of the sample behind the windows, and the Screen Element box will read `Desktop`. Click on any color on the palette, and Windows will show you a sample of your new color scheme. When you have set up the colors the way you like, click on the OK button to exit the Color program and put your new color scheme into effect, or click on the Cancel button to ignore the changes you made.

Mouse

The *tracking speed* of the mouse and the *double-click speed* of the mouse button can also be customized in the Windows environment. The tracking speed of the mouse refers to how far the mouse pointer will move on the screen relative to the distance the mouse moves on its surface. A faster tracking speed means that the mouse pointer will move farther on the screen for every increment of distance you move the mouse on its surface (mouse pad or desk surface). Fast tracking speeds may make the mouse so sensitive that it might become difficult to position the mouse pointer accurately on small objects on the screen. Slow tracking speeds allow you to be very accurate but may require you to use the entire desk to move the mouse pointer from one side of the screen to the other. The ideal is to find the speed where you have good control of the mouse pointer but do not have to move the mouse a great distance to move the pointer across the screen. The mouse tracking speed is normally set halfway between fast and slow, but setting it slower or even to the slowest is desirable under some circumstances. Many computer labs have mice that have been used and abused, losing some of their sensitivity and ease of control. Some users have shaky hands, and certain tasks on the computer require fine movements with the mouse. Those are several reasons to slow the mouse tracking speed.

Mouse

To change the tracking speed and the double-click speed, click on the Mouse icon in the Control Panel. The Mouse window will appear on the screen, as shown in Figure 0.8. The Mouse icon and Mouse window you see may vary depending on what type of mouse is installed on your system.

FIGURE 0.8
The Mouse window

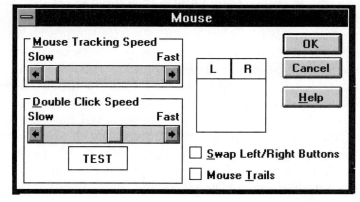

To decrease or increase the tracking speed, click on the left or right arrow in the Mouse Tracking Speed portion of the window. Again, the name of this feature may differ on your system. The sliding box in the bar between the two arrows will move left or right to show you the speed you have selected relative to fast or slow.

The double-click speed is changed in the same manner. The double-click speed of the mouse button can also be customized. Windows recognizes a double-click command when you click twice quickly on an item. If the double-click speed is set too fast, you may not be able to click fast enough to get Windows to recognize what you are doing. If it is too slow, you may inadvertently double-click on an item on the screen without meaning to. Windows allows you to select the setting that is just right for you.

Click on the left or right arrow in the Double Click Speed section of the window to decrease or increase the double-click speed. You may immediately test the new speed by double-clicking on the TEST box. If the box changes colors, the double-click worked. If the box does not change colors, decrease the double-click speed and test it again. Use the fastest speed at which you can click comfortably and easily.

Another important item that can be changed in the Mouse window is which mouse button to use to click on objects on the screen. The mouse is usually set up for right-handed users who hold the mouse in their right hands and click the left button with their index fingers. Lefties may find it more natural to hold the mouse in their left hands and click with their *left* index fingers on the *right* mouse button. To change the functions of the left and right mouse buttons, click on the box next to Swap Left/Right Buttons. An X will appear in the box when the buttons are swapped. Remember, however, that to switch back to the default configuration you will have to click with the right button. When you are through making changes in the Mouse window, click on OK to save or on Cancel to ignore any changes you made.

Desktop

In addition to changing the color of the desktop from the Color window, you may select a pattern or picture to appear as the background (or *desktop*) for a Windows session. A picture used in this fashion is called *wallpaper*. Any picture that you create in Paintbrush (another Windows application available under Accessories) can be used for wallpaper. You may also select a *pattern* to cover the background. Wallpaper is displayed over the background pattern; therefore, a large picture used as wallpaper may completely obscure the pattern. Keep in mind that the computer has to keep up with any pattern or wallpaper that you have selected when you are minimizing and maximizing applications. If any pattern or wallpaper is selected, processes that require window manipulation will occur more slowly. To prevent the computer from slowing down its processing, select a solid black background with both pattern and wallpaper set to (None). More attractive patterns will decrease performance speed but will enhance the visual appeal of the Windows environment.

Desktop

When you double-click the Desktop icon, the Desktop window shown in Figure 0.9 will open. Click on the down arrow in the Wallpaper section to get a list of the standard pictures available. (None) is the current selection. Click on one of the other Wallpaper names. You may scroll through the entire list by clicking on the down and up arrows in the Wallpaper section of the window. Click on OK to exit the Desktop window, and the background you selected will appear behind the Program Manager. To turn the background off, open the Desktop icon, select (None) for the Wallpaper, and exit the Desktop window.

Date and Time

Every computer stamps the time and date when each file is saved. Windows provides an application in Accessories—the Clock—to help you keep track of the time while you're working on the computer. Of course, these are only helpful if the time and date are correctly set on your computer. The date and time can be changed from DOS, but Windows provides an icon in the Control Panel to do this. Double-click on the Date/Time icon to open the window.

Date/Time

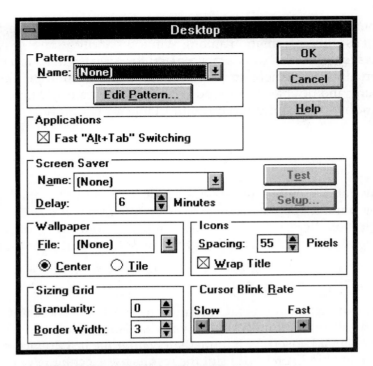

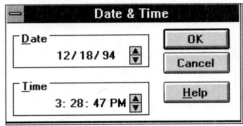

The date is changed by double-clicking on the month, day, or year portion of the date and entering new numbers or clicking on the up or down arrow to increase or decrease the number, as shown in Figure 0.10.

The month portion of the date is highlighted; increase it by one month by clicking once on the up arrow or typing the new number. Return it to its original setting by clicking on the down arrow.

Set the time and date correctly on your computer. When they are correct, click on OK to confirm the changes and exit the window. Click on the minimize button near the top-right corner of the Accessories icon to put it neatly out of the way. To exit Windows, double-click on the Control-menu box in the upper-left corner of the Program Manager. In the dialog box that appears, click OK to exit Windows.

Summary

The Windows environment makes it easier for you to use applications because it is a graphical environment. The drawback for this ease of use is a decrease in performance speed, but as new generations of faster computers become available this decrease is minimal.

Windows provides several advantages. It allows you to

- use common commands and screen elements in every application,

- see text and graphics just as they will be printed,

- run several applications at once, and

- copy text, graphics, or data from one application to another.

Applications in Windows have many commands and components in common. The commands guarantee that you will already know how to open and save files, print documents, and exit the program if you have used any other Windows package. The components allow you to move, size, maximize, minimize, and restore windows as well as copy information among Windows applications.

The Windows environment can be customized to a great extent. You can change the colors of virtually any element on the screen, set a background picture, customize the mouse tracking and double-click speeds, and reset the date and time. This allows you to tailor Windows to a configuration comfortable for you.

Exercises

1. Start Windows and open the Accessories window. Start the Notepad, and type the following phrase. You may change the words to match the terminology used by your institution. Replace "X" with the number of hours or credits received for this class. Replace "Y" with the cost per hour or per credit at your institution.

    ```
    The cost of this class is $X per hour (credit) times Y
    hours (credits) for a total of $.
    ```

2. Minimize the Notepad. (Don't exit, minimize it!) Start the Calculator. Multiply the value you substituted for "X" by the value substituted for "Y". Copy the result to the Notepad, inserting it immediately after the last dollar sign in the phrase you created in Exercise 1. Print the results by selecting File/Print from the Notepad menu.

3. Minimize Program Manager to an icon. On your printout, draw a picture of the button you clicked to perform this step. Restore Program Manager to its original size. Maximize Program Manager. Draw a picture of the button you clicked to perform this step. Restore Program Manager to its original size. Draw a picture of the button you clicked to perform this step.

4. Open the Accessories window and double-click on Clock to display the time. Write down the current time.

5. Click on the word Settings on the menu, then click Digital on the menu that appears. Drag the borders of the Clock window until it is very large. Write down how the appearance of the digits of the time changes when the clock is very large. Minimize Clock. Close Accessories.

6. Open the Main window. Open the Control Panel. Open the Mouse window. Change the settings on the mouse so that the tracking speed and double-click speed are set to your liking. Draw a diagram of the Mouse window showing your settings. Close Mouse.

7. Open the Color window in the Control Panel. Change the color scheme and close the Color window. List various screen elements and describe the color assigned to each.

Review Questions

The answers to questions marked with an asterisk are contained in Appendix B.

*1. What is a window? What kinds of things can appear in a window?

2. What are the advantages and disadvantages of a graphical environment compared with those of a text environment? Give an example of each kind of environment.

*3. What creates the performance differential between graphical and text environments?

4. What component of a window is used to move the window to another location? What component is used to size it? What mouse action is required to do these two procedures?

*5. How are windows maximized and minimized?

6. What is the difference between the way maximized and minimized windows are restored?

*7. What component of the screen is used to copy information between applications?

8. What parts of the Windows environment can be customized? What program group contains the programs used to customize the environment?

Key Terms

The following terms are introduced in this unit. Be sure you know what each of them means.

Active window	Double-click	Pattern
Application	Double-click speed	Pixel
Border	Drag	Point
Click	Graphical user interface	Program group
Clipboard	(GUI)	Restore
Color palette	Icon	Title bar
Control-menu box	Maximize	Tracking speed
Common user interface	Menu bar	Wallpaper
Cursor	Minimize	Window
Desktop	Mouse	Windows application
Disk Operating System	Mouse button	
(DOS)	Mouse pointer	

Documentation Research

Answers to all Documentation Research questions can be found either in the *User's Guide* for Windows or in the on-line Help facility. Select the Help facility by clicking Help on the menu bar or by pressing the F1 key on the keyboard.

1. How do you neatly arrange windows and icons within a window?

2. What is the purpose of the About command under the Help menu?

3. What is another way to switch between applications besides minimizing and maximizing?

Running Start

This unit previews some of the features of Word for Windows and should be used at the computer. Ordinarily you should read the units before attempting to perform the Guided Activities, but this unit is intended for you to use at the computer to introduce you to Word for Windows and show you how simple it is to use a word processor. Some of these tasks can be used in any Windows application. Many steps in these activities will be explained in more detail in later units.

Learning Objectives

At the completion of this unit you should know

1. how to enter and exit Word for Windows,

2. how to create a simple document,

3. how to use buttons and menus.

Using Word for Windows

The best way to appreciate the simplicity and power of a Windows program is to start it and use it. You will need a formatted disk if you want to save the document you will create in the Guided Activities. If you have not installed the software or need to format a disk, consult your Word for Windows documentation for details about these procedures.

Microsoft
Word

To start Word for Windows, find the picture on the screen that represents it—its icon, shown in the margin—and double-click on it. The screen in Figure 1.1 should appear. The Word screen contains certain elements common to every application that runs under Windows. You will see the title bar, the menu bar, the Control-menu box on the upper left, the minimize and maximize boxes on the upper right, and scroll bars on the right and bottom sides. The menu bar shows a list of commands that you can select to manipulate your document. As you select a word on the *menu*, a list drops down, giving you more specific commands.

There are also several features unique to Word. Word displays several *toolbars* just below the menu, which allow you to use certain commands by clicking on their *buttons*. The *ruler* is used to change the margin and tab settings. The *status bar* gives information about your document or about the command you are performing. Word typically displays each of these screen elements when it starts. The following steps will help you set them up if your screen does not match the one in Figure 1.1.

FIGURE 1.1
The Word screen

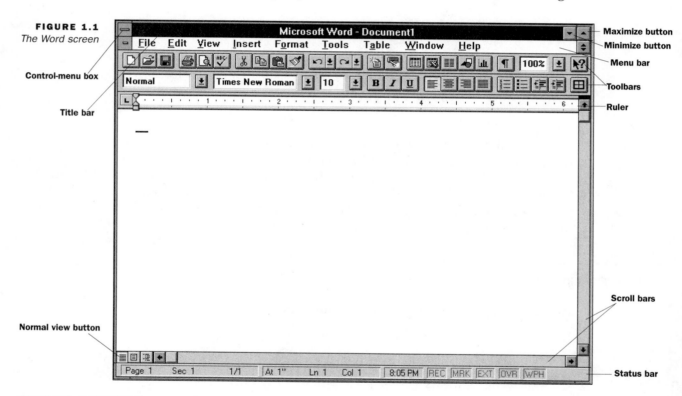

GUIDED ACTIVITY 1.1

Setting Up the Word Screen

1. Click once on the word View on the menu bar. The View menu drops down for you to select another command, as shown on Figure 1.2.

   A list of commands appears below the word View. This list is called a drop-down menu. The area of the screen you clicked is called the menu bar. Menus display the commands available under a menu title such as View. To exit the menu without executing any of the commands, press [Esc] or click on View again. If you ever open an incorrect menu or dialog box, pressing [Esc] will cancel the action. Some

FIGURE 1.2
The View menu

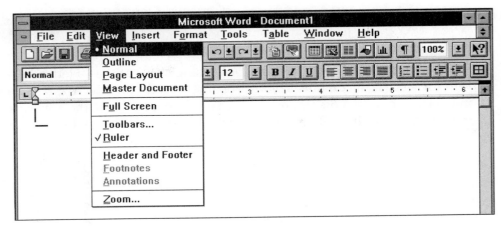

commands in the menus are followed by ellipses (. . .). These commands will cause a dialog box to appear on the screen.

2. If no check ✓ appears next to the word Ruler, click on Ruler, and the ruler will appear near the top of the Word screen.

3. If no toolbars are at the top of the Word screen, select the View menu again, but this time click on the word Toolbars.

4. This time a dialog box appears for you to give additional information, shown on Figure 1.3. Click on the boxes next to the words Standard and Formatting. Those two boxes should contain an X, as should the one at the bottom next to Show ToolTips. Click OK. If the toolbars appear to be floating on the screen, point the mouse at the tiny title bar, and click-and-drag to the top of the screen.

FIGURE 1.3
*The Toolbars
dialog box*

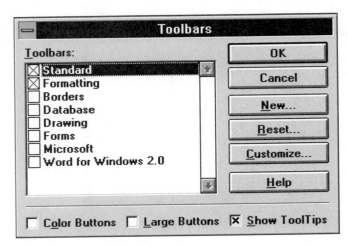

5. Click on the Normal view button on the far left side of the status bar (refer back to Figure 1.1) to make sure you are in Normal view.

6. If a paragraph symbol (¶) appears next to the blinking cursor, click on the ¶ button on the toolbar and the symbol will disappear.

GUIDED ACTIVITY 1.2

Entering Text

Let's begin with a typical word processing application—a letter. When Word for Windows starts, it contains a blank document ready for new text. The cursor, a flashing vertical bar, is in the upper-left corner of the *work area*, the area where text is entered and modified. The finished text will resemble Figure 1.4.

FIGURE 1.4
The letter to create

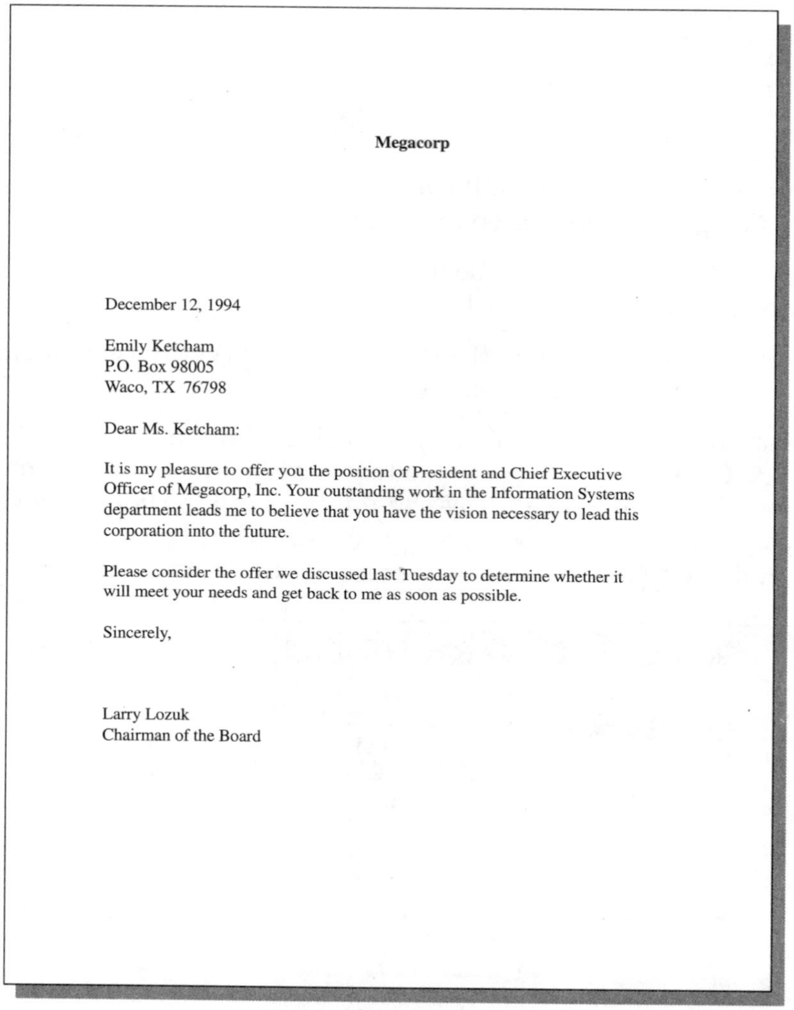

Megacorp

December 12, 1994

Emily Ketcham
P.O. Box 98005
Waco, TX 76798

Dear Ms. Ketcham:

It is my pleasure to offer you the position of President and Chief Executive Officer of Megacorp, Inc. Your outstanding work in the Information Systems department leads me to believe that you have the vision necessary to lead this corporation into the future.

Please consider the offer we discussed last Tuesday to determine whether it will meet your needs and get back to me as soon as possible.

Sincerely,

Larry Lozuk
Chairman of the Board

---

1. Type the name of the company, `Megacorp`.

    If you make a typing error, erase it using [Backspace]. The [Backspace] key erases the character immediately to the left of the cursor.

2. Press [Enter] twice. Type in today's date.

3. Press [Enter] twice. Type in your first and last name. Press [Enter] again.

4. Type in your street address and, on the next line, the city, state, and zip code in which you live.

   You may have figured out that in order to get the cursor to the next line (as you are required to do in the previous step), you press [Enter].

5. Press [Enter] twice to leave a blank line between the zip code and what you are about to type. Type in Dear followed by Mr. or Ms. and your last name plus a colon. Press [Enter] twice again to start a new paragraph.

   You know that [Enter] places the cursor at the beginning of the next line. However, there is no need to use [Enter] at the end of each line within a paragraph. Word processors automatically wrap to the beginning of the next line words that will not fit at the end of the current line. The only time [Enter] is used when typing text is at the end of a paragraph or anytime you want to leave a blank line in your document.

6. Type in the following text, pressing [Enter] only at the end of each paragraph or to leave a blank line.

   ```
   It is my pleasure to offer you the position of Chief Execu-
   tive Officer of Megacorp, Inc. Your outstanding work in the
   Information Systems department leads me to believe that you
   have the vision necessary to lead this corporation into the
   future.

   Please consider the offer we discussed previously to deter-
   mine whether it will meet your needs and get back to me as
   soon as possible.

   Sincerely,



   Larry Lozuk
   Chairman of the Board
   ```

   The text of your letter is now complete. This is the first step involved in creating a word processing document. The preceding Guided Activity would work in most word processors. Sad to say, software engineers have not yet designed the software package that will enter the text for the user with perfect accuracy.

   The next step in preparing the letter involves changing the way the letter appears, which is called *formatting*.

GUIDED ACTIVITY 1.3

Formatting the Letter

   The letters in the document seem too small to be easy to read. The first step in formatting is to indicate what words you wish to change by *highlighting* or *selecting* them.

1. To highlight the document, click on the Edit menu and choose the command Select All. The entire document now appears in reverse color—white letters on black instead of black letters on white.

    Look at the area of the screen above the work area, shown in Figure 1.5. This area of the screen is called the Formatting toolbar, and is used for formatting text. The size of the letters is indicated by the number 10. To make the letters larger, this number must be larger.

2. Move the mouse pointer to the number 10 and double-click. This highlights (selects) the 10.

3. Type 12 (which replaces the number 10, as shown in Figure 1.6) and press [Enter]. Now the entire document is a little easier to read. Compare the sizes on the following sample:

    This is size 10.
    This is size 12.

4. Click the mouse anywhere on the document to remove the highlighting.

    Let's turn the word Megacorp on the top line into the letterhead.

5. Press [PgUp] once or twice, if necessary, so that you are able to see the top line of the document with the word Megacorp.

6. Move the mouse pointer over the word Megacorp in your document. With the mouse pointer touching any part of the word, double-click. Now that word is highlighted.

7. Click on the center button on the Formatting toolbar.

    The letterhead is now centered on the page.

    You may have discovered that, as you point with the mouse at any button on the screen, after a few seconds the name of the button appears, just under the mouse pointer. These are called *ToolTips*.

8. Click on the B (bold) button.

    Megacorp now appears in bold letters and will stand out from the rest of the document.

    The letter is now complete. Although each paragraph is displayed the way it will be printed, the entire page will not fit on the screen. To get an idea of how the page will appear, look at it with the preview screen.

9. Click on the Print Preview button, which has an image of a magnifying glass over a sheet of paper. It appears on the Standard toolbar shown in Figure 1.7.

This is the way your document will look on the page when you print it. The preview screen is meant only to display the position of the paragraphs on the printed page; the text is not really legible.

The body of the letter looks correct, but the text is positioned too high on the page.

10. Click on the Close button at the top of the screen to exit the preview screen.

To lower the document on the page, you must increase the distance from the top of the page to the top margin of the text. One way to do this is to position the cursor above the date and press `Enter` several times, adding blank lines, until the date is low enough on the page.

11. Press ⬇ once to move the cursor to the blank line between the letterhead and the date.

12. Press `Enter` 6 or 8 times to insert some blank lines.

13. Click on the Print Preview button again. The page looks a little more balanced now, but, if necessary, you can repeat the process a few more times until the page looks nicely balanced.

14. Click on the Close button to exit from the preview screen.

Ideally, you are finished; in all probability, someone will want to change the letter. It has been determined that the phrase Chief Executive Officer should actually read President and Chief Executive Officer; therefore, you will need to edit the first paragraph.

GUIDED ACTIVITY 1.4

Changing Text

1. Move the mouse pointer just to the left of the C in Chief, and click once. First press `PgDn`, if necessary, to see the line.

The cursor is now positioned correctly to enter the new text.

2. Type in the new text, President and . Make sure to enter a space after the d in and.

The second editing change to be made is to replace the word previously in the second paragraph with last Tuesday.

3. Double-click on previously to highlight it.

4. Type last Tuesday.

Highlighted or selected text is replaced with whatever you type.

The letter is complete. Now you need to print it.

 5. Click the Print button on the Standard toolbar. A dialog box will appear while the document is being printed, and soon you will have your printed letter (assuming your printer is on and ready to work).

You have successfully entered, edited, and formatted text. The commands used were simple and intuitive. All of the formatting steps were performed by clicking buttons on the screen. Rather than requiring you to speak the computer's language by learning and remembering complicated codes or key sequences, Word for Windows offers the use of commands in a manner that seems natural. Instead of your having to learn to bridge the gap between human and computer, the computer is now capable of doing some of this work for you. This is typical of Word for Windows specifically and of Windows software in general.

Executing Commands from the Keyboard

Any command that you execute with the mouse may also be executed with the keyboard. Users who type quickly may find it faster to use the keyboard for certain commands than to use the mouse, since they can keep both hands on the keyboard. To access the menus, press and release the *Alternate* or Alt key (Alt) on the keyboard. Each menu title contains one letter that is underlined, usually the first letter of the menu's name. You may display that menu by pressing the underlined letter. Each command in the menu will also have one underlined letter or number that can be pressed to execute the command. Any menu command can be executed by pressing three keys: Alt, the menu letter, and the command letter.

GUIDED ACTIVITY 1.5

Executing Commands Using the Keyboard

If you have a mouse and will be using it to execute commands, you need not bother to complete this section. However, if you know how to execute commands from the keyboard as well as with the mouse, you will find yourself using both methods alternately, as convenient. When your hands are already on the keyboard (or if you have the misfortune of being stuck on a computer without a mouse), you will find this method of executing commands most helpful.

To preview the document with the keyboard, select the command File/Print Preview from the menu.

1. Press Alt. Press F.

The File menu drops down. The F in File was underlined, so when you pressed that key, the File menu opened. Both uppercase and lowercase letters are accepted when executing commands from a menu with the keyboard.

2. Press ⓥ.

    The File/Print Preview command is executed immediately.

3. Press Ⓔꜱᴄ to close the preview screen.

    If you do not have a mouse, the toolbars just consume valuable workspace on the screen.

4. Press Ⓐˡᵗⓥ, Ⓣ.

    The Toolbars dialog box appears. You may turn off or on any highlighted check box by pressing the spacebar, Ⓢᴘᴀᴄᴇʙᴀʀ.

5. To turn off the Standard toolbar, press Ⓢᴘᴀᴄᴇʙᴀʀ.

6. Press ⓥ to highlight the Formatting toolbar choice and press Ⓢᴘᴀᴄᴇʙᴀʀ to remove the check and so turn off the Formatting toolbar.

7. If you wish to make the changes, press Ⓔɴᴛᴇʀ to select OK, or press Ⓔꜱᴄ to cancel, and return to the document.

8. Although it is not necessary, you may wish to save the document you created in this unit. To save you must have a formatted disk and place it in drive A:. Click on the Save button (with a picture of a floppy disk), type the file name A:GA1, and press Ⓔɴᴛᴇʀ. This step is optional for this exercise.

9. To exit Word for Windows completely, select File/Edit from the Word for Windows menu. If you skipped the previous step a dialog box will ask if you wish to save your document. Click No. Your computer returns to the Program Manager.

Getting Help

If you need help in using Word, you don't have to find the manual or wait for someone to guide you. Word has help available right on your computer screen. You may get help in several ways:

- Select Help from the menu.

- Press the Ⓕ¹ key.

- Click the Help button on the toolbar.

- Click on Help in any dialog box to get further instructions.

Selecting Help/Contents from the menu or pressing Ⓕ¹ brings up the Help Screen shown in Figure 1.8, which displays the ways you can get help. You can receive step-by-step directions on using Word. You can see visual examples and demonstrations. You can review tips, guides, and other reference material. The bottom choice, technical support, gives you telephone numbers for you to call if you have questions that are not answered in the manual or on screen.

Clicking on the Search button on the Help Screen allows you to get information on a certain key word. If you want information about printing your document, for

FIGURE 1.8
The Help screen

Select File/Exit
to return to your
document.

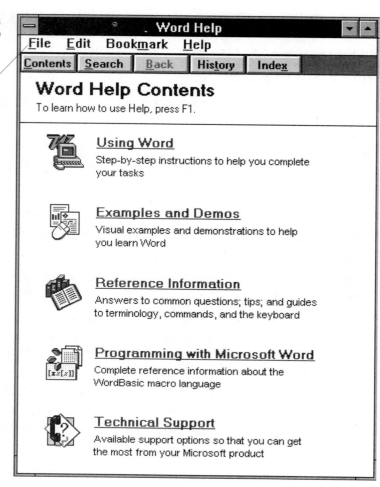

instance, you would type the word `print` in the box on the Search screen, as shown in Figure 1.9. As you type, Word lists all the related topics. You can click on the down arrow next to the topics to see other choices and select the one called Printing documents, then click the Show Topics button. Select the Printing topic, and click the Go To button. This reveals the "chapter" on printing, beginning with an overview. You may click on any topic in the chapter to see relevant information.

Clicking the index button on the Help Screen or selecting Help/Index from the Word menu displays an index of all the topics in Help. To get information about printing from the Index, click on the P button to jump

quickly to the topics beginning with P, as shown in Figure 1.10. Click on ▣ and hold it down until you see the index entry for the Print command.

The Help button on the far right side of the toolbar gives context-sensitive help. When you click on the Help button, the mouse pointer displays an arrow with a large question mark. Whatever you click on next will be the subject of the Help screen.

The help within Word for Windows is comparable to that found in the Microsoft Word *User's Guide*, and is convenient and easy to use. You can access it on screen by selecting from the menu, the keyboard, or by clicking the Help button on the toolbar.

Summary

This unit led you through the steps of double-clicking the icon to start Word for Windows 6.0 and learning about the elements on the Word screen: the buttons on the toolbars, the selections on the menu, and the dialog boxes. You stepped through typing and formatting a simple document, and tried previewing and printing the

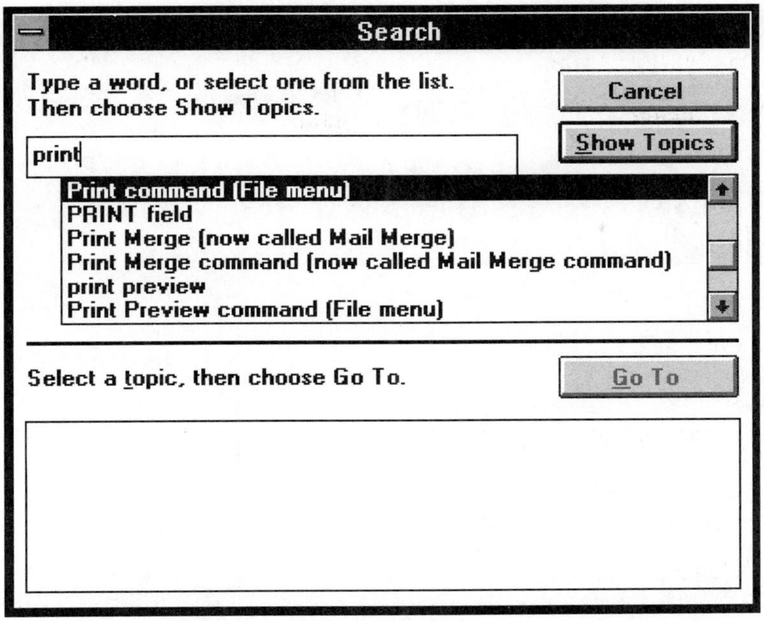

FIGURE 1.9
*The Search
dialog box*

```
┌─────────────────────────────────────────────────────┐
│ ─          Search                                      │
│ Type a word, or select one from the list.  ┌─────────┐│
│ Then choose Show Topics.                    │ Cancel  ││
│                                             └─────────┘│
│ ┌─────────────────────────────────────┐   ┌──────────┐│
│ │ print                               │   │Show Topics││
│ └─────────────────────────────────────┘   └──────────┘│
│ ┌─────────────────────────────────────────┐ ▲        │
│ │ Print command (File menu)               │ █        │
│ │ PRINT field                             │ █        │
│ │ Print Merge (now called Mail Merge)     │ █        │
│ │ Print Merge command (now called Mail Merge command)│
│ │ print preview                           │          │
│ │ Print Preview command (File menu)       │ ▼        │
│ └─────────────────────────────────────────┘          │
│                                                        │
│ Select a topic, then choose Go To.       ┌──────────┐ │
│                                          │  Go To   │ │
│                                          └──────────┘ │
│ ┌─────────────────────────────────────────────────┐ │
│ │                                                   │ │
│ │                                                   │ │
│ │                                                   │ │
│ └─────────────────────────────────────────────────┘ │
└────────────────────────────────────────────────────────┘
```

finished product. You also learned how to use the on-screen Help facility. Later units will give you much more information about each of these procedures.

Review Questions

The answers to questions marked with an asterisk are contained in Appendix B.

*1. What parts of the screen are found in all Windows applications? What parts are found in Word 6.0?

2. What makes Windows software packages different from other packages?

*3. What is the single most important key to remember when executing commands from the keyboard?

Key Terms

The following terms are introduced in this unit. Be sure you know what each of them means.

Alternate	Menu	ToolTips
Button	Ruler	Status bar
Formatting	Select	Work area
Highlight	Toolbar	

FIGURE 1.10
The Help index

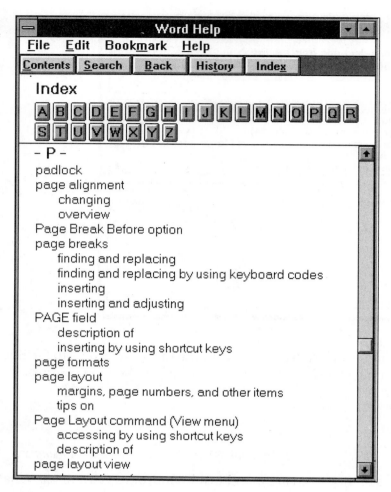

Documentation Research

Answers to all Documentation Research questions can be found either in the Microsoft Word *User's Guide* or in the on-line Help facility. Select the Help facility by clicking Help on the menu bar, or by pressing F1.

1. In addition to bold, what other formats are available from buttons on the Formatting toolbar?

2. What button is used for Help at any point in Word for Windows?

3. What is the difference between using the Print button on the toolbar and selecting File/Print from the menu?

Simple Word Processing

Word processing can be broken into three general procedures.

- Entering and editing text
- Formatting text and paragraphs
- Using advanced features

This unit will cover the first of these procedures. This is the easiest part of word processing and is basically done the same way in any software package. You will learn how typing in a word processor is different from typing on a typewriter, how to correct errors as you type, how to move around in the document after information is entered, and how to manipulate and change text. These procedures are fundamental to word processing and must be mastered before continuing.

Learning Objectives

At the completion of this unit you should know

1. what general procedures are involved in word processing,
2. how to enter, correct, and manipulate text in a document,
3. how to use shortcut menus and shortcut keys.

Important Commands

Edit/Clear

Edit/Copy

Edit/Cut

Edit/Paste

Edit/Undo

Entering Text

Text is entered into a document in much the same way as on a typewriter. There are some differences that will affect the way you enter text. Most of these arise from features designed to make typing faster.

A major difference between word processing and using a typewriter is the use of the *Enter* key (Enter). Most electric typewriters have a carriage return key that is used at the end of each line of text. Many first-time word processor users mistake the Enter key on the computer keyboard for the carriage return on the typewriter and use it to end each line of text. This is unnecessary because of a feature in word processors called *word wrap*, which automatically adjusts the text to fit between the margins. As you approach the end of a line, the word processor monitors the length of each word that you type. When you enter a word that will go beyond the current right margin, that word is automatically moved to the beginning of the next line. There is no need to manually force the cursor to the beginning of the next line within paragraphs. The only time Enter is used is at the end of a paragraph or when the user wants to leave a blank line in the text.

The word wrap feature is invaluable because it allows you to concentrate on what you are typing without having to worry about how close the text is to the end of each line. This leads to faster typing speeds and minimizes the amount of time spent entering the document. Word wrap is also important when it comes to editing the text. Whenever you add or remove text, change the size of the typeface, or alter the margins, text flows between the margins. Pressing Enter at the end of each line would cause the lines to break at odd places after making changes like these.

Whatever your typing accuracy, you will eventually make an error as you enter text. If you notice the error when you make it, you can easily correct it by pressing the *Backspace* key (Backspace) on the keyboard. The Backspace key always performs exactly the same function: it erases the character immediately to the left of the cursor.

If you notice an error farther back in the document, there are several ways to correct the mistake. You may use either the *arrow keys* (←, ↑, →, ↓) or the mouse to move the cursor to the error. If you position the cursor immediately to the right of the mistake, you can erase it by pressing Backspace once for each incorrect character. After the incorrect text is removed, simply type the correct letters to fix the passage. If the error is more than two or three lines away from the current cursor position, it may be more efficient to use the mouse to position the cursor to the right of the incorrect text. When the mouse pointer is moved into the work area, it will appear as an *I-beam* so that it can be easily positioned between characters. Move the mouse pointer to the right of the incorrect text, and click once. The cursor will appear at the location of the mouse click. The procedure to correct the error is identical whether you use the arrow keys or the mouse to position the cursor.

GUIDED ACTIVITY 2.1

Entering Text

1. Start Word for Windows. For this activity you will be typing an article. While it is usually inappropriate to double-space a letter, most teachers prefer that students turn in papers double-spaced. To set up a document so that it will be automatically double-spaced, hold down the ⌷Ctrl⌷ key and press 2.

2. Type the three paragraphs of text before this Guided Activity (beginning with A major difference...) as a new document.

    If you notice any keystroke errors as you type, correct them by pressing ⌷Backspace⌷ until the error disappears, and retype the text correctly. Remember not to press ⌷Enter⌷ at the end of each line. Let the word wrap feature take you to the next line instead. If you do press ⌷Enter⌷ inadvertently, press ⌷Backspace⌷. At the end of each paragraph, press ⌷Enter⌷ once to end the paragraph and a second time to leave a blank line before starting the next paragraph.

    In a word processor, an ⌷Enter⌷ character is like any letter on the keyboard in that it can be added or deleted. This character is not displayed on the screen. You can display it by clicking the Show/Hide ¶ button, which appears on the toolbar. When you click this, ⌷Enter⌷ characters appear as a ¶ (paragraph symbol), and spaces between words appear as small dots. If this makes the screen too cluttered, click the Show/Hide ¶ button again, and these symbols will disappear.

Reviewing the Document

When you are done entering the text, the next step will usually be to read back through what you have done to proofread the document. This step often involves adding, deleting, modifying, or moving text and can be considered your "second draft." An important element in editing text is moving around in the document. In essence, the screen is a window that allows you to look at only a portion of your text at once; thus, it is important to know how to manipulate the window.

The easiest way to move through your text is to use the arrow keys on the keyboard. If the cursor is at the top of a document, you can move down by repeatedly pressing the Down Arrow key (⌷↓⌷). The cursor will move down one line at a time for each time you press ⌷↓⌷. Though this is a simple method to remember, it is cumbersome to read long documents one line at a time. A more efficient method to review your text is to press the *Page Down* key (⌷PgDn⌷). This key will scroll down a document one screen length at a time and allow you to skim a few paragraphs at once. Rather than pressing ⌷↓⌷ once for each line of text, ⌷PgDn⌷ allows you to press a single key every 8 or 10 lines of text. This is less tiring for reading long documents and allows you to move much more quickly through several pages. The Up Arrow key (⌷↑⌷) and the *Page Up* key (⌷PgUp⌷) work like the ⌷↓⌷ and ⌷PgDn⌷ keys, except that they scroll up through the document rather than down.

GUIDED ACTIVITY 2.2

Moving Within a Document Using the Keyboard

1. The cursor should still be at the end of the last paragraph you typed. Press `PgUp` until the cursor reaches the top of the document.

2. Press `↓`. The cursor will move down one line. Continue pressing `↓` until the cursor is on the last line of the screen.

    So far the screen has not moved at all. All of the movements of the cursor have fit on one screen.

3. Press `↓` one more time. This time the screen will scroll down one line.

    This is a good way to move a few lines of your document onto the screen, but not a good way for scrolling long distances in the text. The `PgDn` key is better for this.

4. Press `PgDn`.

    Rather than moving down one line at a time, the screen has moved down to display the next 8 or 10 lines.

5. Press `PgUp` until the cursor reaches the top of the document.

    Each time you press `PgUp`, the screen moves up 8 to 10 lines.

6. Press the *End* key (`End`) on the keyboard. The cursor moves to the end of the current line. Press the *Home* key (`Home`) to move the cursor back to the beginning of the line.

    You can now move quickly up and down through the document and to the beginning and end of lines. It is also helpful to be able to quickly move to the middle of a line using the arrow keys. Use the *Control* or Ctrl key (`Ctrl`) in conjunction with the arrow keys to move along a line one word at a time.

7. Move the cursor to the top of the document. Hold down `Ctrl` and press `→` five times. The cursor moves a distance of five words along the first line.

    This is a much faster way to move through text than just using the `→` key.

8. Press `↓` one time to get to the next line. Hold down `Ctrl` and press `→` several times until the cursor moves to the last word of the first line. Press `Home` to get the cursor to the beginning of the line.

9. Since using `Ctrl` with arrow keys augments their effect, you see that adding `Ctrl` to the `Home`, `End`, `PgDn`, and `PgUp` keys will increase or exaggerate their effect as well.

10. Press `Ctrl` `End` and the cursor jumps immediately to the very end of the document.

11. Press `Ctrl` `Home` and the cursor jumps immediately to the very beginning of the document.

    Table 2.1 lists all the keys and their effect on the location of the cursor within a document.

TABLE 2.1
Movement keys

PRESS	TO MOVE
↑	up one line
↓	down one line
←	left one character
→	right one character
PgUp	up one screen
PgDn	down one screen
End	to end of the line
Home	to beginning of the line
Ctrl →	one word to the right
Ctrl ←	one word to the left
Ctrl ↑	to beginning of the paragraph
Ctrl ↓	to beginning of the next paragraph
Ctrl PgUp	to top of the screen
Ctrl PgDn	to bottom of the screen
Ctrl Home	to beginning of the document
Ctrl End	to end of the document

The functions of the arrow keys and the PgUp and PgDn keys can be duplicated by mouse movements. The *scroll bar* is used to move the screen position with the mouse.

An important point to remember when using the mouse to move through your document is that, unlike when you use the keyboard, you are not changing the location of the cursor within the document. When you press ↓ or PgDn on the keyboard, you are forcing the cursor beyond the bottom of the screen; therefore, Word for Windows scrolls down to show you the new cursor position. This is not the case when you use the mouse to move through the document. Using the mouse changes the part of the document being displayed but does not affect the position of the cursor *until* the left mouse button is clicked with the mouse pointer in the work area. The cursor then moves to the position of the pointer when the mouse was clicked.

The scroll bar allows you to move three ways through a document: one line at a time, a screen at a time, and globally (through the entire document). To move up or down a line at a time, click the scroll bar's up arrow or down arrow, respectively. This is equivalent to pressing the keyboard's ↑ or ↓ arrows and is useful for moving short distances but inefficient for scrolling through large segments of text.

Elevator box

The functions of the PgUp and PgDn keys can also be duplicated by using the mouse with the scroll bar. Between the scroll bar's up and down arrows is a vertical strip with a box in it. The box is called the *elevator box* and represents the position of the screen you are viewing relative to the rest of the document. In the sample scroll bar, the user is viewing a screen of text approximately one-third of the way through the document. To perform the Page Up function, click anywhere in the vertical strip between the scroll bar's up arrow key and the elevator box. Page Down is performed by clicking between the elevator box and the scroll bar's down arrow. The screen will move up or down one screen height, respectively, and allow you to view other portions of your document.

One move function is available with the mouse and scroll bar that cannot be duplicated using the keyboard. The elevator box can be dragged directly with the mouse to any position in the vertical strip between the scroll bar's up and down arrows. You can immediately go to the top or bottom of the document, or anywhere in between, by dragging the elevator box to the top or bottom of the strip. This is called a *global move* and is very useful for moving large distances quickly.

GUIDED ACTIVITY 2.3

Moving Within a Document Using the Mouse

1. Click on the down arrow at the bottom of the scroll bar. The screen shifts down one line.

   When you use the scroll bar, the movement of the screen is independent of the location of the cursor. The cursor is still at the same position in the document.

2. Click in the area between the elevator box and the down arrow at the bottom of the scroll bar. The screen shifts down just as though you had pressed PgDn on the keyboard.

3. Click on the up arrow at the top of the scroll bar.

   The screen moves back up one line at a time.

4. Click in the area between the elevator box and the up arrow at the top of the scroll bar.

   This is the equivalent of pressing the PgUp key. Continue clicking in this area until the top of the document is displayed.

When using the scroll bar to move through a document, you are not using the cursor to move the screen. When you scroll using the scroll bar, the cursor remains in the last spot on the screen where you inserted or deleted text. If you edit a sentence on the last page and use the global move to move to the beginning of the document, although the first page is displayed, the cursor is still on the last page where you finished editing the sentence. This is the one major difference between using the keyboard and using the scroll bar to move through a document. When you use the scroll bar, the cursor remains at its last position until you click with the mouse pointer somewhere in the work area.

A touch typist can move around a document more quickly using the keyboard than the mouse, although using the mouse is more intuitive. Rather than having to remember what keys perform a function, many users find the mouse functions easier to recall.

Selecting Text

Many editing procedures will require you first to highlight (or select) various combinations of letters, words, lines, and paragraphs. Selecting may be done with the keyboard or the mouse.

When any amount of text is selected, any key that you press will replace the selected text. If that was the desired result, this feature is not a problem and is often beneficial. However, occasionally you may accidentally press a key with a large block of text highlighted, and the selected text will be replaced by the key you pressed. Do not panic. Should this happen, the deleted text may be retrieved with the Edit/Undo command or by clicking on the *Undo* button on the toolbar. Large blocks of selected text must be treated carefully to avoid losing them.

GUIDED ACTIVITY 2.4

Selecting Text Using the Keyboard

1. Make sure the cursor is just to the left of the letter A at the beginning of your document. Hold down the *Shift* key and press ⇥ once. The A is highlighted.

   At this point you could format the character by making it bold or underlined or by changing its font or point size. You could delete the character or replace it with other text.

2. Press ⇦ to remove the highlighting. Moving the cursor automatically removes the highlighting from text.

3. Hold down Shift and press ↓ to select the line. Keep holding down Shift and press the ↓ key or ↑ key to see how the highlighting is extended. Try holding down the Shift key and pressing PgUp and PgDn.

4. Remove the highlighting by releasing the Shift key and pressing any arrow key.

   Selecting text with the keyboard can take many taps of the arrow keys, but it is useful because of its precise control. Selecting text with the mouse is faster, but the user sometimes feels less control over the process.

GUIDED ACTIVITY 2.5

Selecting Text Using the Mouse

To highlight a single letter, position the mouse pointer to one side of it and drag to the other side of the character. The character will appear highlighted.

1. Select the letter m in the word major in the first line of your document. Position the mouse pointer directly to the left of the letter m and drag the pointer to the right of the letter. Remember that dragging requires that you hold down the mouse button while moving the mouse pointer. It may be difficult to highlight a single character using the mouse.

There is no difference between text selected with the arrow keys or with the mouse. At this point you could format the letter m by making it bold or under-lined or by changing its font or point size. You could delete the character or replace it with other text.

2. Double-click on the word major near the top of your document.

Individual words can be selected by positioning the mouse pointer anywhere over the word and double-clicking. Again, a word may be highlighted with either the arrow keys or the mouse.

To extend a selection, simply continue dragging the mouse.

3. Place the mouse over the middle of the word difference and begin dragging to the right. As you drag to extend the highlight into the next word, the highlight automatically extends back to the beginning of difference and continues to extend the highlight a word at a time. Remove the highlighting by clicking any-where on the document.

Some selection procedures require you to use [Ctrl].

4. Select the first sentence in your document by holding down [Ctrl] and clicking any-where on the sentence.

5. A single line of text is selected by clicking in the area to the left of the line. Click in this area to highlight the first line in your document.

 This selection technique requires you to click on the far left edge of the screen, outside the text area. You can tell when you are in the correct area because the mouse pointer will change from an I-beam to an arrow pointing up and to the right.

6. Select several lines in the document by clicking on the far left side of the screen and dragging carefully downward. *Watch out:* a fast mouse and a fast computer may quickly select more than you intend!

7. Double-click in the far left side of the screen to select an entire paragraph at once.

8. *Triple*-click on the far left side of the screen to highlight the entire document, or hold [Ctrl] and click in the left margin. This technique with the mouse has the same effect as selecting the command Edit/Select All.

9. Click once anywhere in the document to remove the highlighting.

A summary of the mouse actions to select certain parts of a document is given in Table 2.2.

Editing Text

Editing is the part of the word processing procedure that involves adding, delet-ing, modifying, and moving text that is already entered into a document. Editing

TABLE 2.2	TO SELECT	MOUSE ACTION
Selecting text with the mouse	Any amount of text	Drag over the text.
	Word	Double-click on the word.
	Sentence	Ctrl click on the sentence.
	Entire line	Click on left side of screen.
	Paragraph	Double-click on left side of screen or *triple*-click on the paragraph.
	Entire document	*Triple*-click on the left side of screen or Ctrl click on the left side of screen.

requires the two skills you have already learned in this unit: moving around the document and selecting text.

Once you have moved the screen to view an area of text that needs editing, the cursor is positioned by clicking with the mouse pointer in the work area. To add text, click on the point where the new text will be inserted, and begin typing. All characters to the right of the cursor will shift to the right to make room for the new text. The word processor is in the ***insert mode*** because the new text is inserted at the location of the cursor.

If you want the new text to replace the characters to the right of the cursor, you could use the ***overtype mode***. In the overtype mode, each character you type will replace the character to the right of the cursor. To change between the insert and overtype modes, press the ***Insert*** or Ins key (Ins) on the keyboard. When the word processor is in the overtype mode, the letters OVR appear in dark letters on the status bar at the bottom of the screen, as shown on Figure 2.1. Another way to change between overtype and insert mode is to double-click the OVR on the status bar. Use the mode that requires the fewest keystrokes and is most suited to the editing that you are doing.

FIGURE 2.1
Status bar showing OVR mode

Double-click to change mode.

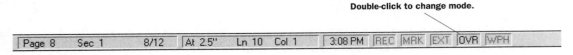

| Page 8 | Sec 1 | 8/12 | At 2.5" | Ln 10 | Col 1 | 3:08 PM | REC | MRK | EXT | OVR | WPH |

The bottom line on the screen is the status bar. It gives several different items of information used periodically during editing. The first area gives information about the text that is visible on screen. The second box shows the position of the cursor on the page. The third box shows the current time, keeping you from working on your document past your bedtime, and the last area has indicators for several modes, including the overtype mode just discussed.

GUIDED ACTIVITY 2.6

Overtype and Insert

1. Position the cursor to the left of the word The that starts the last sentence in your document. Make sure the letters OVR appear gray (dimmed), and not dark on the status bar. If they are dark, press ⟦Ins⟧ once to make OVR turn gray (dimmed). (Make sure the **Num Lock** key ⟦Num Lock⟧ is off if ⟦Ins⟧ is combined with a number key on the numeric keypad portion of the keyboard.)

2. Type in your name.

   The last sentence in the paragraph shifts to the right to make room for the new text you have typed in. This is the insert mode.

3. Switch to the overtype mode by pressing ⟦Ins⟧ once, or by double-clicking on the status bar where the gray letters OVR appear. Now OVR appears in dark letters on the status bar.

4. Watch the screen to see what happens during this step. Type in the following text:

   The word wrap feature is invaluable because it allows you to concentrate on what you are typing without having to worry about line endings.

   The last sentence in the document was replaced by the new text you entered. The overtype mode is very helpful when you want to replace old text with new in a single step.

Delete and Undo

After you have reviewed your document, you may want to delete a large block of text. You could use ⟦Backspace⟧ to remove the text one character at a time, but this is a slow way to work. A faster way is to remove the text all at once. This can be done easily by selecting the text and pressing the **Delete** or Del key (⟦Del⟧) on the keyboard.

The ⟦Del⟧ key can also be used to remove individual characters. However, it is different from the ⟦Backspace⟧ key in that it deletes characters to the right of the cursor instead of to the left.

One of the nicest features of most Windows applications is the first command located under the Edit menu. The Undo command allows you to change your mind and reverse the action. For example, if you delete a large segment of text and subsequently decide that you needed that text after all, you could select Edit/Undo to recover the text. The Undo command works to reverse formatting, changes, deletions, cuts, and pastes, and even typing. The action verb after the word Undo changes, based on the last thing you did.

The Undo button may be clicked once to undo the last action, or several times to undo the last several actions. If you click on the down arrow next to the Undo button, a list will drop down, showing the last 100 editing actions that you may undo in reverse order. Next to the Undo button is the Redo button that works in a similar way. If you Undo an action and change your mind, a single click on the Redo button reverses the undo. Clicking on the down arrow next to the Redo button drops down a list of actions. You can use the Undo and Redo buttons with typing, editing, and formatting actions, but not with some commands, such as printing and saving.

GUIDED ACTIVITY 2.7

Deleting and Undeleting

1. Highlight the entire last paragraph in your document. (Double-click in the area to the left of the paragraph.)

2. Press [Del] or choose the command Edit/Clear.

    The paragraph has been erased. If you change your mind, you can still retrieve it.

3. Click once on the Undo button.

    The paragraph reappears exactly as it was before [Del] was pressed. It is still high-lighted and ready for the next function you will perform.

Cut, Copy, and Paste

Several commands are used often in copying and moving highlighted portions of a document. To copy or move, first select the text, then issue the command Edit/Copy or Edit/Cut. Move the cursor to the new location where you would like the text to appear, and issue the command Edit/Paste.

These commands—Edit/Cut, Edit/Copy, and Edit/Paste—are so commonly used that Word provides four different ways to access these commands. The first way, of course, is to choose them from the Edit menu on the menu bar. Another way is to click on the buttons on the toolbar: Cut, represented by scissors; Copy, represented by two identical documents; and Paste, represented by a document on a clipboard.

Because these commands are so commonly used, Word also provides these on a *shortcut menu*, which is accessed by clicking the *right* mouse button within the document, as shown in Figure 2.2. In addition, for speed typists, there are key combinations, called *shortcut keys*, that can quickly perform certain commands. You already used the one for double-spacing: [Ctrl] 2. Many shortcut keys appear on the drop-down menus to the right of the command. The shortcut keys for Cut, Copy, and Paste are shown in Table 2.3. Word provides several methods for you to perform these common tasks, and you will likely learn to use the one that is simplest for you to remember and use.

Word includes a feature that allows you to move and copy text without using any menu or button commands. This feature is known as *drag-and-drop*. To move text using this method, you must first highlight it. Move the mouse pointer over the highlighted area so that it changes shape from the typical I-beam to an arrow. Drag the selection to a new location, and drop it there by releasing the mouse button. To copy instead of moving the selected text, press the [Ctrl] key on the keyboard while dragging the highlighted text.

FIGURE 2.2
The shortcut menu

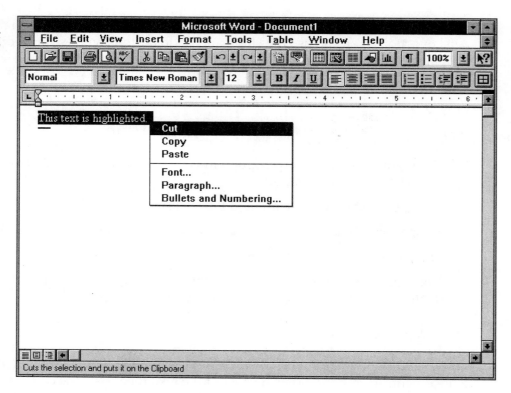

TABLE 2.3
Shortcut keys

TOOLBAR BUTTON	SHORTCUT KEY	COMMAND
	Ctrl X	Edit/Cut
	Ctrl C	Edit/Copy
	Ctrl V	Edit/Paste

GUIDED ACTIVITY 2.8

Copying and Moving

1. If the last paragraph is not highlighted, select it now.

2. Choose the command Edit/Copy.

   A copy of the paragraph is stored in the Clipboard.

3. Position the cursor at the beginning of the first line of the document. To insert at this location a copy of the material in the Clipboard, select Edit/Paste.

4. Click on the Undo button twice. Redo steps 2 and 3, accessing the commands from the shortcut menu by clicking the right mouse button with your middle or ring finger.

5. Press ⌨Enter once to leave a blank line between the paragraph you inserted and the original first paragraph in the document.

6. Position the cursor at the end of the last paragraph in the document. Press ⌨Enter twice to leave a blank line after this paragraph.

7. Click on the Paste button.

    The same paragraph you pasted at the beginning of the document is now duplicated at the end. You can paste as many copies of the text contained in the Clipboard as you like. Simply place the cursor where the new copy is to be inserted, and choose the Paste command or click on the Paste button.

    The Edit/Cut command works like Edit/Copy except that it does not leave the original in place. It removes the selected text and stores it in the Clipboard.

8. Select the second paragraph in the document (it should begin with `A major difference`). Select Edit/Cut.

    The paragraph disappears, but it has not been deleted. The Clipboard now contains the paragraph that was just cut. It will stay there until some other piece of text is cut or copied or until you exit Word for Windows. (Unlike Undo, the Clipboard holds only one block of text at a time.)

9. Position the cursor at the end of the line in the last paragraph in the document. Press ⌨Enter twice to leave a blank line.

10. This time use the shortcut key for Paste. Hold down ⌨Ctrl and press ⌨V.

    The paragraph that was cut in step 8 has been moved to the end of the document.

    Edit/Copy and Edit/Cut both place the selected text in the Clipboard. The text can then be pasted to the location of the cursor in the document. Edit/Copy does not affect the original selected item, whereas Edit/Cut removes it.

11. Highlight the paragraph that was pasted in step 10.

12. With the mouse directly over the highlighted text, press and hold down the left mouse button. Notice that the mouse pointer looks like an arrow with a dotted rectangle attached, as in Figure 2.3. With the mouse button held down, carefully drag the mouse pointer upward. As you do so, you will notice a dotted or gray insertion point move upward. Move this gray insertion point until it is just above the next paragraph. When you let go of the mouse button, the highlighted text is inserted at the location of the gray insertion point.

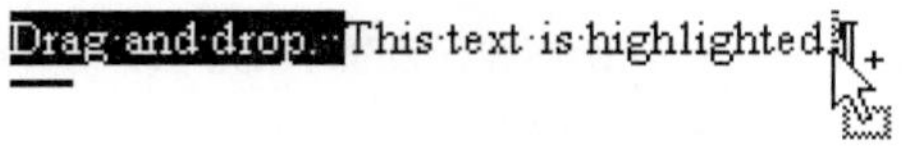

FIGURE 2.3
Using
drag-and-drop

Drag and drop. This text is highlighted.

Summary

In this unit you have learned that text is entered in much the same way it is typed on a typewriter. Errors made as you enter text can be corrected immediately with the [Backspace] key, or later with the [Del] key. After the text is entered, you can review the document by scrolling through it with the keyboard or the mouse. The arrow keys ([↑] [↓] [←] [→]) and page keys ([PgUp], [PgDn], [End], [Home]) are used to move with the keyboard. The scroll bar is used to navigate through a document with the mouse. Text can also be selected with the [Shift] and arrows keys or with the mouse. There are shortcuts for selecting words, lines, sentences, paragraphs, and the entire document, with the mouse.

Text is added to a document in the insert mode. The text will be inserted at the location of the cursor in the work area. Characters can be replaced by new text if the word processor is placed in the overtype mode.

The [Del] key is used to erase large blocks of selected text. Deleted text can be recovered with the Edit/Undo command or by clicking on the Undo button.

Finally, large blocks of text can be copied or moved to other locations in a document. The Edit/Copy command is used to make a duplicate of the selected characters to the Clipboard. The Edit/Cut command removes the selected text and places it in the Clipboard. Edit/Paste copies the contents of the Clipboard to the document at the location of the cursor. These commands may also be accessed from the shortcut menu, from buttons on the toolbar, and through shortcut keys. In addition, Word allows you to drag-and-drop text to a new location without using any menu commands or buttons.

Exercises

Each of the following exercises requires you to print. Before you print, make sure that a printer is attached to your computer and that the printer is on and has paper in it.

1. Create a new document by selecting File/New and clicking OK. Enter the following paragraph. Duplicate the paragraph twice. Print the document by clicking on the Print button on the toolbar.

    ```
    Word provides several ways to accomplish many commands. Com-
    mands are easily accessible from the menus at the top of
    the screen. Buttons on toolbars represent many common
    tasks. Shortcut menus contain some commands that are
    accessed without even reaching for the menu bar. Speed typ-
    ists may prefer to use shortcut keys to perform tasks with-
    out removing their hands from the keyboard.
    ```

2. Modify the top paragraph by changing the word accomplish to perform. Change the word several to various, using the overtype mode. Print the result.

3. Using Cut and Paste, move the entire sentence starting with `Buttons` to the end of the paragraph. Delete the second and third paragraphs from the document by highlighting both at the same time and pressing `Del`. Restore the deleted text without typing, then print the result.

4. Delete the extra paragraphs over again by using the Redo button. Enter a title at the bottom of the document on a line of its own: `Four Ways to Choose Commands`. Print the result.

5. Using drag-and-drop, move the title to the top of the document. Place a blank line between the title and the paragraph. Print the result.

Review Questions

*1. What are the three general procedures in word processing?

2. How is entering text on a word processor different from typing text on a typewriter?

*3. What keys are used to move through a document using the keyboard? What are their functions?

4. What screen area is used to move through a document with the mouse? How do the parts of this screen area work? What movement can you perform with the mouse that you cannot perform with the keyboard?

*5. What key is used in conjunction with the arrow keys and the page keys to select text with the keyboard?

6. What is the shortcut method to highlight a word with the mouse? To select a line? To select a sentence? To select a paragraph? To select the entire document?

*7. What is the difference between the insert and overtype modes? When is each used?

8. How is a block of text deleted? How can the action be reversed?

*9. Explain the functions of Edit/Cut, Edit/Copy, and Edit/Paste. What is the Clipboard?

10. What is the difference between using delete (Edit/Clear) and Edit/Cut?

*11. What are four methods to execute many commands?

Key Terms

Arrow keys   Global move   Page Up
Backspace   Home   Scroll bar
Control   I-beam   Shift
Delete   Insert   Shortcut key
Drag-and-drop   Insert mode   Shortcut menu
Elevator box   Num Lock   Undo
End   Overtype mode   Word wrap
Enter   Page Down

Documentation Research

1. What information appears on the status bar?

2. What is the shortcut key for the Edit/Undo command?

3. What is the horizontal scroll bar used for?

Documents and Disks

In the previous unit you entered and edited text in a document. This unit will cover how to use the File menu to create new documents, save completed documents, and retrieve previously saved documents from the computer's disk drives.

The first section will discuss what types of disks there are and the advantages of each type, how disks are prepared, and what conventions DOS requires for saving *documents*, called *files*, on disk.

The second section covers the commands available in the File menu used to manipulate Word for Windows documents on disk.

Learning Objectives

At the completion of this unit you should know

1. what kind of disks documents can be stored on,

2. how to prepare these disks for use,

3. how to use the File menu to create, open, close, and save files,

4. the parts of a dialog box,

5. how to work with several files at once.

Important Commands

Disk/Format Disk (this command is found in File Manager, not Word)

File/Close

File/New

File/Open

File/Save

File/Save As

Window/*filename*

Disks and File Names

Computers store information on magnetic storage devices called **disks**. Almost every application has some way to store the work you have done so that it does not have to be re-created every time the computer is turned back on. Using a computer disk is a fast, convenient way to store your work after it is created.

The computer reads a disk by placing a magnetic head very close to the disk's surface to read the information stored on it. Any contaminants on the surface of the disk will get caught between the surface and the head and will make a scratch on the disk. This will cause the disk to be damaged and information to be lost. Substances that can contaminate disks are dust, smoke, hair, and water. Just touching the surface of the disk can place skin oils on the disk surface that will damage it when the head passes over that point. It is very important to handle disks carefully to avoid damaging the surface.

Because a disk is magnetic, placing the disk near a magnetic field may damage the information stored on it. Magnetic fields may be found near many electrical devices such as vacuum cleaners, televisions, ringing telephones, and even improperly shielded computers and monitors.

Disks must be maintained in a temperature- and humidity-controlled environment. Hot temperatures will cause the disk to warp and the chemicals on its surface to degrade. Cold temperatures will destroy the lubricants inside the disk's outer case, preventing it from spinning correctly. Excessively dry or wet atmospheres will also adversely affect the disk and its case. Even taking a disk from a cold area to a hot one can cause condensation to form on the disk surface, creating potential problems if the disk is used immediately.

Finally, disks fail with age. After several years of continuous use a disk can lose information without warning. After the same surface is written to and read from many times it loses its ability to be magnetized properly.

After all this is known, it seems incredible that anyone would trust a valuable document to such a volatile storage medium. In reality, disk storage is extremely reliable. Billions of disks are used on a daily basis for years without any failure. However, you must remember the limitations of the storage media. The likelihood of loss of information can be reduced to almost zero by keeping a backup copy of your document on a different disk. You will learn to save your files on multiple disks in this unit.

Types of Disks

The two kinds of disk are removable disks and fixed disks. *Removable disks* (also called diskettes or floppy disks) are portable and can be used in many different computers. *Fixed disks* (also called hard disks) are attached to the inside of the computer and cannot be easily removed.

Removable disks come in two popular sizes, 3.5-inch and 5.25-inch. The 5.25-inch format has been popular for many years and is still available on many personal computers. The 3.5-inch format was introduced more recently and gained rapid popularity in the computer market. Purchasers of new computers usually have the option to install two *disk drives,* one each of the two sizes of floppy disks. Popular software is available on both sizes of disk, usually for no extra charge. Each size of removable disk also has two capacities, *high-capacity* and *low-capacity*, which will be discussed for each size below.

A *5.25-inch disk,* as shown in Figure 3.1, comes in a flexible exterior case and can hold either 360,000 characters or 1,200,000 characters. The capacity of computer storage devices is abbreviated, using metric suffixes. The letter K (for kilo) stands for 1,000 in the metric system, while the letter M (for mega) stands for 1,000,000. Roughly, a single character (such as any character that can be typed from the keyboard) equals a byte, abbreviated B. Using the abbreviations for kilobytes and megabytes, the capacities for the two kinds of 5.25-inch disk are 360KB (360,000 bytes) and 1.2MB (1,200,000 bytes), respectively. (All of these values are approximate—1KB, for example, is actually equal to 1,024 characters—but for convenience these numbers have been rounded to thousands and millions.) To get the higher capacity, you must purchase high-density disks. The large majority of the computers that can run Windows 3.1 and have 5.25-inch disk drives will be able to take advantage of the high-density disks.

FIGURE 3.1
5.25-inch disk

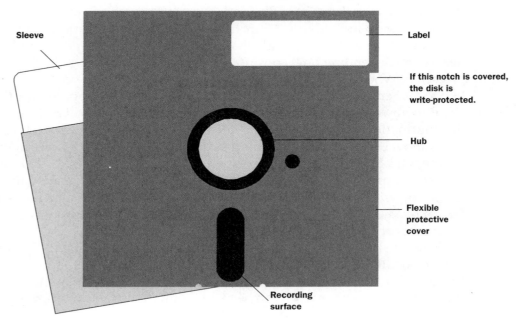

Sleeve

Label

If this notch is covered, the disk is write-protected.

Hub

Flexible protective cover

Recording surface

An advantage of using 5.25-inch disks is the large base of 5.25-inch drives that already exist in currently available microcomputers, plus the cheap price of the disks. However, the 3.5-inch disks hold more information and have a rigid exterior case, which makes them more durable. The outer case cannot be bent, unlike the 5.25-inch case. Additionally, when the 3.5-inch disk is removed from the computer, the disk itself is completely enclosed by the outer case, whereas parts of a 5.25-inch disk are always exposed to damage. The 3.5-inch disks are also smaller, which makes them easier to store and transport.

A *3.5-inch disk*, shown in Figure 3.2, also offers two capacities: 720KB and 1.44MB. You can tell that the disk in Figure 3.2 is high-density (1.44MB) from the letters "HD" and the extra square hole in the corner, which do not appear on a low-density disk. Unlike 5.25-inch disks, 3.5-inch disks when removed from the computer have a metal shutter that covers part of the otherwise exposed disk surface: when the disk is inserted into the drive, the shutter moves back to expose the disk to the drive head.

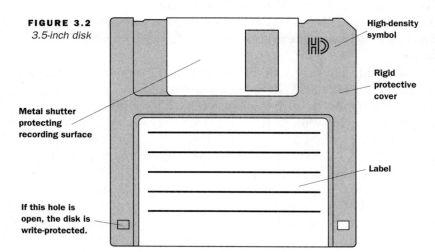

FIGURE 3.2
3.5-inch disk

High-density symbol

Rigid protective cover

Metal shutter protecting recording surface

Label

If this hole is open, the disk is write-protected.

Both disk formats have a mechanical means of preventing information from being written to or erased from the disk. To be able to write on a 5.25-inch disk, you must ensure that there is a notch on the side of the disk called the write-protect notch. To protect the information on the disk, you cover the notch with an adhesive strip. A disk with the strip in place over the notch is *write-protected*, that is, you cannot save information to it. A 3.5-inch disk may also be write-protected. On the back of the disk is a small plastic slide that either covers or uncovers a small hole in the disk cover, depending on its position. If the hole is uncovered, the disk is write-protected. When the slide is moved and the hole is covered, you can write information to and erase information from the disk. The disk can be permanently write-protected by removing the slide tab from its hole: the hole will be left uncovered and the information on the disk will be safe as long as the disk is in good condition.

Removable disks are useful for transferring information from one computer to another and for making backup copies of documents. However, fixed disks can retrieve information more quickly and hold much more information than removable disks. You will spend less time waiting for a document to be saved to or retrieved from a fixed disk than a removable disk. The fixed disk spins more quickly; thus, the computer can get the information from it in less time.

Fixed disks come in many different sizes, from 20MB (roughly 20 million characters) to 300MB, 600MB, and even larger sizes. This is many times more storage than that found in a removable disk. However, the fixed disk is not removable from the computer. Unless your work can be moved onto removable disks, you must complete it on the same computer. Not all computers have a fixed disk, but you can use Windows on a computer only if the computer has such a disk.

Preparing Removable Disks for Use

Before you can use a new removable disk, you must *format* it. Formatting prepares a disk so that the drive in the computer can read from and write to it. If a disk is not formatted, the computer will be unable to use it for storage.

There are two ways to format disks on your computer, from the Windows File Manager and from DOS (the IBM-compatible Disk Operating System). Both methods will prepare the disk exactly the same way.

GUIDED ACTIVITY 3.1

Formatting Disks

CAUTION   *Formatting erases all information on the disk, so do not do this activity if you have data on your disk you wish to keep.*

1. Start Windows. If you have already started Word for Windows, minimize it by clicking on the down arrow at the top-right corner of the screen.

2. Restore the Program Manager if it is minimized to an icon by double-clicking on it.

3. Open the Main program group by double-clicking on the Main icon in the Program Manager.

Main

4. Double-click on the File Manager icon to start the File Manager, as shown in Figure 3.3. What you see listed will not match the figure.

FIGURE 3.3
File Manager

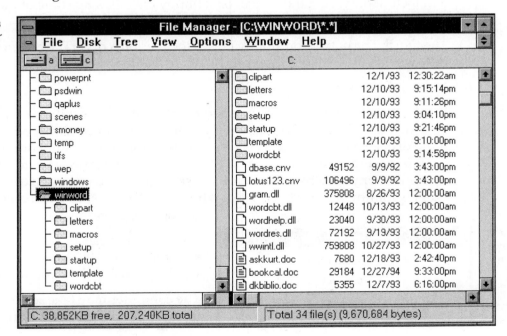

File
Manager

There are many functions available in the File Manager. We will use File Manager only to format a disk.

5. Select Disk/Format Disk from the menu bar of the File Manager.

The Format Disk dialog box will appear, as in Figure 3.4.

Drive A: is usually the left or top drive on the computer.

File Manager now offers you the option to create a low-capacity or a high-capacity disk in any of the drives available on your computer. Depending on the size of your disk, you may select either 1.44MB or 720KB (for 3.5-inch disks) or 1.2MB or 360KB (for 5.25-inch disks). To format a 5.25-inch disk using the high- capacity option, the disk itself must be high-density. This term will appear on the box the disk came in or on the manufacturer's label. Disks formatted to the lower capacities will be accessible to most computers. To make sure a disk can be used in a particular computer, format the disk in that computer.

FIGURE 3.4
The Format Disk dialog box

Format Disk		
Disk In:	Drive A: ↕	OK
Capacity:	1.44 MB ↕	Cancel
Options		Help
Label: [ ]		
☐ Make System Disk		
☐ Quick Format		

The Make System Disk option is used to format the disk as a *system disk*; that is, operating system files are incorporated into the disk while it is being formatted. A system disk, placed in drive A: before the computer is turned on, is capable of starting the computer. Since the computer that you are working on probably starts from a hard disk, you will ordinarily not need to format disks with the system included. Placing the system on a floppy disk uses up some of the storage capacity that would otherwise be available on it.

The Quick Format option simply erases the files on a disk. The command will only work if the disk has been previously formatted.

6. Insert your disk and click on OK.

If your disk has not been previously formatted, Windows will begin formatting your data disk in the drive, showing you the dialog box illustrated in Figure 3.5. If the disk has been formatted before, you will see the Confirm Format Disk dialog box, asking if you are sure you want to format the disk. Since formatting the disk erases any data contained on the disk, it gives you one more chance to change your mind before formatting. If you click on Yes, you will then see the dialog box in Figure 3.5.

FIGURE 3.5
The Formatting Disk dialog box

If you want to cancel, click on Cancel to stop the format. If you do cancel, the disk will be unusable until you format it again.

The computer may take several minutes to format your disk. It is checking the entire

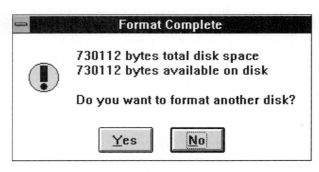

usable surface of the disk for imperfections. If it finds any spots on the disk that are bad, it will inform you (and quarantine them from being used). When the computer has successfully formatted the disk, Windows will ask if you have another disk to format, as in Figure 3.6.

7. Click on No and close the File Manager by double-clicking on the Control-menu box in the upper-left corner of the File Manager window.

The disk is now formatted and prepared for the computer to store information on it.

Files and File Names

Files are identified on disk by the *file name* and *extension*. The file name is usually a word that represents something about the file being stored, one unique to that file. For example, the first assignment for a class may be saved as CLSASG1. The more representative of the file the file name is, the easier the file will be to find and retrieve later.

DOS limits file names to no more than eight characters, and some characters cannot be included in the file name. Certain symbols, such as %, space, and period (.), cannot be part of a DOS file name because they have special significance for DOS. In general, limit your file names to letters, digits, dashes, and underscores. When you type in an invalid file name, Word for Windows will warn you and request another name.

The extension is the second item that identifies your file on disk, and consists of up to three characters. Unlike the file name, extensions are not unique to individual files. Extensions often serve to group files into categories. For example, all Word for Windows documents have the extension .DOC. Excel spreadsheets have the extension .XLS.

The file name and extension, separated by a period, are put together to identify files on disk. If you created a letter in Word for Windows and called it LETT1, DOS would identify it by LETT1.DOC on disk. However, when you are saving documents in Word for Windows, you will not have to enter the extension. The word processor appends the extension .DOC automatically to the name you give the file.

The File Menu

The Word for Windows commands dealing with files are located on the File menu, as shown in Figure 3.7. This menu allows you to create new documents, open documents already on disk, save documents you have created or edited, and close documents. These commands are also represented in graphical form, accessible with a click of the mouse, and with shortcut keys, summarized in Table 3.1. These commands are listed in a certain logical order, but people may actually use these commands in a different order. Word starts with a blank document on screen, and users often just begin typing. The first command needed, then, is File/Save, to keep a permanent copy of a document.

File/Save

The File/Save command saves the active document being viewed on the screen under the name that appears in the window title bar. However, when you first create a document, it does not have a name. Word for Windows gives it the default name Document1. When you select File/Save for a document that does not have a name, Word for Windows executes instead the File/Save As command.

Notice on the File menu that the Save As command is followed by ellipses (. . .). This means that Word will open a *dialog box*, shown in Figure 3.8, asking for further information before it can perform the command.

Dialog boxes occur with many commands, and have several elements that are commonly found. You will generally see *command buttons*, which perform an action (such as OK or Cancel), or which open yet another dialog box (such as Help). A *text box* allows you to type or edit information. *List boxes* appear already displayed or will drop down as you click on an arrow. Not shown in the dialog box in Figure 3.8 are *tabs* to see other sets of options and *check boxes* and *option buttons* you may click to select or clear an option.

File/Save As stores the document in the active window under a name supplied by the user. You must type a name in the File Name text box in the Save As dialog box in order to name the document and save it to disk. The name that you enter is then placed in the Word for Windows title bar. Subsequent File/Save commands will save the document under the same name.

The File/Save As command is also used when you have opened an existing document from disk, have modified it, and now want to save it under a different name. If you selected File/Save, the original document on disk would be replaced by the modified version. To preserve the original, use the File/Save As command to store the modified document under a different name. The File/Save As dialog box allows you to enter a name for the file and choose what disk drive to store it on, as in Figure 3.8.

File	Edit	View
New...		Ctrl+N
Open...		Ctrl+O
Close		
Save		Ctrl+S
Save As...		
Save All		
Find File...		
Summary Info...		
Templates...		
Page Setup...		
Print Preview		
Print...		Ctrl+P
Exit		

TABLE 3.1
Shortcut keys

SHORTCUT KEY	COMMAND
Ctrl N	File/New
Ctrl O	File/Open
Ctrl S	File/Save

FIGURE 3.8
The File/Save As dialog box

Text box

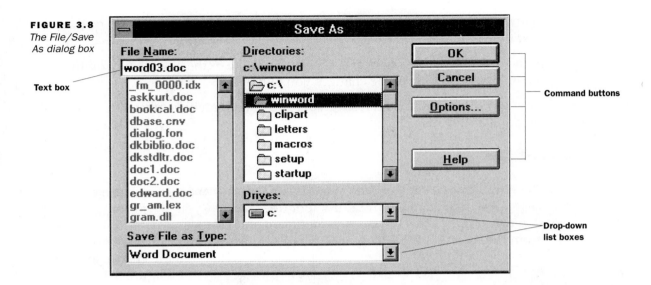

Command buttons

Drop-down list boxes

GUIDED ACTIVITY 3.2

Saving Files

1. Start Word for Windows. Place your formatted disk in drive A:.

   A new document is displayed. It has not been saved, so it has no name. The title bar displays Document1 to reflect this.

2. Enter your name.

   Word for Windows knows that you have now made changes to this document. The word processor will not let you close the document without warning you that the changes will be lost unless the document is saved.

3. Select File/Save.

   Instead of selecting the command from the menu, you may click on the File/Save button or use the shortcut key Ctrl S . Word for Windows checks for the name of the document. When it discovers that the document is not yet named, it executes instead the File/Save As command.

4. Enter the file name ONE, then select drive A: in the Drives box. To do this, click on the down arrow to drop down the list of available drives. The drives are listed in alphabetical order. You may need to use the scroll bar to display drive A:. Click on a: to highlight it and press Enter or click on OK. If the Summary Information dialog box appears, click OK.

   As the file is saved, the status bar displays a message and a graphical representation of the save process from start to finish. After the file is saved, the cursor returns to the place you left it in the document. In the title bar, the name ONE.DOC appears. The file was saved on the disk in drive A: because you selected that drive. You could have selected any of the disk drives from the list available. However, placing a document on the hard disk of a computer other than your own is not recommended, because the document may not be there the next time you are.

5. In the document, press [Enter] and type in the name of the city where you live. Select File/Save to save the changes you just made.

    Now Word for Windows can save your file immediately because the document already has a name.

File Close

The File/Close command removes the active document from the screen. This does not erase the document from disk, nor does it cause you to exit from Word for Windows. It simply takes the current document and removes it both from memory and from the screen. If the document has not yet been saved, Word will give you one more chance to save, as in Figure 3.9.

FIGURE 3.9
The save changes dialog box

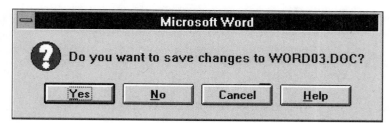

If you click on No to close the document without saving it, the document will be permanently erased or any changes you made since last saving it will be lost.

If you click on Yes, and the document already has a name, Word for Windows will execute the File/Save command and save the document before closing it. If the document has not yet been saved and does not have a name, the File/Save As command will be executed, and Word for Windows will prompt you for a name for the file and the disk drive on which to save it before closing it.

GUIDED ACTIVITY 3.3

Closing Files

1. Press the [Spacebar] to make a change to the document, then close the document by selecting File/Close.

    Word for Windows attempts to close the document, discovers that it has not been saved, and gives you a chance to save the changes.

2. Click on Yes.

    Word saves the file and removes the ONE document from the screen.

    Now that the document has been closed, Word is left with no document to work with. Consequently, the only menu commands that are available are File and Help. All the other commands are used only within documents.

File Open

The File/Open command is used to retrieve a document that has previously been saved to disk, as shown in Figure 3.10. It can be accessed from the menu bar or with the File/Open button on the toolbar, or with the shortcut key Ctrl O. Notice that the command is followed by ellipses (. . .), which means you will need to supply additional information in a dialog box.

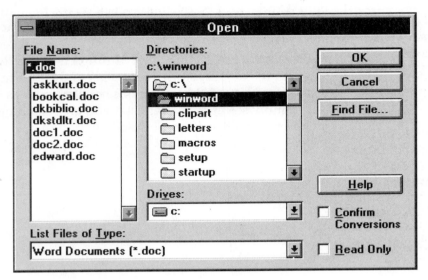

FIGURE 3.10
The File/Open dialog box

The Open dialog box contains these main areas: a File Name text box containing a description of the type of files being displayed, a list of files matching the description, a list of available directories, and a list of available drives.

The text box that describes the files being listed contains the characters *.DOC. The asterisk (*) is called a *wild card* and can be replaced by any file name. This means that in the File Name box Word will display all file names with a .DOC extension. Word for Windows documents all end with the extension .DOC, so this description will display Word for Windows documents. Files created with another word processor could be listed by changing the extension in the description. For example, a list of Microsoft Works documents could be displayed with the extension *.WPS because .WPS is the extension used with Works documents. You may type into the text box the name of the file you wish to open, but it is often easier to select the file name directly from the list box.

NOTE *File names and extensions are shown in lowercase letters in the Open dialog box. In this book, they are printed in uppercase for readability.*

The File Name box displays a list of files matching the description in the text box. You may scroll through the list of files by clicking on the up and down arrows to the right of the File Name box or by dragging the elevator box up or down the scroll bar.

The Directories box shows what directories are available for document storage and the current directory.

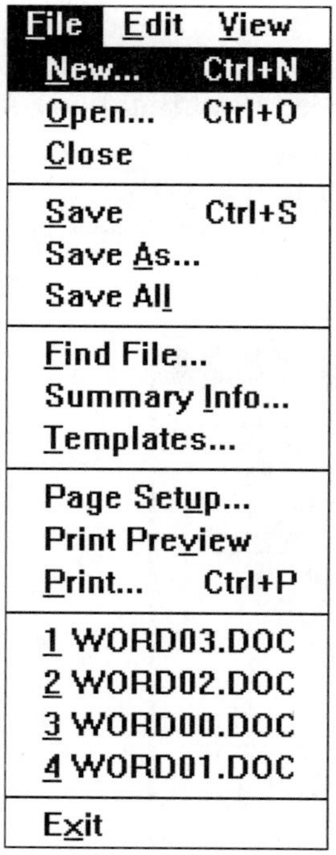

FIGURE 3.11
*The four most
recently used
files*

File	**Edit**	**View**
New...		**Ctrl+N**
Open...		**Ctrl+O**
Close		
Save		**Ctrl+S**
Save As...		
Save All		
Find File...		
Summary Info...		
Templates...		
Page Setup...		
Print Preview		
Print...		**Ctrl+P**
1 WORD03.DOC		
2 WORD02.DOC		
3 WORD00.DOC		
4 WORD01.DOC		
Exit		

The Drives box shows which drives are available on your computer. Probable disk drives will be A:, B:, C:, or D:. Computers attached to a local area network may have more drives available.

Once you have selected the proper drive and directory, and see the name of the file you wish to open on the list, all you need to do to open the file is click on the file name to highlight it and click OK, or double-click on the file name.

Word provides users many handy shortcuts for working. Users commonly modify a document that was recently closed. Rather than forcing you to look through lists of drives, directories, and file names, Word keeps a list of the four most recently used documents at the bottom of the File menu, as in Figure 3.11. Simply select from that list if you are searching for a document recently created or modified.

GUIDED ACTIVITY 3.4

Opening Files

1. Select File/Open.

2. When the Open dialog box appears, select drive A: in the Drives box by clicking on the arrow next to the Drives box and selecting a : .

3. When the list of documents on drive A: appears, double-click on ONE.DOC in the File Name box, or you may click on the file name, then click OK.

   You opened the file ONE from the disk in drive A:. You could have viewed a list of the files on any drive by selecting the disk drive, and then double-clicking on the name of the file to open.

4. Press [Spacebar] once.

   Although this is just a single character, it is a change to your document. Word for Windows will not let you close this document without its first warning you to save the changes.

5. Double-click on the Control-menu box in the top-left corner of the Word for Windows window to exit the word processor.

   Exiting Word for Windows automatically closes your document, so Word for Windows gives you a warning.

6. Click on Yes to save the document.

   Word for Windows will close, returning you to the Program Manager.

7. Start Word for Windows again.

8. Select the word File on the menu to drop down the File menu.

    At the bottom of the menu, above the Exit command, is a list of recent documents.

9. Select the top one—ONE.DOC— by clicking on it.

    Now the document is open on the screen again.

File New

Word for Windows allows you to have several documents open at the same time. You may view them one at a time or simultaneously, depending on your needs. When you are working on a document and need to create a new one, select the command File/New, which opens the New file dialog box, shown in Figure 3.12.

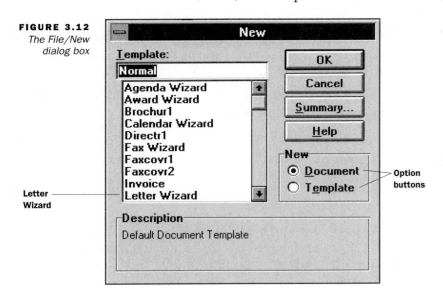

FIGURE 3.12
The File/New
dialog box

Letter
Wizard

The first section in the dialog box determines what kind of file will be opened. A document is a normal word processing file, one that will be unique and used for only one purpose. A *template* is a form document that is used many times and has spaces in it for variable information. A form letter that is sent on a regular basis can be saved as a template, allowing you to enter the name and address of the person to whom it is being sent without having to type the rest of the letter.

When you select the File/New command from the menu to begin a document, Word suggests the NORMAL template, an empty template that sets up normal margins, page size, font, and size. Word provides several other templates that allow you to create and format documents quickly. Many of these templates come with wizards. Using a *wizard* is probably the simplest way to create a document. A wizard asks a series of questions and sets up the document according to your specifications.

 The File/New button on the toolbar immediately opens a document using the NORMAL template without viewing the dialog box. The shortcut key Ctrl N acts the same way as the button.

Using File/New or File/Open while a document is already in the work area opens an additional document without closing the first one. The original document is merely hidden behind the *active document*, or latest document. Commands on the Window menu, shown in Figure 3.13, allow you to view the names of all the *open documents*, to bring another document to the front so that it becomes the active one (the New Window option), and to display more than one document at a time in the work area (the Arrange All option). The file names are listed with the most recently opened document listed first. The active document is marked with a check ✓ next to its name. Having more than one document open makes it simple for you to copy information from one document to another.

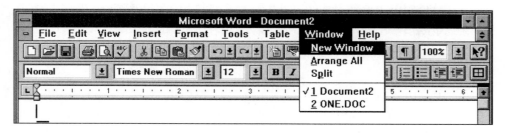

GUIDED ACTIVITY 3.5

Working with More than One Document

1. With the ONE.DOC file already on the screen, select the File/New command to create a new document. Press 🄴🄽🅃🄴🅁 to use the NORMAL template.

   A blank document appears on the screen. Your other document is not gone from the screen; it is simply hidden behind the new one.

2. Enter your street address.

   You now have two documents open at the same time. The Window menu will show you what documents are open.

3. Click on the Window menu.

   The bottom of the menu displays the names of the two documents you have created. You can tell that one has not been saved because it has the name given by Word for Windows: Document, followed by a number. You can also tell which document is active by the check.

4. Select the file name ONE.DOC by clicking on it.

   Immediately, ONE.DOC becomes the active document and is displayed on screen, hiding the other document from sight.

   You can copy information from one document to another using Edit/Copy and Edit/Paste.

5. Select the text in the document and select Edit/Copy.

6. Click on the Window menu and switch to the other document, Document2, by clicking on its name.

7. With the new document now the active one, issue the Edit/Paste command, and the information is transferred to the new document.

8. To view both documents at once, select the command Window/Arrange All.

Both documents are visible on screen. Each document is contained in a separate window with separate title bars, rulers, and scroll bars. You can tell which document is the active document by the color of the title bar.

With both documents visible, you can use drag-and-drop to move information from one document to another.

9. Highlight text in the active document and, with the mouse pointer over the highlighted area, drag it to the document in the other window.

10. To view only one document on screen at once, click on the maximize button at the right side of the title bar of the desired document.

The Automatic Save Feature

Anyone who has worked on personal computers for any length of time knows that, for one reason or another, on occasion, they temporarily stop working. You may call this "freezing," or "locking up," or any of several other colorful terms. Power may even suddenly go out. When this happens, the information you were working on, regardless of the application, is usually gone, and you will need to completely redo any work you have done since the last time you saved. This often causes wailing and gnashing of teeth, and, at worst, tragically loses what you wrote in a rare flash of brilliance.

Word for Windows has a feature called Automatic Save, accessed from the File/Save As dialog box. This feature automatically saves your document after a time period you determine. If you turn on the feature and select five minutes, every five minutes Word will save your document. The time period you pick is entirely up to you. If you are a fast typist, the period should probably be relatively short. If it takes you several minutes to type a sentence or paragraph, the period could be longer.

To turn on Automatic Save, select File/Save As, and click on the Options button on the dialog box. The Save tab of the Options dialog box appears, as shown in Figure 3.14.

Click the up or down arrow in the box to the right of the Automatic Save Every____ Minutes section to set the number of minutes in the Automatic Save period. Click OK to exit the Options dialog box and click Close to exit the Save As dialog box. Your document will now be saved automatically after every time period you specified.

You must still save the file yourself when finished with it (or before you answer the phone or go to lunch) by selecting File/Save or clicking the Save button on the toolbar. Using Automatic Save will just prevent the tragedy of lost information in case of unforeseen circumstances.

GUIDED ACTIVITY 3.6

Using Automatic Save

1. Open a new document and type your name. Select File/Save As, and click on the Options button.

FIGURE 3.14
*The Save
Options
dialog box*

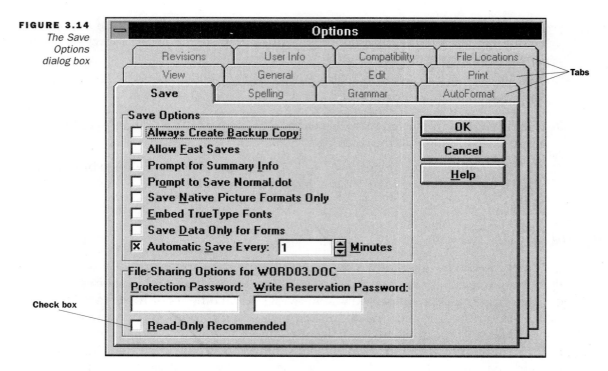

2. Set the Automatic Save period to 1 minute and click OK. Click on Close (not OK) to exit the Save As dialog box.

3. Wait at least two minutes without touching the keyboard or mouse. The status bar will briefly display a message telling you it is autosaving. After this occurs, turn off the computer.

4. Turn the computer back on and start Word for Windows.

   Your document will appear in the work area, and the title bar will show that the document was recovered. You may now save the document under any name you like.

   The Automatic Save feature will prove to be invaluable. It is a fast, efficient means of making sure that you lose very little information in case of a power failure or a personal computer mishap. It is recommended that you set this feature once and leave it on permanently.

5. Choose File/Close as many times as you need to close all the open documents.

Summary

Disks are a magnetic storage medium used to store information from computer applications. Two types of disks are available: removable and fixed. Many environmental factors cause a disk to fail, although proper handling and backups can virtually eliminate data loss.

Removable (floppy) disks come in two popular sizes, 3.5-inch and 5.25-inch, and various densities. Many computers offer drives in both sizes. Removable disks can be taken easily from one computer to another. Fixed (hard) disks are installed in only one computer and are not easily transportable, but they hold much more information than removable disks. The information on a fixed disk can be retrieved more quickly than information from removable disks.

DOS identifies files by two items: the file name and the extension. The file name is unique to each file, and the extension is often used to group types of files together.

Word for Windows manipulates files by commands in the File menu. File/New is used to create new documents and to access templates and wizards. File/Open opens a file that was previously saved to disk. File/Close removes the current document from the screen and from memory. File/Save saves the current file under the name in the title bar of the window. File/Save As saves the current file under a new name that you supply. The Automatic Save feature automatically saves your document to keep you from losing any changes if your personal computer shuts down for any reason.

Exercises

1. Try out the Letter Wizard by selecting the File/New command from the menu, and double-clicking on Letter Wizard. Select a prewritten business letter, then click on the Next button. Select the letter of your choice, or choose Letter to Mom and click Next. On the next screen, click on the Plain Paper and then the Letterhead selections to see the difference in the sample document. Click Next twice, then type the return address and the recipient's address in the boxes provided, then press Next. Select the Classic look, then click on the Finish button. View the document on screen and replace the information in square brackets or underlined to customize the letter and print. Save the document as A:EX3_1 (for Exercise 1 in Unit 3, stored on a floppy disk in drive A:) and close it.

2. Open the file A:EX3_1, which you created in Exercise 1. Place your name and the date on a new line at the top of the document. Save the file as A:EX3_2. In the Save As dialog box, click the Options button and turn on the Always Create Backup Copy feature. Click OK to return to the Save As dialog box, and click OK again to save the document under the new name.

3. This exercise will demonstrate the method used to recover a file from a backup created by the Create Backup feature. With the document from Exercise 2 open, highlight the entire document and press [Del]. Save the document.

    You have now stored the changes that you made (deleting text in the document). You cannot open A:EX3_2 to restore the original document because you saved the changes to disk. However, if Create Backup is turned on, Word for Windows saves the previous version of the document under the same file name with the extension .BAK. Open the document with the name A:EX3_2.BAK. This name will not appear in the list because it does not have a .DOC extension. Type the entire file name, A:EX3_2.BAK, in the File/Open dialog box and press ⌜Enter⌝. The text that you "accidentally" deleted has been restored.

A disadvantage of using the Create Backup feature is that each file is stored twice on disk, so only half as many documents will fit in the same amount of disk space.

4. Create a new, blank document. Arrange both documents on screen at once, using the command Window/Arrange All. Use drag-and-drop or Edit/Cut and Edit/Paste to move the text of the letter in the file EX3_2.BAK to the new document. Print the result. Close the documents, and do not save any changes.

5. You decide to begin a catalog of your videotape library. Each videotape will be stored in an individual file using the following format:

```
Title:
Director:
Starring:
Year Produced:
Rated:
Length:
Summary:
```

Create a document template containing the above information so that you do not have to enter it each time you add a videotape to the library. To save a document as a template, from the File/Save As dialog box, choose Document Template from the list under Save File as Type. Use the name VIDEO to save the file. Close the file after saving it.

Create a new document that uses the new template you created by selecting VIDEO from the list of templates instead of NORMAL. Fill in the information for a movie you have seen, and save the file under a file name representative of the title of the movie. Close the file.

Create files for four different movies. Print each file before saving and closing it.

6. Make a backup copy of your removable disk using the Disk/Copy Disk command in the File Manager. You will need a second disk that is blank and formatted. This step should be repeated periodically to make sure you don't lose information if your primary removable disk fails.

Review Questions

*1. Why are disks used to store information? So you can retrive info.

2. What is the difference between removable and fixed disks? Is one better than the other? 3.5 5.25

*3. What types of removable disks are available? What are the advantages and disadvantages of each type? How much information can be stored on each type?

4. What types of environmental factors can damage a disk?

*5. How can you prevent information from being erased from or changed on removable disks? *write protect notch*

6. What is the significance of the Make System Disk check box in the Format Disk dialog box of the File Manager? What is the difference between a high-capacity and a low-capacity format? What program group is the File Manager in?

*7. What limitations does DOS place on file names? *8 char. no special char.*

8. What are extensions often used for? *gives you options*

*9. What is the difference between the File/New command and pressing the File/New button on the toolbar? *normal*

10. What happens when you attempt to close a file that has not been saved? What command does Word for Windows execute if you then elect to save the file?

*11. What command does Word for Windows execute if you select the command File/Save for a document that has not been saved (that is, does not have a name)? *asks you if you want to save.*

12. What is a wizard? What wizards are available with File/New?

*13. What is a template? Why would you want to create a template? *common doc. easier - like a outline*

14. What are some elements of a dialog box?

*15. What part of the File/Save As dialog box and File/Open dialog box contains a list of the drives available on the computer? *The list of drives available on comp.*

Key Terms

3.5-inch disk	Extension	Option button
5.25-inch disk	File	Removable disk
Active document	File name	System disk
Check box	Fixed disk	Tab
Command button	Format	Template
Dialog box	High-capacity disk	Text box
Disk	List box	Wild card
Disk drive	Low-capacity disk	Wizard
Document	Open document	Write-protected

Documentation Research

1. How do you save a document into the WordPerfect file format?

2. How can you protect a document so that others cannot make changes?

Using Basic Word Processing Skills

1. Create a new document. Select an article from a newspaper or magazine that contains at least two pages of text, and enter it into your document.

    When entering the text, do not press `Enter` at the end of each line. Let the word wrap feature automatically move the text to the next line when it will not fit on the current line. Use `Enter` only at the end of paragraphs.

    If you need to correct a word you have just typed, use `Backspace` to delete characters and retype the word.

    You may make mistakes and not catch them until you are a few lines down in the document. Rather than use `Backspace` to delete all the text back to the error, use the arrow keys or the mouse to position the cursor at the location of the error. Use `Del`, `Backspace`, and `Ins` appropriately to correct the error. Remember that `Backspace` erases characters to the left of the cursor, while `Del` removes text to the right of the cursor.

2. Highlight the first paragraph and delete it. Use the Edit/Undo command to bring it back. Edit/Undo tries to undo the last command you performed, regardless of its nature.

3. The first paragraph should still be highlighted. Copy it to the end of the document.

4. Move the second paragraph to the beginning of the document. Make sure to adjust paragraph symbols (¶) so that there is one and only one blank line between all the paragraphs in the document.

5. Save the document by selecting File/Save and typing A:APPA as the file name. Type the file name with no spaces between the characters. This command will require a formatted disk in drive A: of the computer. If you are storing files on the hard disk of the computer, type C:APPA for the file name. Remember that storing files on a hard disk that is not yours is risky at best, since the files may not be there when you need them later. Make sure to save the document before performing the next step. It is always a good idea to save before attempting any other major function.

6. After saving, print the document (assuming that your printer is ready) by selecting File/Print and pressing `Enter`.

Proofing Tools

After you have entered and edited a document, Word for Windows 6.0 gives you the ability to check the spelling of every word typed. This automates one of the proofreading tasks you need to perform when creating a document. The spelling checker has a large dictionary against which it checks each word.

While a document is being written, in the flurry of creativity, it is easy to make grammatical errors. While the spelling checker picks up most spelling and typographical errors, it ignores even the most obvious grammatical error. Word provides a grammar checker to uncover not only mistakes in grammar, but also errors in style, and to give suggestions for changes.

Using certain words many times throughout a document can make the text seem repetitive. A thesaurus can be used to find synonyms for words that are used often in a document. Word for Windows has a built-in thesaurus to give help finding synonyms.

All of these features make it easier for you to create a better document. They will not guarantee an error-free document for you, but each makes the proofreading process go more smoothly. This unit will cover the use of the spelling checker, the grammar checker, and the thesaurus.

Learning Objectives

At the completion of this unit you should know

1. how to check the spelling of a document in parts or in its entirety,

2. how to use the AutoCorrect feature,

3. the limitations of the spelling checker,

4. how to use the grammar checker,

5. how to find synonyms for words.

Important Commands

Tools/AutoCorrect

Tools/Grammar

Tools/Spelling

Tools/Thesaurus

The Spelling Checker

When a document is first created, it is easy to miss simple typographical mistakes that occurred when entering the text. Part of the proofreading procedure should be to thoroughly review the document for these mistakes. For some reason, however, it is difficult to spot mistakes on the computer screen. To reduce the number of errors that you must catch, Word for Windows provides a *spelling checker* to check single words, a selected part of a document, or an entire document.

The spelling checker will check a segment of selected text. If no text is selected, the spelling checker will check every word in a document. Word for Windows compares each word against entries in its *dictionaries*, and if it finds a word in the document that does not occur in its dictionaries, a dialog box appears. At this point the user can type in the correct spelling, select from suggested alternatives, ignore it (that is, accept it), or add the word to the dictionaries. Word uses two types of dictionaries to search for correct spellings: the main dictionary and a custom dictionary. The standard custom dictionary is CUSTOM.DIC, but you may use a different custom dictionary that you create or purchase.

The spelling checker is accessed through the command Tools/Spelling, or by clicking the Spell Check button.

Checking a Single Word

1. Start Word for Windows. Type in the following text exactly as it appears. There are some errors. Do not correct them while you type.

   In Great Britain, one of the hihgest grossing films of the late 80's was the British-made science ficttion thrilller *Modavi Registrar*. In the United States, the choice was *Life of Kilarney*, a ronantic comedy set in Boston. Both movies won international acclaim, yet neither film was a financial success outside its home country. Futhermore, on a list of the top ten movies of the 80's, neither filme earned a spot. Success at home was not enough to overcome weakneses in the international market.

```
The topgrossing movies of the 80's were films with appeel
to audiences all over the world, regardless of differences
in economics or sociel structure. In this paper, we'll look
at some of those films, audiance reactions to them, and pos-
sible reasons for their intwrnational success.
```

2. After entering the text, you discover that you are unsure of the spelling of the word `neither` in the third sentence. Select `neither` by double-clicking with the mouse pointer anywhere on the word.

3. Select the command Tools/Spelling.

    You may also press the Spell Check button on the toolbar anytime to replace the Tools/Spelling command. Word looks up the word in both its standard dictionary and any custom dictionaries selected.

    Since the word was found in the main dictionary, it is spelled correctly.

4. Word now asks whether you wish to continue to check spelling, as shown in Figure 4.1. Click on No.

FIGURE 4.1
Spell check finished

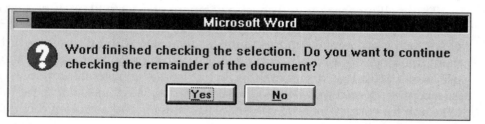

5. Double-click the misspelled word `ronantic` in the second sentence.

6. Select Tools/Spelling or click the Spell Check button on the toolbar.

    Since the word is misspelled, it was not found in the spelling dictionaries. Word for Windows offers a list of suggestions for the word you intended to type, as shown in Figure 4.2. Most of the time, the first word in the list is correct. If there is more than one suggestion, you can click on the up and down arrows to the right of the Suggestions box to scroll through the list of possibilities.

FIGURE 4.2
The Spelling dialog box

Spelling: English (US)

Not in Dictionary:	ronantic
Change To:	romantic
Suggestions:	romantic

Ignore   Ignore All
Change   Change All
Add   Suggest

Add Words To: CUSTOM.DIC

AutoCorrect   Options...   Undo Last   Cancel   Help

7. Click on Change, and click No when Word asks if you want to check the remainder of the document.

> The suggestion you selected has replaced the incorrectly spelled word.

> Each time the spelling checker tries to find suggestions for a misspelled word, it must pause as it looks through the dictionary. To speed up the process, you may tell Word for Windows not to make suggestions for every mistaken word. For simple mistakes, you may wish to make the changes to the error yourself.

8. Highlight the misspelled word filme in the fourth sentence. Select Tools/Spelling and click Options.

9. Click on the check box next to Always Suggest to turn this feature off. The X should disappear from the box. Click OK to continue, and Cancel to close.

10. Start the spell checker to check the word again.

> The Spelling box appears again, but more quickly, because the spelling checker does not have to look up suggestions for the misspelled word. If you would like to see suggestions for the correct spelling, that option is still available.

11. Click on the Suggest button.

> The list of suggestions reappears. However, the next time you check the spelling of a word the list will not appear unless you again click on Suggest.

12. Since the correct spelling of the word in the Suggestions box is already selected, click on Change. Click No to stop checking the spelling.

> In addition to checking the spelling of a single word, you may use the spelling checker to check any selected segment of text, or the entire document.

GUIDED ACTIVITY 4.2

Checking a Segment of Text

1. Select the first paragraph by double-clicking to the left of the paragraph. Select Tools/Spelling. Word begins checking the highlighted segment of text.

> For each word the spelling checker does not find in the dictionary, the Spelling dialog box will open to give you a chance to review the word.

2. The first misspelling found is hihgest. Type the correct spelling, highest, in the Change To box. Click on the Change button to replace the word. Continue spell checking the entire paragraph. For each misspelled word, either type the correct spelling in the Change To box, or click on Suggest and pick the correct spelling from the list and then select Change.

> One of the words that does not appear in the dictionary is Modavi. This word is not an error; it is a proper name.

3. When this word appears in the Spelling dialog box, click on Ignore All to tell the spelling checker that this and all subsequent occurrences of the word in the current document are not misspellings.

   Use the same procedure with `Kilarney`, since it is also a proper name.

4. At the end of checking the paragraph, click No to stop the spell checker.

   Occasionally, you will find a word in documents you create that is not in the spelling dictionary. A perfect example of this is your last name. While common names may appear in a spelling dictionary, `Ketcham` is included in very few. To avoid Word's having to list this as a misspelling in every document where it appears, it can be added to a special dictionary. This option is only available when CUSTOM.DIC is in the Add Words To box.

5. Enter your last name at the end of the first paragraph. (You may wish to use another name if yours is a common English word.) Select Tools/Spelling.

   Spell check the paragraph again. There should be fewer misspellings this time.

6. When your last name appears in the Spelling dialog box, click on Add to add it to the dictionary. If CUSTOM.DIC is not available, click Ignore.

   Your last name is added to the custom dictionary named CUSTOM.DIC. Whenever a document is checked that contains your last name, the spell checker will not consider this a misspelling.

7. Continue to correct the errors in the second paragraph. When the spell checker reaches the end of the document, it begins at the beginning of the document. The spelling checker stops when it reaches the position of the cursor from which you first started checking, and displays a dialog box telling you the spelling check is complete. Click OK.

8. Save the document as A:4_A.

AutoCorrect

Word for Windows 6.0 includes a new feature called *AutoCorrect*. This feature can be customized to fix your most common typographical errors while you type, without running the spelling checker. AutoCorrect may also change straight quotation marks (like ") to "curly" ones and fix certain capitalization errors. If you find yourself making the same typographical errors time after time, you can have Word correct them automatically while you type by clicking the AutoCorrect button in the spelling checker. You can also manage what errors are automatically corrected by selecting the command Tools/AutoCorrect from the menu.

GUIDED ACTIVITY 4.3

Customizing the AutoCorrect Tool

1. Select from the menu Tools/AutoCorrect.

2. In the text box under Replace, type directotr, as in Figure 4.3.

FIGURE 4.3
*The AutoCorrect
dialog box*

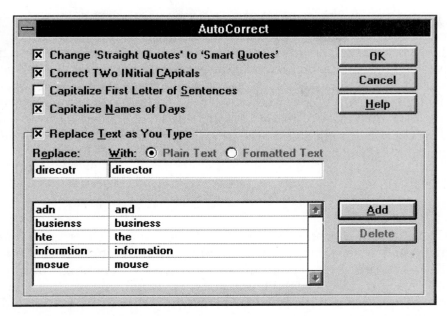

3. Press [Tab] to move the cursor to the With text box. Type director.

4. Click the Add button to add these to the list, and then OK.

5. Press [Enter] at the bottom of the document. Type the following words and watch Word automatically correct the mistakes: "ONe award-winning directotr is Martin Scorsese."

The straight quotes are changed to curly ones, the capitalization is corrected, and the spelling of directotr is changed while you type.

Some words or phrases are simply long and difficult to type, such as Environmental, even with Word correcting typing errors for you. AutoCorrect can also be used to automatically expand certain abbreviations into a word, phrase, or sentence.

6. Select Tools/AutoCorrect, in the Replace box type callif, and in the With box type Please call if you have any further questions. Click Add.

Of course, you must be careful to use a unique word in the Replace box. In this case, using the word call would automatically expand to the phrase even if you didn't intend it to.

7. Add another abbreviation in the Replace box: EPA. In the With box, type the full name: Environmental Protection Agency. Click Add and then OK to close the dialog box.

8. Type callif and EPA and watch AutoCorrect expand the word to the phrase or sentence. Type a space after each word for AutoCorrect to happen.

Limitations

The spelling checker and AutoCorrect can be very useful when creating and checking a document, but there are limitations to what they can correct. While the spelling checker finds words that do not appear in its dictionary and suggests alternative spellings, and AutoCorrect fixes specified typographical errors, neither can find every mistake in a document. For example, the word of may be typed incorrectly as or, but Word for Windows will not find this error because both words appear in its dictionary. You cannot assume that a document is correct simply because the spelling checker does not find any misspelled words. You must read each document you create to find such mistakes.

Grammar Checking

The ***grammar checker*** is useful for spotting grammatical errors and identifying elements of a weak writing style. Furthermore, the grammar checker finds misspelled words, so you can perform two functions with one step. The grammar checker also provides readability statistics to let you know whether you use too many big words or complex sentences. Through the use of the command Tools/ Grammar, you can choose to check the entire document or a single selection.

Just as when checking spelling, Word normally checks the entire document beginning at the location of the cursor. When it finds a sentence with questionable grammar, style, or spelling, it displays the sentence in the dialog box. Directly underneath the questioned sentence is a box containing a suggested way to correct the error. The buttons on the right side of the dialog box give you several alternative ways to deal with the grammar checker's findings—Ignore, Next Sentence, Change, Ignore Rule, Cancel, and Help.

The grammar checker follows certain grammatical and stylistic rules. It may be quite permissible to use language informally for personal letters, but usually not for business writing. To select whether the grammar checker should be strict or lenient, choose Options and set your preferences. Even so, in some cases the grammar checker questions phrases that you think are correct. The Explain button gives an explanation of the suspected error. Choosing Ignore causes the grammar checker to skip the questioned word or phrase without making any changes. Choose Ignore Rule, on the other hand, to skip this and similar occurrences for the remainder of the document. Next Sentence causes the grammar checker to leave the entire sentence unchanged. If you have made an error, you may accept the suggested correction by selecting Change. If the Change button is unavailable, type your correction in the Sentence box, then click Change and continue checking the remainder of the document.

GUIDED ACTIVITY 4.4

Using the Grammar Checker

1. Change the last sentence of the second paragraph from `their interna-`
`tional success` to `there international success`.

2. Highlight the second paragraph by double-clicking with the mouse pointer in the left margin next to the paragraph.

3. Select the command Tools/Grammar. The spelling checker highlights an unknown word, then when you click Ignore, the dialog box in Figure 4.4 appears.

FIGURE 4.4
The Grammar dialog box

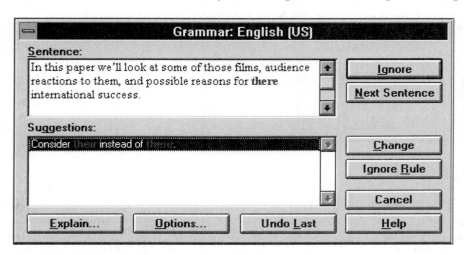

4. Click Change to make the suggested changes. Click No and OK to finish.

Readability Statistics

The grammar checker also provides information about the readability of a document. At the end of the grammar checking process, Readability Statistics are displayed, as shown in Figure 4.5. These indexes measure how many long words and complicated sentences are in the document. Several of the indexes are referenced to grade level. A Flesch-Kincaid Grade Level of 7, for instance, would be considered readable by the average reader who has completed seventh grade. Thus, the higher the number, the more difficult the material is to read.

The Flesch Reading Ease figure is the only exception. This score ranges from 100 (corresponding to a fourth grade reading level) to 0 (which is college graduate level or very difficult reading). This score tells the number of people who can readily understand the document, so a higher number here means that the document is less difficult to read.

The grammar checker can be customized for several different kinds of text, including formal, business, and casual writing. The customization can be performed by clicking Options in the Grammar Checker box to reveal the dialog box shown in Figure 4.6. Additional customization is available by clicking Customize Settings.

FIGURE 4.5
Readability statistics

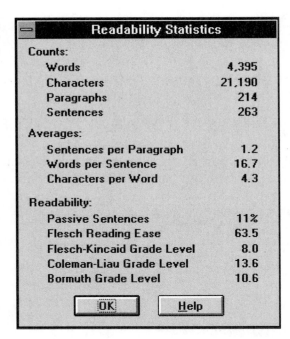

The Thesaurus

A thesaurus is used to find synonyms for words in a document. The thesaurus tool in Word is very (*extremely, quite, remarkably*) useful when a word is repeated many times and needs to be replaced by another word with the same or similar

FIGURE 4.6
Grammar Options

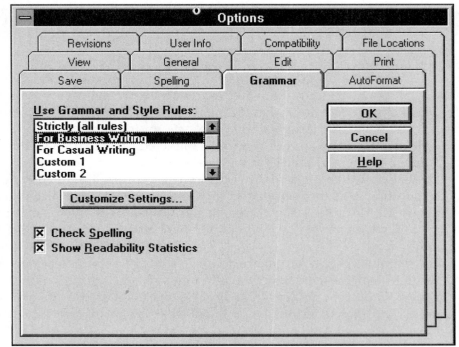

meaning. Sometimes you are searching for a word with a particular shade of meaning. To use the thesaurus, highlight a single word and select Tools/Thesaurus.

GUIDED ACTIVITY 4.5

Using the Thesaurus

1. Select the word acclaim in the first paragraph of your sample document. Select Tools/Thesaurus to see the dialog box shown in Figure 4.7.

FIGURE 4.7
The Thesaurus dialog box

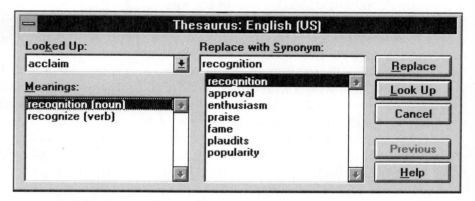

Word for Windows provides a list of alternatives in the Replace with Synonym box to the right of this dialog box. All of these words loosely match the definition in the Meanings box. However, acclaim is not always a noun.

2. Click on the verb definition in the Meanings box to see more definitions for the word acclaim.

   New synonyms now appear in the Replace with Synonym box. Acclaim has several synonyms as a verb in addition to its synonyms as a noun. These are the synonyms for acclaim when it is used as a verb.

3. Click on the noun definition in the Meanings box.

   The original synonyms appear in the Replace with Synonym box.

4. Highlight praise in the Replace with Synonym box and click the Replace button.

   Word returns to the work area and replaces acclaim with praise.

   The thesaurus allows you to find all of the possible definitions of a selected word, to select from the definitions the correct one, and to choose an alternate word. This will help reduce repetition of commonly used words in your documents, although you should still use discretion when substituting synonyms to avoid the writing fault called "elegant variationism."

Summary

Word for Windows has a spelling checker that can check a single word, a segment of text, or an entire document. The spelling checker can offer alternatives to words it cannot find in the dictionary, but it takes time to compile a list of these alternatives. You may select one of the alternatives or type in the correct spelling yourself. You may also add words (such as your name or technical words) to the dictionary that are not already there but that may appear in many of your documents. AutoCorrect is useful for correcting specific typographical errors and for automatically expanding abbreviations into words or phrases.

The grammar checker goes one step further. It will help correct simple grammatical mistakes and flag text with questionable style. If you use the grammar checker, it performs the spell check function at the same time.

The thesaurus offers synonyms for repetitive words in a document. This allows you to replace these words with other words of roughly the same meaning. The thesaurus in Word for Windows maintains all the possible meanings for each word in the dictionary and offers a different list of synonyms for each one.

The spelling checker, the AutoCorrect feature, the thesaurus, and the grammar checker will not correct all the errors in a document for you. It is still your responsibility to make sure that there are no errors in the text before giving the document to its intended recipient.

Exercises

1. Enter the following paragraph into a new document. There are intentional spelling errors in the text. Type the errors as they appear. Correct the document, using the spelling checker, and print it. Save the file as A:EX4_1.

```
Spelling checking is available two diferent ways. This
function can be accesed either from the Toolbar or with the
command Tools/Spelling. The spelling dialog box appearss
when the spelling checer finds a word that does not match
any word in the main dictionary or in any custom dictionar-
ies you selected. You can ask for suggestions for alterna-
tive spelling, add the word to one of the custom dictionar-
ies (like CUSTOM.DIC), correct the word, or leave the word
as it is.
```

2. Open the file A:EX4_1. When you checked this document previously, the word CUSTOM.DIC was one of the "misspelled" (actually, unknown) words. Check the document again, but first create a custom dictionary by selecting Tools/Options and picking the Spelling category by clicking on its tab at the top of the dialog box. Click New to add a new dictionary. Call the dictionary A:EX4_2.DIC. Click OK in the two dialog boxes to exit them. Check the document again. When the spelling checker finds the "misspelling," add it to the new dictionary you created by selecting the name of the new dictionary in the Add

Words To box. Check the document again. This time, CUSTOM.DIC should not appear as a misspelling.

Open the file A:EX4_2.DIC. Since this file name does not have a .DOC extension, you will need to type the entire name in the File/Open dialog box. Print the file.

3. When using a word processor on a public-access computer (for example, one in a student computer lab), any custom dictionaries available to the word processor may be corrupted by users who have inadvertently added *incorrectly* spelled words. When these words appear in one of your documents, Word for Windows will not catch the misspelling because the word appears in the dictionary. You can avoid this problem by always using your own custom dictionary—avoiding the possibility of being penalized for others' mistakes!

    Create a custom dictionary by selecting Tools/Options, selecting the Spelling tab, and clicking the New button. Type in the name of the new custom dictionary, A:PERS.DIC. Click OK.

    Type your name and address into a new document and spell check it. If any words appear in your name or address that are not in Word's dictionary, add them to your personal dictionary by selecting A:PERS.DIC in the Add Words To section of the Spelling dialog box, and clicking Add.

    Open the file A:PERS.DIC. Print the file.

4. A common problem with documents is an author's tendency to use words that would not be used under normal circumstances. The Tools/Thesaurus command can help you find alternate, more common forms of many words. Type in the following column of pretentious or obscure words. On a new line under each word, type a definition for the word and replace it with a more common word of the same meaning. Print the document.

    ```
    nefarious
    obfuscate
    effectuate
    recompense
    recollect
    rebut
    mettlesome
    ```

5. Enter three paragraphs from a current newspaper or magazine into a new document. Type the paragraphs quickly without looking at the screen. Print the result.

    Spell check the document and use the thesaurus to replace at least five words with synonyms. Check the grammar of the document. Print the result.

Review Questions

*1. How do you check the spelling of a single word?

2. How do you check the spelling of a single sentence?

*3. How do you check the spelling of an entire document? How does the position of the cursor affect this command? Is the cursor position a limitation when checking an entire document?

4. Give the procedure for handling words that are correctly spelled but not found in the dictionary.

*5. Why is there an option to turn off the suggestions in the spelling checker?

6. What is the purpose of the grammar checker? What other functions does it perform?

*7. Why is it a waste of time to spell check a document after using the grammar checker?

8. Is everything that is highlighted by the grammar checker in error? Why or why not?

*9. What functions does the thesaurus perform?

10. What should you do if the synonyms that are listed under the first definition in the Meanings box do not match the usage of the word in the document?

Key Terms

AutoCorrect	Grammar checker	Thesaurus
Dictionary	Spelling checker	

Documentation Research

1. What function keys are the equivalents of Tools/Spelling and Tools/Thesaurus?

2. What extension is required for custom dictionary file names if they are to appear in the dictionary list in the Spelling dialog box?

Printers and Printing

The goal of word processing is to get a document on paper. You know how to create documents on the screen. This unit will discuss how to print documents that you have created in Word for Windows.

Before you print for the first time in Word, you must connect a printer to your computer or to the network to which your computer is attached. Second, you must install a printer driver through the Windows Control Panel or Windows Setup. Third, you must select which printer you will use for a particular document, if there is more than one printer available.

The first section discusses the types of printers that are available to you. The printer that you use will determine the quality of the printed document and the fonts and point sizes available.

The second section covers the way the printer is attached to your computer. It is important to understand how your computer communicates with the printer and the name of the connection to the printer, as well as how Windows handles the printing for all applications.

Finally, the Word for Windows print commands will be covered in this unit.

Learning Objectives

At the completion of this unit you should know

1. what types of printers are available,

2. what kind of printer you have,

3. how printers are attached to computers,

4. how to set up Windows for different printers,

5. how to preview and print documents and envelopes.

Important Commands

File/Print

File/Print Preview

Tools/Envelopes and Labels

Types of Printers

Several popular types of printers may be attached to your computer. They are generally classified by how they print characters on paper and the quality of the print they produce. The printer to which you have access will determine the quality of the output you produce and the fonts and sizes that are available to you for use in documents.

Dot-matrix printers produce characters by printing a series of dots in the shape of letters. For example, the letter ɱ when greatly enlarged would look like Figure 5.1.

FIGURE 5.1
Dot-matrix character

At their actual size the dots are so small that the eye does not distinguish between them. When you look at a character, you simply see the shape created by the dots, not the dots themselves. The more dots a printer can place in a specific location on a page, the smoother the characters will appear. This is the same principle as the pixels on a computer monitor. A finer image can be produced by making the dots or pixels smaller and placing them closer together.

Most early dot-matrix printers created characters no more than nine dots high. These printers are called 9-pin printers. Inexpensive and widely available, they were the standard printer used with most applications. Dot-matrix printers are still sold, but the popular models now are 24-pin printers, capable of producing characters with 24 vertical dots. The appearance of these characters is much better than that of 9-pin text because the dots are much smaller and closer together. These printers are called *NLQ* (near letter quality) because their text closely resembles that of a typewriter. Most NLQ printers are also capable of printing graphics in addition to text. The print heads pass across the page line by line to print the document, and it takes several minutes to print each page.

Though more expensive to operate than dot-matrix printers, *laser printers* soon became the standard. The laser technology, similar to that of a photocopy machine, increased both print speed and print quality. Although these printers also create letters by joining a series of dots, the dots are so minute that they are indistinguishable to human eyes. Typical laser printers can print 300 or 600 dots per inch (dpi) and can print 4 to 16 pages per minute.

Laser printers come in many varieties, but the most popular is the LaserJet series, produced by Hewlett-Packard. This company produced so many printers that the LaserJet became a standard copied by many other manufacturers. Laser printers quickly became extremely popular, but they were still limited in the size and number of fonts that they could print. More fonts could be added only by plugging cartridges into the printer. Beginning with the Hewlett-Packard LaserJet III, laser printers came with *scalable fonts* built in, which meant that fonts of any size could be printed without adding cartridges. The scalable fonts available in Windows, called TrueType fonts, allow both older and newer laser printers to print any style and size of letters, since the fonts reside in the software, rather than in the printer itself.

The final printer type is the *inkjet printer*, some models of which print in color as well as black ink. Inkjet printers work by injecting black or different colored inks onto the paper surface. This requires special ink cartridges and sometimes special types of paper. Inkjet printers are less expensive to purchase and use than laser printers, so they are increasingly popular. Color inkjet printers now are quite reasonably priced, making the ability to print in color quite attractive. Word for Windows allows you to format text in different colors and to include pictures and graphics to take advantage of color printers.

Computer Connections

Peripherals, such as printers, scanners, and modems, are connected to computers by plugging them into *ports* (plug-in sockets) on the back of the computer. There are several different kinds of ports, but printers can be connected either into *parallel ports* or *serial ports*. The large majority of printers attach to parallel ports, but a few attach to the serial port. Since the configuration of different computers varies so much, it is impossible to tell exactly where the parallel and serial ports will be on your computer. To find these ports, you must consult the documentation for the particular computer you are using, although you may be able to tell by looking. A parallel port on the back of a computer is typically around 1½ inches long and ¼ inch wide, and contains 25 holes in two rows, as in Figure 5.2. A serial port, on the other hand, may be approximately the same size but instead of 25 holes it contains 25 pins in two rows. Some serial ports are only half as long and have only 9 pins in two rows, as in Figure 5.3.

FIGURE 5.2
Parallel port has 25 holes.

FIGURE 5.3
Serial port has 9 pins.

The computer has names for each of the ports available in its configuration. The parallel port is called *LPT1:* and the serial port, *COM1:*. If the computer has more than one parallel or serial port, these additional ports have the same name with the number increased by one. For example, if a computer had three parallel ports, the second and third ports would be called LPT2: and LPT3:, respectively. If the computer had a second serial port, it would be called COM2:.

You can determine to which port your printer is connected by tracing the cable that attaches the printer to the computer, noting the location of the port where it is attached, and consulting your computer's manual to find out what port it is. This information will be necessary to properly set up Windows to use the printer and to make sure your printouts go to the right printer when you select the Print command.

You may be able to use a printer that is attached not to your computer but to another computer on a *network*. A computer network allows several computers to be connected to each other so that they may share information and peripherals. It is cost-effective to buy one expensive printer, attach it to a network, and share it with 20 or 30 other computers. If you use a printer from a network, it may appear to the computer that you are using an LPT2: or LPT3: even though your computer may not even have these ports. You may not have to set up the software yourself to make your computer communicate with a network, but you should know how to tell what printer Windows has set up on which port on your computer.

Windows maintains a list of printers available for use in all Windows applications. Every Windows application has access to the same set of printers. Printers are defined from the Control Panel program in the Main program group in the Program Manager. The original Windows 3.1 installation disks are required to set up printers in the Control Panel if you are adding a new printer. If you are just changing the port to which a printer is attached, the disks will not be necessary.

GUIDED ACTIVITY 5.1

Setting Up Printers in Windows

Printers

1. Start Windows. Double-click on the Main program group in the Program Manager. Double-click on the Control Panel. Double-click on the Printers program icon.

    The Printers dialog box appears, showing a list of currently installed printers, as in Figure 5.4. From this dialog box you can add and delete printers, change the ports to which they are assigned, and tell Windows which printer is the default.

FIGURE 5.4
The Printers dialog box in Windows

Printers	
Default Printer IBM Proprinter II on LPT1:	Cancel
Installed Printers: IBM Proprinter II on LPT1:	Connect...
	Setup...
	Remove
Set As Default Printer	Add >>
☒ Use Print Manager	Help

You will not actually add or delete printers at this point because Windows has probably been set up for the printers attached to your computer. However, you can easily change the port to which the printer is assigned without permanently damaging the setup.

The first (and possibly only) printer listed in the Installed Printers box should be selected. If it is not, click on it once to highlight it.

2. Click on Connect, to reveal the dialog box shown in Figure 5.5.

The Connect box is used to change the port to which a printer is connected.

Make a note of which port is selected in the Ports box so that you can change the printer back to the correct port later.

3. Click on one of the ports that is not selected (such as COM1: or LPT2:). Press ⏎Enter or click on OK.

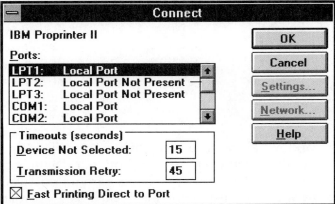

FIGURE 5.5
The Printers Connect dialog box

Windows returns to the Printers box. The list of printers in the Installed Printers box is still the same, but the port next to the printer you selected has been changed. Whenever you select this printer from any application and print to it, Windows will attempt to send the information for the printout to this port.

Since this is not actually the correct port for this printer, change the port back to its original setting.

4. Click on Connect to change the port back.

5. Click on the original port to which the printer was connected in the Ports box.

6. Press ⏎Enter or click on OK.

The selected printer is now changed back to the original port.

7. Click Close, then close both the Control Panel and the Main windows.

Print Commands

Once you have correctly set up the printers in the Control Panel, you are ready to print from any Windows application. The commands in this section relate specifically to Word for Windows, but you will find them in many different Windows applications in nearly the same form. If you know how to print in Word for Windows, you know how to print in almost any Windows application. The File/Print command contains several features that give the user control over the printing function.

Since Word for Windows will format and display your document based on the printer that you have selected, the next step is to verify which printer will be used to print the document.

To select or verify which printer will be used, click on the Printer button within the File/Print dialog box, shown in Figure 5.6. The Print Setup dialog box that then appears, shown in Figure 5.7, closely resembles the one in the Control Panel. Double-click the name of the printer you wish to use in printing your document, click Close, then Close again.

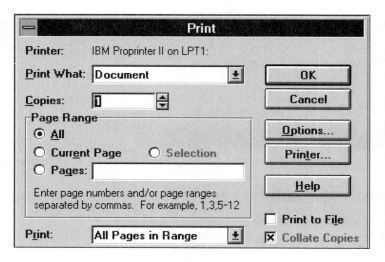

Once the printer is selected, you could print the document to see what it looks like. However, to do this is frequently a waste of paper. In anything but the simplest document there are minor changes that need to be made to produce a document that looks right. Some of these needed changes can be seen when you view the entire document on the screen before printing it. Word for Windows allows you to do this with the File/Print Preview command. Print Preview will show you what each page of your document will look like. The actual text in the document cannot usually be seen from Print Preview, but the shape of the paragraphs and their position on the printed page are displayed. This is a very useful feature that shows whether individual pages in a document appear correct and balanced, and whether what you intend to be a one-page letter fits on one page.

After you preview the document on the screen and make any changes that are necessary, you are finally ready to print. The File/Print command sends the document to the printer. Word provides several options for printing one or more copies of the entire document, certain pages, or a highlighted selection.

Located under the Tools menu is a selection that allows you to print an envelope or mailing labels with ease.

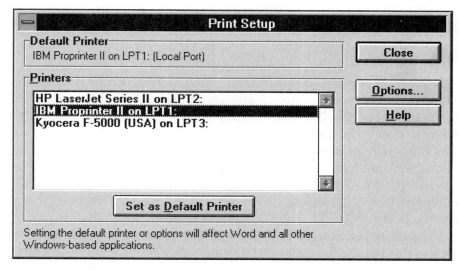

Preparing the Printer

1. Start Word for Windows.

2. Select File/Print. At the top of the dialog box Word shows the selected printer and the port to which it is connected.

3. Click on the Printer button.

   The Print Setup dialog box appears, as shown in Figure 5.7, with a list of the printers that have been selected and configured from the Control Panel. This box is used to select which of the available printers will be used as the default.

4. Double-click the printer you want to use. The name of that printer now appears as the default printer. Click Close, and click Cancel to exit the dialog boxes.

   The printer is now ready to produce your document. However, before putting your document on paper you should preview it on the monitor.

Previewing and Printing a Document

This Guided Activity will require a sample document. If you have created a document that is more than one page long and is saved on your disk, open and use that document. You may be able to use the file you created in Exercise 3.1 (A:EX3_1) and add a few paragraphs to it. If you have not created a document, find an article or paper that is more than one page long and enter it into the word processor.

1. Position the cursor at the top of your document. Select File/Print Preview.

   Word creates a picture of how the entire page will look, and displays a new toolbar with buttons specific to the Preview mode, as shown in Figure 5.8.

2. You can see what the paragraphs will look like when you print the document. However, the actual text is not legible. Your mouse pointer now appears as a magnifying glass.

3. Click on the document with the magnifying glass to examine the text at a legible size.

   If you have additional corrections you need to make before you print the document, you can make them here in Preview.

4. Click on the Magnifier button to change the mouse pointer into an I-beam, and click on the page to place the cursor back in the document. Make changes to the text as desired.

5. Click on the Magnifier button to turn the mouse pointer into the magnifying glass, then click on the document to zoom back out to see the entire page.

FIGURE 5.8
Print Preview

Magnifier button

One Page button

Multiple Pages
button

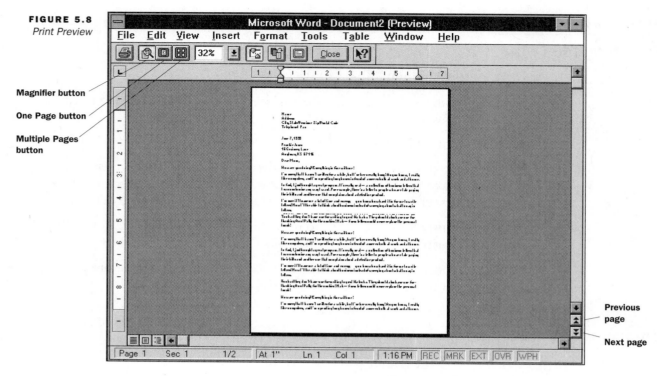

Previous
page

Next page

6. Click the next page arrow on the scroll bar at the right of the screen (or press the
    PgDn key) to view the second page of your document, then click the previous
    page arrow (or press the PgUp key).

7. To view more than one page at a time, click the Multiple Pages button on the tool-
    bar. Highlight the number of pages you wish to view at once by dragging across
    the sample pages, as shown in Figure 5.9.

FIGURE 5.9
*Viewing multiple
pages*

8. Change the preview back to a single page by clicking on the One Page button.

9. You could print one copy of the entire document on the default printer by click-
    ing the Print button on the toolbar, both in Print Preview and in Normal view.
    Instead, click Close to return to Normal view.

10. Select the command File/Print from the menu, and the dialog box in Figure 5.6
    appears.

    You should note two important pieces of information in the dialog box. The first
    is the number of copies to be printed. The default is 1, but you could enter a

different number before continuing. Since the Copies box is already highlighted, it is not necessary to position the cursor on the box to change the number of copies. You could either type in the number of copies to print, or use the mouse to increase or decrease the number of copies by clicking on the up or down arrows next to the box.

For this Guided Activity, leave the number of copies at 1.

The second important piece of information in this dialog box is the range or amount of the document to print. There are three options you can select. The default is to print the entire document: the option button next to All is filled in. The second option is to print only the page where the cursor is located by clicking on the option button next to Current Page in the print box. The third option is to specify certain pages of the document to print. For this Guided Activity, print all pages of the document.

11. Make sure your printer is ready, then click on OK to print the document.

If Print Manager is turned on in Windows, Word handles printing in the background. That is, the printing is handled by the fixed disk and the CPU (central processing unit) without making you wait until the job is finished before you can continue to work on a document. To let you know how the background printing is proceeding, the status bar shows a tiny, animated picture of pages coming off a printer next to the number of the page currently being printed. If Print Manager in Windows is disabled, you will instead see a dialog box on screen while the document is printing.

If your printer is set correctly and ready to print, the document should begin to print within a few seconds. Network printers may take longer to print, depending on how many other people have printouts in the queue ahead of you.

Another way to print is to click the Print button on the standard toolbar, as shown in Figure 5.10. Pressing this button bypasses the Print dialog box and immediately sends the entire document to the selected printer. It is the fastest way to print a single copy of your document.

FIGURE 5.10
Standard toolbar with Print button

Print

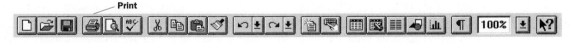

Printing Envelopes

Since printing a letter is a common task, Word makes it simple to print the envelope or mailing labels to go along with the letter. To create and print an envelope, simply choose Envelopes and Labels from the Tools menu, and then click on the Envelopes tab. Word examines the letter to find text that is most likely an address, and inserts it into the Envelopes and Labels dialog box, as shown in Figure 5.11. From this dialog box you may change the recipient and the return address. Click on Options to change what direction the envelopes feed into the printer. If you are using

FIGURE 5.11
*The Envelopes
dialog box*

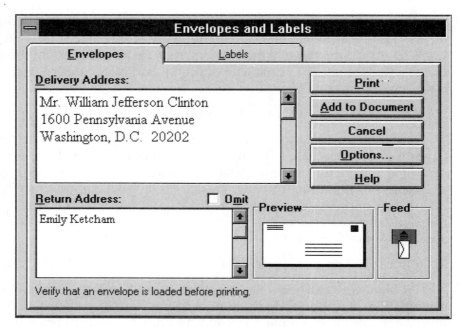

envelopes with a preprinted return address, click in the check box next to Omit to keep from printing over it. Note that a sample of the elements to be printed is shown in the Preview area.

Summary

Several types of printers are available, including dot-matrix, laser, and inkjet printers. Each produces a different kind of print quality and is used for different purposes. Printers are attached to the computer by means of ports located on the back of the computer. There are two kinds of ports: parallel and serial.

Windows maintains a list of printers that are available to all Windows applications. The list of printers is maintained from the Printers window in the Control Panel. From the Control Panel, you may add, delete, or configure printers by changing the port to which they are attached. Network printers may be available to you even though they are not physically attached to your computer.

Printing in Word for Windows is a simple process. To view or change the default printer, check the Print Setup dialog box through File/Print Printer. Print Preview is used to view the document on the monitor to check that the appearance of each page is correct. Use File/Print to specify what portion of the document and how many copies to produce. Click on the Print button on the toolbar to bypass the dialog box and print a single copy of every page in the document.

Exercises

1. Open the file A:EX4_1. Print the file on each printer available to your computer.

2. Continue using the file from Exercise 1. Insert a page break (press Ctrl Enter) after the paragraph. Type your name followed by Exercise 5-2. Print only the second page of the document.

3. Address and print an envelope using the Envelopes and Labels tool. Consult your printer documentation if necessary to determine how to feed the envelope.

Review Questions

*1. What types of printers may be attached to a computer? What kind of printer are you using?

2. What are the two kinds of ports to which printers may be attached? How is yours attached?

*3. How does Windows keep track of printers?

4. What are the three steps necessary when preparing to use the printer for the very first time?

*5. What is the difference between pressing the Print button on the Preview toolbar and pressing the Print button on the Standard toolbar?

6. What are the advantages to using Print Preview?

Key Terms

COM1:	LPT1:	Peripheral
Dot-matrix printer	Network	Port
Inkjet printer	NLQ	Scalable font
Laser printer	Parallel port	Serial port

Documentation Research

1. How does the Shrink to Fit button on the Print Preview toolbar function?

2. When is draft output used, and how can you access that option?

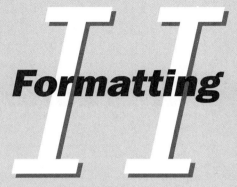

Formatting

■ **PART TWO** of this manual helps you change documents to ensure that the reader gets the meaning you intended to convey. Every formatting command can be used to help you put your message across in a better way to the reader. Different formats affect the way the reader's eyes move across a page of text and can enhance the reader's comprehension and retention of a document. Different character sizes and attributes such as bold, italics, and underline can draw attention to important words or letters in a document. Changing the way a paragraph looks can emphasize a section of text by making it stand out from the rest of the document. You can use formatting commands to make more or less information fit on a page, to give a certain impression, or to follow specific styles required by some organizations.

Useful documents can be created without using any formatting commands. However, formatting will make documents more effective and can be the single most important step that you can take (aside from creating the text) to make sure that your document communicates your intended message.

Formatting Characters

There are three levels of formatting: character, paragraph, and document. These formatting commands affect only text that is currently selected or text that is typed immediately after selecting the command. Because formatting is done so often, Word makes the commands easily accessible. Formatting commands are found on the Formatting toolbar, on the Format and shortcut menus, and through shortcut keys. This unit covers the first of the three levels of formatting commands.

The first and most specific level of formatting is character formatting. Once the actual text in a document has been established, the way the words look may be changed to emphasize their meaning. Characters may be made **bold**, <u>underlined</u>, or *italic*, or may be ^{super}scripted or $_{sub}$scripted. Character formats may be combined for added effect.

Learning Objectives

At the completion of this unit you should know

1. how to format existing or new text,

2. what character formats are available,

3. how to apply character formatting,

4. how to copy formats,

5. how to change the default font,

6. how to insert special characters into a document.

Important Commands

Format/Font

Insert/Symbol

Formatting Characters

Selected characters are formatted using commands located on the Formatting toolbar, the Format menu, and the shortcut menu, or by using the shortcut keys. The most commonly used commands are located on the Formatting toolbar for the fastest access. Other character format commands are accessed by selecting Format/Font.

The format commands can be used in two different ways. Text may be formatted either after it has been entered or as it is typed into the work area. To format text that is already entered, you must first highlight it before executing the format command. As you select the command, the highlighted characters will display the format. This formatting method, known as *direct formatting*, is ordinarily used when you are trying different format attributes on a portion of text to see which will best convey the message the passage is meant to send.

If you already know which format a word or sentence should have, it can easily be applied to the text before you enter it. With the cursor positioned where the text is to be inserted, turn on the desired format and begin typing. Every character typed will have the format attribute you selected. Eventually, you will probably want to type text without this formatting. To continue typing text without the selected format attribute, you turn off the format again. This method of formatting is known as *indirect formatting*.

Font and Point Size

The first and most common character attributes formatted are the font and point size. Word for Windows uses the word *font* as a name for the shape of a character. While the actual name of the shape of a character is its typeface, for the sake of consistency with the program it will be called a font. Different fonts are used to convey different messages with the same text. Fonts affect the legibility of a document and give a certain image to a document. Styles in fonts change over the years, just as styles in colors do. The *point size* of a font is its size. One vertical inch is equal to 72 points; the normal point sizes of text in documents are 10 and 12.

Fonts are classified into two broad categories, *serif* and *sans-serif*. A serif is a small line used to finish off a main stroke of a letter, as at the top and bottom of the letter M. Paragraphs of text are easier to read in serif fonts because the serifs guide the reader's eyes along the line of text. They are often used in books and newspapers with long, narrow columns to read. Examples of serif fonts include Times Roman, Times New Roman, Palatino, and Courier. Sans-serif fonts, without the serifs, are slower to read. That is what makes them good for titles, headings, and STOP signs because, in slowing the eye, they stand out better. Helvetica and Arial are examples of sans-serif fonts.

Fonts are further classified as *proportional* and *nonproportional*. If a font is proportional, each of the letters in that font has a different width. These fonts are very pleasing to look at because each character has an individual shape and width. Capital letters in a proportional font are much wider than lowercase letters.

Nonproportional fonts, by contrast, force every character to be exactly the same width. While these fonts are not beautiful, they are easy to work with when creating tables or any other application that requires letters to be vertically aligned. The example in Figure 6.1 illustrates the difference between widths of characters in the Times Roman and Courier fonts. The characters in both samples are the same point size.

FIGURE 6.1
Font samples

Courier:
```
The quick brown fox jumped over
THE QUICK BROWN FOX JUMPED OVER
```

Times Roman:
The quick brown fox jumped over
THE QUICK BROWN FOX JUMPED OVER

All the Courier characters line up. There are 31 characters on each line of the Courier sample. The capital letters are the same width as the small letters. Because nonproportional fonts have a fixed spacing, they are often measured in characters per inch (CPI), rather than points.

In the Times Roman sample, neither line matches the other or the lines in the Courier sample, even though they are the same point size. The Times Roman uppercase letters are much wider than the lowercase letters, and the W is more than four times wider than the I because of its shape. When you are working with a document that will require you to line up characters in any kind of tabular form, it is easier to use a nonproportional font, although paragraphs of text look more attractive—and are more legible—in a proportional font.

Many different fonts and sizes are available for use in documents. Windows provides several fonts called *TrueType* fonts, including Times New Roman, Arial, Courier New, and Symbol. These fonts are scalable, that is, they can be made any size. TrueType fonts appear the same on screen as they will on the printed page, which is termed *WYSIWYG* (what you see is what you get). Other fonts are unique to the printer you use, and still others are appropriate for on-screen use but not for printing. These may be limited in the sizes available.

Any good word processor will allow you to change the font and style of text in a document. Many will let you select format commands from a menu so that you do not need to remember complicated keystrokes. Word allows you to format text instantaneously by clicking on areas of the Formatting toolbar or by using the shortcut keys, and also through the Font dialog box by using the shortcut menu available by clicking the *right* mouse button.

Times New Roman is the **default** font in Word, and 10 points is the default size. A default is the normal setting that is used in the program unless you specify another. The font and size can be easily changed from the Formatting toolbar. As you click on the arrow next to the font name Times New Roman, an alphabetical list of other fonts appears. You can tell which fonts are TrueType, screen, or printer fonts by the symbols next to the font name, as in Figure 6.2.

FIGURE 6.2
The Formatting
toolbar displays
font choices.

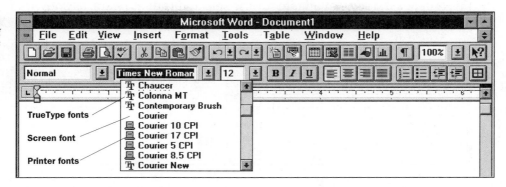

GUIDED ACTIVITY 6.1

Changing Font and Size

1. Start Word.

The default font is displayed in the Font box on the Formatting toolbar, as in Figure 6.2. The default point size is in the Points box.

2. Type the words `This is Times New Roman.`

Any text that you enter will be in the font and point size listed on the Formatting toolbar. You may select any font or size by selecting from the drop-down list.

3. Press `Enter` twice. Click on the down arrow to the right of the Font box.

The list of fonts is displayed in alphabetical order. If the list is too long to fit in the Font box, a scroll box will appear to the right of the box to allow you to scroll through all the available fonts. The most recently used fonts are listed above the alphabetical list.

4. Select Arial as the new font by clicking on Arial in the font list. Type `This is Arial.`

The words appear in a new font. Using this method, you may position the cursor anywhere in a document and begin typing in any font available on this list.

5. Press `Enter` twice. Type the words `new text.`

These words appear in the same font as used in the previous line. However, you can change this.

6. Select the entire line you just typed (click to the left of the line). Click on the down arrow next to the Font box to see the list of fonts again. Select Courier New.

The words on the last line change to the Courier New font. You could just as easily have changed them to any other font on the list.

In addition to changing the font, you may also select a different size.

7. Select the first line in the document. Click on the down arrow next to the Points box.

A list of the sizes available for the selected font appears, as shown in Figure 6.3. The current size is listed in the box at the top of the list and is highlighted in the list itself.

FIGURE 6.3
*The Formatting
toolbar with
drop-down list of
point sizes*

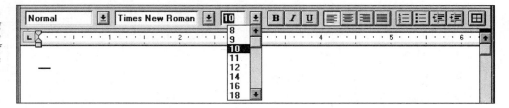

8. Select a different size from the list in the Points box by clicking on any size in the list.

Because Word is a WYSIWYG word processor, you can actually see the text change sizes on the screen after you change the format. The printed output will match the document's on-screen appearance.

To see a sample of the fonts before applying them to text, you may also use the Format/Font command.

9. Position the cursor at the end of the document by clicking anywhere below and to the right of the bottom line. Press Enter twice to start a new line. Select Format/Font to see the dialog box shown in Figure 6.4.

FIGURE 6.4
*The Format Font
dialog box*

Font

Font	Character Spacing

Font:
Times New Roman

Ŧ Subway
Ŧ Symbol
System
Terminal
T Times New Roman

Font Style:
Regular

Regular
Italic
Bold
Bold Italic

Size:
12

8
9
10
11
12

OK
Cancel
Default...
Help

Underline:
(none)

Color:
Auto

Effects
☐ Strikethrough ☐ Hidden
☐ Superscript   ☐ Small Caps
☐ Subscript   ☐ All Caps

Preview

Times New Roman

Font
sample

This is a TrueType font. This same font will be used on both your printer and your screen.

You may select a new font and size from the Font dialog box using the same method as the one you used with the Formatting toolbar.

10. Change to the Symbol font, and look in the Preview window. Is this what you were looking for? Unless you wanted Greek letters, it is not. Are you curious just how large the font can be? Scroll down the list of sizes and pick a very large number and preview the effect. Select other fonts or sizes to preview how the font appears in the Preview box, and when you see one you like click OK or press Enter. Type the sentence This must be easy if I can do it.

Word keeps track of the names of the most recently used fonts. They are listed at the top of the drop-down list of available fonts in addition to being listed alphabetically.

It's a good idea to limit the number of fonts in a document. One serif and one sans-serif font offer plenty of contrast and variety, simply by varying point sizes and changing to bold, italic, or both. Too many fonts cause confusion and clutter, and can be in bad taste just like mixing plaid, checks, and stripes in clothing.

In addition to changing the font in small segments of text, it is possible to change the basic font for the document. As you know, the default font for Word is Times New Roman, 10 points. As you experiment, you may find that you prefer a slightly larger size or an entirely diffferent font for your documents. Change the default font and size setting by making the selections you want and then clicking on the Default button in the Font dialog box.

Bold, Italics, and Underline

In addition to changing the font and point size of text, the Formatting toolbar has three other formatting attributes to choose from. These are normally used to make certain characters stand out from the others around them. Because they are the most frequently used character format attributes, they are available from the Formatting toolbar, shown on Figure 6.5.

FIGURE 6.5
The Formatting toolbar

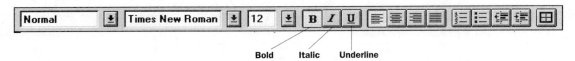

The attribute buttons on the Formatting toolbar normally appear to be three-dimensional, that is, to stick out from the surface of the toolbar. When one of the attributes is selected, its button, like the Bold button in Figure 6.5, will appear to be pressed in. The buttons themselves also give you a quick preview of the function they perform. The B on the Bold button is itself bold, the I on the italics button is italic, and the U on the Underline button is underlined. These visual reminders and cues are made possible by the Windows graphical environment.

The *bold* attribute makes letters darker by making the lines that make up the letters thicker. Bold words will immediately stand out on a printed page, so they are easy to find. Highlighted text in Word can be easily made bold by clicking once on the Bold button on the Formatting toolbar. *Italics* also make words stand out from the text around them, though not as much as the bold attribute. The italics attribute slants characters to the right. To make words appear with the italics attribute, click once on the Italics button on the Formatting toolbar.

Sample text regular:	sample
Sample text in bold:	**sample**
Sample text in italics:	*sample*
Sample text in bold italics:	***sample***
Sample text with underline:	<u>sample</u>

Many writing style manuals indicate that bold or italics may be used in place of underlining when creating references like footnotes or endnotes for passages from other texts. This is desirable because underlining certain letters alters their appearance. The strokes of characters that extend beneath the line of text (as in the letters g and p) are called *descenders*. Descenders can be overwritten by the underline attribute, as shown on the sample text with underline; therefore, it is advantageous to use bold or italics whenever possible to avoid underlining text.

The *underline* button is used to add or remove the Single underline attribute from selected text. There are three other kinds of underlining, available only in the Font dialog box, shown in Figure 6.6. The Word Only underline attribute places a single underline only under the actual characters selected, excluding spaces. The Double underline attribute places two lines under selected text. Another option is to use a Dotted underline.

Sample text underlined:	<u>This text is underlined.</u>
Sample text word underlined:	<u>This</u> <u>text</u> <u>is</u> <u>underlined</u>.
Sample text double underlined:	This text is underlined.
Sample text dotted underlined:	This text is underlined.

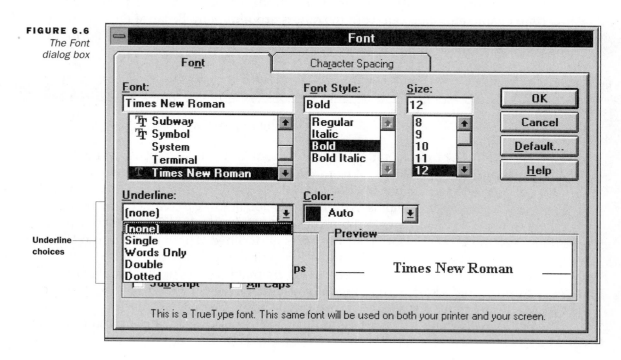

FIGURE 6.6
The Font dialog box

Underline choices

GUIDED ACTIVITY 6.2

Applying Bold, Italics, and Underline

1. Highlight Times in the first line in your document. Click on the Bold button on the Formatting toolbar to make the word bold. Click somewhere else in the document to remove the highlighting from the word.

2. Highlight the second line and make it italic by clicking on the Italics button.

3. Highlight the fourth line of text in the document and underline it by clicking on the Underline button.

   As with the font and point size format commands, you may either format existing text or type in new, formatted text.

4. Position the cursor at the end of the document by clicking anywhere below and to the right of the last line. Turn off the underline by clicking on the Underline button. Click on the Bold button to turn on Bold and press [Enter]. Type in your name.

   Using the shortcut keys turns attributes on and off and makes the buttons appear pushed in, just as if you clicked the button.

5. Press [Enter] twice. Hold down [Ctrl] and press [B] to turn off the bold attribute. You will notice that the button does not appear pushed in anymore. Hold down [Ctrl] and press [I] to turn on the italics. Type in your name again.

6. Press [Enter] twice. Turn off the italics with the [Ctrl][I] shortcut key, and use [Ctrl][U] to turn on the underline. Type in your name a third time.

7. Highlight the first line with your name on it. Click on the Underline button on the Formatting toolbar to underline it.

   The entire line is underlined, including spaces.

8. Highlight the second line with your name on it. Select Format/Font, and from the Font dialog box in the Underline section select Words Only and click OK. This turns on the word-underline attribute.

   All letters on the line are underlined, but spaces are not.

   You also may use the shortcut menu to quickly access the Font dialog box.

9. Highlight the third line with your name on it. With the mouse pointer over the highlighted text, press the right mouse button to access the shortcut menu. When the menu appears, click on Font using either mouse button.

10. From the Font dialog box, select Double from the Underline section to turn on the double-underline attribute. Click OK.

    The entire line is double underlined. The attributes that are in effect at the location of the cursor will continue to be in effect as you type in new text.

11. Press [→].

The highlighting on the last line disappears, and the cursor should appear at the end of the line. The double underline attribute is still on. As you type new text, it will be double underlined.

12. Press ⏎Enter twice. Type Accountants often use double underline for final totals.

13. Highlight the words double underline. Select (none) in the Underline section of the Font dialog box to remove the double underline for these two words. Click OK.

The Underline button may also be used to turn off all types of underlining.

14. Highlight the entire sentence beginning with Accountants. Click on the Underline button twice to turn off all underline formats.

Commands in the Font Dialog Box

Several other character format commands are found only in the Font dialog box. These functions are not often used and therefore are not included on the Formatting toolbar. They are special-effect attributes that are rarely used in most documents.

The Color selection in the dialog box allows you to select a color for text in a document. Using color is an excellent way to get words to stand out in a document, and some very attractive effects can be achieved by matching colored text with pictures.

A second feature available only from the Font dialog box is the ability to change certain effects to the formatted font. These effects include *strikethrough*, used in marking revisions; *superscript* and *subscript*, used in formulas; and *hidden* text, used in making comments that will not appear in the printed version. Characters that have been typed in lowercase may appear in all *capitals* or in *small capitals*, which combines normal-sized capital letters with all lowercase letters converted to capitals in a smaller point size. Clicking in the check box next to the attribute desired will make an X appear in the box. When you then click OK, the format attribute will be in effect. You may format text that has been highlighted or may execute a command and enter new text that has the format attribute.

Sample text with strikethrough:	~~Sample text~~
Sample text superscripted:	x^2
Sample text subscripted:	H_2O
Sample text in all caps:	SAMPLE TEXT
Sample text in caps and small caps:	SAMPLE TEXT

Superscripting is often used when referencing a passage from another author's text. A superscript number, keyed to a note at the foot of the page or at the back of the text, is placed at the location in your document where you wish to give credit to another person or source. Word handles footnote and endnote marks automatically, so there is no need to use superscripting for this purpose. (For an explanation of footnotes, see Unit 14.) However, superscripting and subscripting are both commonly used when creating mathematical expressions in a document. When raising a number to a power, it is necessary to use superscripting. The variable expression x^2 is created using superscripting. The number 2 is superscripted and automatically formatted to a smaller size. The formula H_2O is created by subscripting the number 2, which automatically makes the font smaller. There are other uses for superscripting and subscripting, but these are the most common.

The Character Spacing Tab

The Format Font dialog box contains a tab for setting *character spacing*. This section of the dialog box gives you control over both the vertical and horizontal spacing of highlighted characters. To change the vertical position, select Raised or Lowered in the Position box. The normal distance a superscripted or subscripted character is raised or lowered from the line of text is 3 points. You may change this number on the Character Spacing tab. Select a higher value next to Position By, as shown in Figure 6.7, to move the character further from the line, or to a lower number to move it closer to the line.

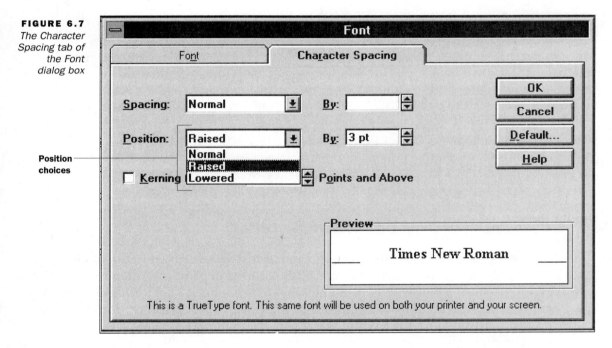

FIGURE 6.7
The Character Spacing tab of the Font dialog box

Position choices

To *condense* or *expand* a series of characters, you choose Expanded or Condensed in the Spacing box, as in Figure 6.8. Selecting Expanded puts spaces between the selected characters. The default amount of space by which to expand each character is 1 point. The higher the number in the By box, the more space is added between each character. Condensing text removes space from around selected characters. The higher the number in the By box, the more space is removed. *Kerning* is a method to force letters to fit more closely together. It is often used to improve the appearance of letters with diagonal strokes, in headings, or in large fonts.

Sample raised by 1 point: x^y

Sample raised by 3 points: x^y

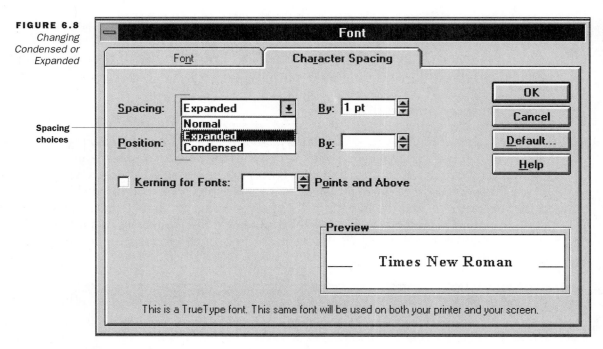

Spacing
choices

Sample raised by 5 points: x^y

Sample condensed by 1 point: Sample condensed text

Sample expanded by 1 point: Sample expanded text

Sample text without kerning: AWAY

Sample text with kerning: AWAY

Changing from Capital to Lowercase Letters

By mistake you may find yourself typing text in a document with the [CapsLock] key turned on, or you may have typed in a title or heading and forgotten to capitalize it. Word provides a handy way to change the case of letters. The Format/Change Case command is a real time-saver, allowing you to select the correct case from a dialog box and keeping you from having to retype the material.

The dialog box shown in Figure 6.9 shows the choices of case you may apply to highlighted text. Sentence case applies a capital letter to the first letter highlighted and lowercase to the rest. The lowercase and UPPERCASE choices change the high-

lighted material to all uppercase or all lowercase letters. Title Case capitalizes the first letter of each highlighted word and places the other letters in lower case. The tOGGLE cASE choice changes all capital letters to lowercase, and all lowercase letters to capitals. The shortcut key to *toggle* (switch between several choices) the case is [Shift][F3].

GUIDED ACTIVITY 6.3

Changing the Case of Text

1. Use the text from the previous Guided Activity. Highlight the top line with the words This is Times New Roman.

2. Select the command Format/Change Case. In the dialog box that appears, choose lowercase.

   The words change to resemble this: this is times new roman.

3. Select the command Format/Change Case. In the dialog box that appears, choose Sentence case.

   The result looks like this: This is times new roman.

4. Select the command Format/Change Case, and select Title Case. Now the text appears as this: This Is Times New Roman.

   Next use the shortcut key to toggle the case.

5. With the words still highlighted, hold down the Shift key and press the F3 key. Now the sentence appears in all capital letters: THIS IS TIMES NEW ROMAN.

6. Repeat the last step again, using the Shift F3 shortcut key. The letters all appear in lowercase.

7. Hold down the Shift key and press F3 6 or 7 times, while observing the effect on the highlighted characters. The case of the letters cycles through three choices. This process is called toggling.

Copying Formats with Format Painter

If you have gone through several steps applying formats to a segment of text, it can be troublesome to repeat the steps to format another portion of the document. You may think that using Edit/Copy could accomplish the task, but that command copies actual text and not the formatting only. Word provides an easy method to copy only the formats of characters to other text. The Format Painter button on the Standard toolbar may be used to pick up and apply character formatting.

Copying character formatting involves three steps. First, highlight the text with the formats you wish to copy. Second, click on the Format Painter button. At this point, the mouse pointer displays a paintbrush. Finally, highlight the text you wish to format. The text is formatted and the mouse pointer automatically changes back to normal.

To apply the formats several times, double-click on the Format Painter button in the second step. This allows the mouse pointer to keep the paintbrush and apply formatting to everything you highlight until you click again on the Format Painter button to turn it off.

GUIDED ACTIVITY 6.4

Using the Format Painter

1. Continue working with the document from the previous Guided Activity.

2. Select a few characters from the middle line of your name. This line has received formatting that changed the font name, and added words-only underline.

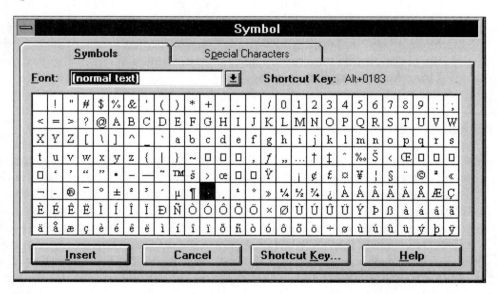

3. Click on the Format Painter button on the Standard toolbar. The mouse pointer changes to display a paintbrush next to the I-beam.

4. Highlight the text that says new text with the I-beam part of the mouse pointer. The character formatting now matches the other text.

Inserting Special Characters

Word provides numerous special characters in addition to the letters, numbers, and punctuation marks shown on the keyboard. You may wish to type letters with accent marks, fractions, cent signs, or trademark or copyright symbols. The command Insert/Symbol reveals a dialog box, shown in Figure 6.10, that provides these special characters and more.

FIGURE 6.10
The Symbol
dialog box

The dialog box has information under two tabs: Symbols and Special Characters. The symbols available under the Symbols tab depend upon the font selected. The (normal text) choice provides letters with accents (diacritical marks) for whatever font is used, as well as common fractions and British pound and Japanese yen symbols. Changing the font to Symbol reveals Greek letters and several mathematical symbols, such as summation and infinity. The Wingdings font provides small shapes and pictures to add sparkle to the page. Select the symbol desired and click Insert.

The Special Characters tab in the dialog box, shown in Figure 6.11, shows several common items used to give text a professional look. Although it may sometimes be acceptable to use two hyphens for a dash--such as these, for example--notice how much more polished the text looks with a real *em dash*—as shown in this sentence. Dates and page ranges are generally connected with *en dashes* rather than hyphens (as in 1994–95).

FIGURE 6.11
The Special Characters dialog box

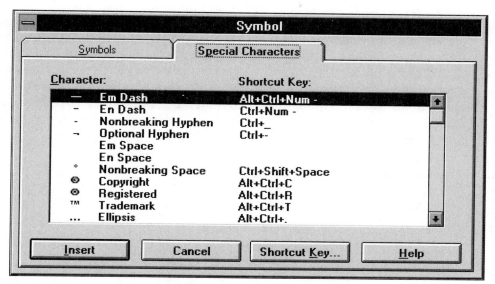

GUIDED ACTIVITY 6.5

Inserting Special Characters

1. Start a new document. Type the following text, leaving out the symbol.

   `Windows® is a registered trademark of Microsoft Corporation.`

2. Place the cursor just to the right of the word `Windows` but before the space.

3. Select Insert/Symbol, then select the Symbols tab.

   If (normal text) does not appear after Font, drop down the list and select it.

4. Some of the symbols are too small to see clearly. As you click on a symbol, Word doubles its size. Select the ® symbol.

5. Click on Insert, then click Close to exit the dialog box.

6. You can insert more than one symbol at a time. Type the following text on a new line, leaving out the quotation marks.

   `These are "curly" quotation marks.`

7. Select Insert Symbol, and click on the Special Characters tab.

8. Scroll down through the list of characters until you find Double Opening Quote. Highlight it and click on Insert. Instead of closing the dialog box, highlight the

Double Closing Quote and click on Insert. Select Close to return to your document.

Your text now appears like this:

`These are curly quotation marks.""`

9. Using cut-and-paste or drag-and-drop, move the symbols to their proper position.

As you inserted the symbols from the Special Characters tab, you probably noticed the shortcut keys that allow you to insert these symbols without opening the dialog box. In fact, there are many shortcut keys for character formats. You used the shortcut keys for bold, italic, and underline, which are simple to remember. Other shortcut keys are not quite as easy to remember, but if the formats are something you use often, shortcut keys can save you time. Shortcut keys for many character formats are given for reference in Table 6.1.

TABLE 6.1
Shortcut keys for character formatting

SHORTCUT KEY	FORMAT
Ctrl Shift F	Change font
Ctrl Shift P	Change point size
Ctrl Shift >	Increase font size to next size larger
Ctrl Shift <	Decrease font size to next size smaller
Ctrl]	Increase font size by 1 point
Ctrl [	Decrease font size by 1 point
Ctrl Shift A	All capitals
Ctrl B	Bold
Ctrl U	Underline
Ctrl Shift W	Word underline
Ctrl Shift D	Double underline
Ctrl Shift H	Hidden text
Ctrl I	Italicize
Ctrl Shift K	Small capitals
Ctrl =	Subscript
Ctrl Shift =	Superscript
Ctrl Spacebar	Plain text
Shift F3	Toggle case

Summary

Character formatting is the most specific of the three formatting levels (character, paragraph, document). Formats may be applied in four different ways:

- Click on buttons on the Formatting toolbar.
- Select the Format/Font command.

- Use the shortcut menu to select Font.

- Use shortcut keys.

The Formatting toolbar allows you to change the font and point size and add bold, italic, and underline formatting with a click of the mouse.

The Font and Point Size boxes change the actual appearance of the characters by allowing the user to select the shape and size of the letters. The use of bold, italics, or underline does not change the shape of the characters, but adds emphasis to them to make them stand out on a printed page. Several types of underlines and other formats such as color and customized character spacing are available from the Font dialog box. These commands are seldom used and therefore are not included on the Formatting toolbar.

Word provides several other tools to make complex formatting simple. Character formats may be copied from one selected segment of text to another with the Format Painter button. You can also choose from an array of special characters and symbols to insert into your document.

Exercises

1. Enter the following paragraph into a new document.

   ```
   The Formatting toolbar displays the font, point size, and
   other formats of the text at the insertion point to help
   you remember what formatting you have applied. In addition,
   the buttons on the Formatting toolbar make it easy to apply
   formatting with the mouse. Press the Ctrl key with the icon
   letter to format with the shortcut keys.
   ```

   Use each of the following format attributes on a different word in the text: bold, italic, underline, word underline (apply this format to three consecutive words), double underline, superscript, and subscript. Print the result. Save the file as A:EX6_1.

2. Use the document from Exercise 1. Format each of the sentences in the paragraph to a different font and point size. Print the result.

3. Change at least four words in the document to different colors. Print the result. What happens if you haven't got a color printer?

4. Format the first two sentences to condensed text. Format the third sentence to expanded text. Print the result.

5. Use the Format Painter to apply the format from the condensed area to a word in the expanded area. Print the result.

6. Open a new document. On separate lines, type the names of several fonts available within Word. Highlight each font name and apply the format. Next to each name specify whether the font is serif or sans-serif, and proportional or

nonproportional. Tell also whether the font is a TrueType font, a printer font, or neither. Save as A:EX6_6 and print the result.

7. Demonstrate what happens to descenders when they are underlined, by typing the letters `qpgjy`, underlining them, and printing the result.

8. Type the following text into a document, using symbols and special characters wherever needed. Use the en dash between the years.

```
piñata      résumé      98.6°F
Area of a circle = πr²      Area of a triangle = ½bh
©copyright 1994    1915–1985
```

Review Questions

*1. What are the three levels of formatting?

2. What is the difference between using the Formatting toolbar and using the Font dialog box to format text? What determines which method you use to execute a command?

*3. What is the difference between formatting text that already exists and formatting text that is being typed?

4. What is the difference between a proportional and a nonproportional font? Between a serif and sans-serif font? What uses are appropriate for each?

*5. Why are some commands included on the Formatting toolbar, while others are only available from the Font dialog box?

6. What commands are available only from the Font dialog box?

*7. What is the default font for Word? How may it be changed?

8. What is kerning?

*9. How may words be expanded or condensed?

10. What is the Format Painter used for?

*11. What special characters are available in Word, and how are they accessed?

Key Terms

Bold	Font	Small capitals
Capitals	Hidden	Strikethrough
Character spacing	Indirect formatting	Subscript
Condensed	Italics	Superscript
Default	Kerning	Toggle
Descender	Nonproportional	TrueType
Direct formatting	Point size	Underline
Em dash	Proportional	WYSIWYG
En dash	Sans-serif	
Expanded	Serif	

Documentation Research

1. How can you find or replace a certain font throughout a document?

2. How is hidden text made visible?

7
Formatting Paragraphs

The second level of formatting is paragraph formatting. Paragraph format commands are used to change the way a paragraph looks. This may be done by changing the indentation, the alignment, the spacing, and other specific paragraph attributes. These commands affect the paragraph where the cursor is located or any paragraphs that are partially or completely highlighted. This unit covers paragraph formatting using the toolbar, the ruler, and the Format/Paragraph command. You will also learn to copy these attributes and to combine them into a style.

Learning Objectives

At the completion of this unit you should know

1. how to format existing or new paragraphs,
2. what paragraph formats are available,
3. how to execute paragraph format commands from the toolbar, from the ruler, and from the menus.

Important Commands

Format/Borders and Shading

Format/Bullets and Numbering

Format/Paragraph

Format/Style

Format/Tabs

Formatting Paragraphs

The paragraph format commands are accessed in the same way as character format commands. Many of these commands are available on the Formatting toolbar, which you have already used, and on the ruler, found immediately below the toolbar. Paragraph format commands may be used to format one or more existing paragraphs. If there is no text currently highlighted, only the paragraph where the cursor is located will be affected by the command. If a paragraph is partially or completely highlighted, the entire paragraph will be changed to reflect the format command. This is known as direct paragraph formatting.

In addition to formatting paragraphs that have already been entered, you may also select the format command before typing. If you already know how the paragraph is to be formatted, this is usually faster than entering the text and formatting it later. This method of formatting, indirect formatting, is accomplished by selecting the desired format attribute as you start a new paragraph, and then typing the text. Indirect formatting stays in effect as you start new paragraphs until you turn it off.

Several paragraph formats may be changed from the Format/Paragraph dialog box. Alignment, spacing, and indentation are all found under the Indents and Spacing portion, shown in Figure 7.1. Other options are found under the Text Flow tab. Just like the Format/Font command, the Format/Paragraph command is found on the shortcut menu, accessed by clicking the *right* mouse button with the middle (or ring) finger.

FIGURE 7.1
The Indents and Spacing tab of the Paragraph dialog box

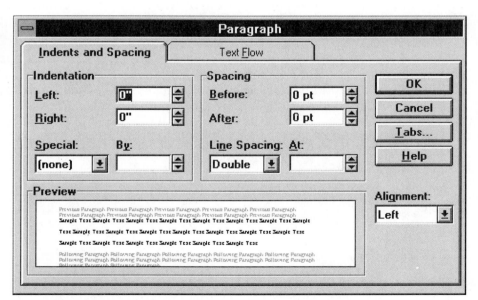

Alignment

Alignment of a paragraph refers to how paragraphs are aligned relative to the page margins. A paragraph may be aligned against the left margin, the right margin, or both margins, or it may be centered between the margins. These alignment options are changed with buttons on the Formatting toolbar, shown in Figure 7.2.

FIGURE 7.2
The Formatting
toolbar

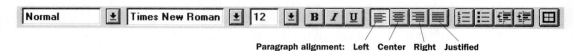

Paragraph alignment: Left Center Right Justified

When a paragraph is left-aligned (like this one), the left edge of the paragraph is even against the left margin of the page and the right edge is not even (also called *flush left* or "ragged right"). This alignment method is commonly used in letters and reports.

Justified paragraphs (like this one) are aligned against both left and right margins so that both edges of the paragraph are straight. If a line of text is not exactly long enough to fill the space between the two margins, space is added between the words to make the line longer. However, this alignment method does not increase the length of documents. Most newspapers, magazines, and books are justified.

Center alignment is usually not used for long paragraphs. This alignment method is used for titles, dates, and other short items that need to be centered between the left and right margins. Centering is done by clicking on the Center button on the toolbar.

This paragraph is centered.

Right alignment causes paragraphs to be flush along the right margin of the document (also called *flush right* or "ragged left"). It is not generally used to align long paragraphs.

This paragraph is right-aligned.

The alignment options can also be selected from the Format/Paragraph dialog box in the Alignment section, as shown in Figure 7.3. Select the alignment desired

FIGURE 7.3
Changing
alignment from
the Paragraph
dialog box

Paragraph
Indents and Spacing / Text Flow

Indentation
Left: 0"
Right: 0"
Special: (none) By:

Spacing
Before: 0 pt
After: 0 pt
Line Spacing: Single At:

OK
Cancel
Tabs...
Help

Preview

Alignment: Left
Left
Centered
Right
Justified

Alignment choices

from the drop-down list in the dialog box and click on OK to execute the command. The shortcut keys for alignment are fairly easy to remember: [Ctrl][L] for Align Left, [Ctrl][E] for Center, [Ctrl][R] for Align Right, and [Ctrl][J] for Justify.

GUIDED ACTIVITY 7.1

Aligning Paragraphs

For this activity you will need a segment of text at least two paragraphs long, such as A:4_A from Unit 4. If you do not have this file, you may type information from another book, a newspaper, or any other source you want. Each paragraph should be several lines long.

1. Start Word. Open the file or enter the segment of text you have selected for this exercise.

2. Position the cursor at the very beginning of the document. Press [Enter] twice to leave two blank lines above your text. Press [↑] twice to get the cursor back to the first line.

3. Enter today's date. Click on the Center button on the toolbar.

    The date, which started out on the left margin, moves to the center of the page.

4. Position the cursor anywhere in the first long paragraph of text. Click on the Align Left button to make sure the document is left-aligned.

    It may already be left-aligned, depending on how your version of Word is set up.

5. Now click on the Justify button.

    Now both edges of the paragraph are lined up with the document margins.

6. Position the cursor anywhere in the last paragraph. Click on the Align Right button to right-align the paragraph.

    The paragraph does not look very good right-aligned and may be difficult to read. Right alignment is not intended to be used for full paragraphs of text several lines long.

7. Position the cursor at the end of the last paragraph. Press [Enter] twice to leave a blank line.

8. Check the toolbar to make sure that the Align Right button is pressed in. If it is not, click on it now. The cursor should appear on the right side of the document.

9. On separate lines enter your name, street address, city, state, and zip code. Save the document as A:7_A.

    Right alignment is used to align several short lines of text along the right-hand side of a document. For example, when you create a business letter without letterhead it is common to add your name and address at the top of the letter. These lines could be aligned against the right margin by formatting them with the Align Right button.

Line Spacing

In addition to the alignment, you may also change the *line spacing*. The line spacing refers to the space between one line of text and the next. Single-spacing places lines of text close together and allows you to get the most information on a page. Double-spacing places a full blank line between each line of text. While this takes up more space on a page, it is easier to read and is the required format for many documents.

Word allows the user to format the line spacing from the Format/Paragraph dialog box, as shown in Figure 7.4. The first setting, Single, is the default mode for Word. Single-spacing allows just enough height to contain the font size selected and to separate it from the lines above and below it. If the size of even one letter on a line is larger, the spacing automatically increases to accommodate it. Spacing is measured either in lines, relative to the largest letter on the line, or in points, which is exact. You may recall that there are 72 points to the vertical inch. Double-spacing makes the lines twice as high, 1.5 Lines spacing allows a line and a half, and Multiple is used to select triple-spacing or larger.

FIGURE 7.4
Changing line spacing from the Paragraph dialog box

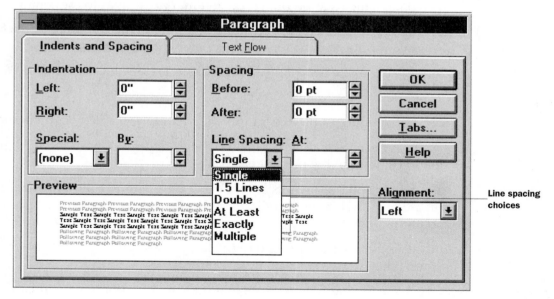

You might think that single-spacing of a line of 10-point text would have 10-point line spacing. As a matter of fact, Word gives an extra bit of white space between each line to increase legibility. This extra white space is known as *leading* (pronounced *ledding*) because in the days of hot-metal typesetting typesetters used to place a thin strip of lead between lines of type. Leading is typically 20 percent of the base points. Thus, a line of 10-point text has 12-point line spacing, 12-point text has a little more than 14-point line spacing, and so on. To achieve a true single space, specify exactly the number of points in the At box.

The At Least setting allows you to set the minimum number of points for the line height. Objects taller than the minimum setting will make the line higher. Problems arise when, in the midst of nicely flowing text, you have a few lines that are widely spaced because of a large object on the line. The Exactly selection overcomes this effect, making each line exactly the line height you specify, regardless of the height of objects on the line. The shortcut keys are [Ctrl][1] for Single spacing, [Ctrl][5] for 1.5 Lines spacing, and [Ctrl][2] for Double spacing. (Use the number keys at the top of the keyboard, rather than those on the keypad at the right side of the keyboard, since using [Ctrl] with the [5] on the keypad is the shortcut key for selecting the entire document.)

GUIDED ACTIVITY 7.2

Setting Line Spacing

1. Position the cursor anywhere in the first long paragraph. Make sure the spacing is set to Single by using the shortcut key [Ctrl][1].

2. Position the cursor in the second long paragraph. Change the spacing to Double by using the shortcut key [Ctrl][2].

   A full blank line is inserted after each line in the paragraph. The paragraph takes up twice as much room as before but is easier to read because the lines are farther apart.

3. Position the cursor in the third long paragraph. Select Format/Paragraph.

4. Under the Line Spacing section of the dialog box, select Multiple. Check that the At box is set to 3 lines. Notice the sample of this triple-spacing in the Preview window. Click OK.

   The height of each line of text is now 3 spaces. There are two full blank lines between each line of text.

   Another spacing option available in Word is to automatically place a space before each paragraph. This is a useful feature when you are entering a long single-spaced document and do not want to press [Enter] twice after each paragraph. The word processor automatically adds a blank line before each paragraph. To turn on this option, use the Spacing section of the Format/Paragraph dialog box, shown in Figure 7.5. You may also turn this feature on and off with the shortcut key [Ctrl][0] (zero).

   Additionally, you may change the amount of space added above the paragraph or may elect to place the blank line after the paragraph rather than before. Use the up or down arrows to the right of the Before or After box and enter the amount of space in points to leave before or after each paragraph. Click on OK to execute the command.

FIGURE 7.5
*Adding a blank
line before each
paragraph*

![Paragraph dialog box]

Paragraph

Indents and Spacing   Text Flow

Indentation

Left: [0"]   **Spacing**

Right: [0"]   Before: [12 pt]   OK

After: [0 pt]   Cancel

Special: **By:**   **Line Spacing: At:**   Tabs...

[(none)] [ ]   [Single] [ ]   Help

Preview

Alignment:

[Left   ▼]

Tabs

A *tab* is a marker that you define to allow you to move quickly to a specific horizontal position in a document. Tabs are used to align text at a location measured from the left margin of a document. When aligning a column of text or numbers formatted to a proportional font, you will find it is more accurate to use a tab than to try to line up the characters by pressing the [Spacebar] repeatedly. If you always use tabs to align numbers and text, you will save time later if you decide to change the font or point size of characters in the document, or if you modify column widths.

By default, if you press the [Tab] key, the cursor will jump one-half inch to the right. The arrows in Figure 7.6 indicate where the [Tab] key has been pressed. It is displayed in the same way as the Enter character, by clicking on the Show/Hide ¶ button on the toolbar. The tabs by default are set every half-inch along the ruler,

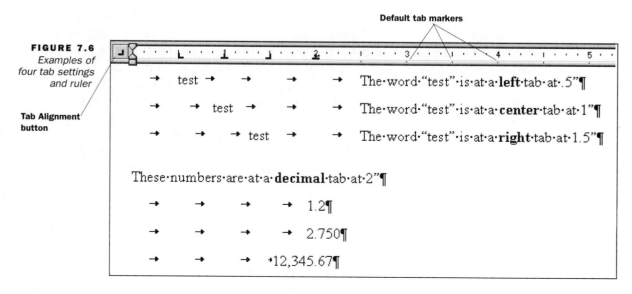

Default tab markers

FIGURE 7.6
*Examples of
four tab settings
and ruler*

**Tab Alignment
button**

→   test →   →   →   The·word·"test"·is·at·a·**left**·tab·at·.5"¶

→   → test →   →   →   The·word·"test"·is·at·a·**center**·tab·at·1"¶

→   →   → test →   →   The·word·"test"·is·at·a·**right**·tab·at·1.5"¶

These·numbers·are·at·a·**decimal**·tab·at·2"¶

→   →   →   →   1.2¶

→   →   →   →   2.750¶

→   →   →   ·12,345.67¶

indicated by small dots at the bottom edge of the ruler, shown in Figure 7.6. You may use the *default tabs* to align columns of information by pressing the [Tab] key once or several times, or you may create custom tab settings.

Custom tabs are placed on the ruler by clicking along the ruler's bottom edge under the measurement marks. Four kinds of tabs can be set from the ruler. The first and most commonly used is a left tab. A column of text typed from a left tab will be left-aligned (aligned along its left side) at the location of the tab. Right tabs are used to right-align a column of words (that is, to align it along its right side) at the location of the tab. Center tabs are used to center columns of text at the location of the tab stop. Decimal tabs align a column of numbers by their decimal points at the tab location. The type of tabs is selected by clicking on the Tab Alignment button on the left side of the ruler until the desired tab is displayed. (The four tab markers available are shown in the left margin.) The picture of the screen in Figure 7.6 gives examples of each of the four types of tabs.

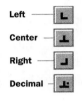

To place a tab on the ruler, check to see that its marker is displayed on the Tab Alignment button. If it is not, click on it to select the type of tab, and then click on the bottom edge of the ruler at the location where the tab is to be set. A marker representing the type of tab will appear at the bottom of the ruler at that location.

Remember that only the paragraph containing the cursor, or any paragraphs highlighted completely or partially, will be affected by the new tab settings. Before setting a tab for an entire document, you must highlight the entire document, by selecting Edit/Select All, or by triple-clicking in the left margin. Another method is to set the tabs before you begin typing.

GUIDED ACTIVITY 7.3

Creating Tabs

1. Open a new document by selecting File/New and clicking on OK. If the ruler is not visible, select View/Ruler to turn it on.

2. Click on the Tab Alignment button 3 times to select a decimal tab. Click on the bottom edge of the ruler directly below the number 2.

   The default tab markers from the left margin to your tab, which were located every half-inch on the ruler, are now gone. When the tab is removed from the ruler, the default tabs will return.

3. Press [Tab] on the keyboard.

   The cursor jumps to the location of the decimal tab.

4. Enter the number 3.1415. Press [Enter] and press [Tab] again.

   The cursor again lines up directly below the tab marker you inserted on the ruler.

5. Enter the number 100.5. Press [Enter], press [Tab], and type the number 0.386. Press [Enter] twice.

All the numbers you have just typed are aligned with their decimal points directly below the decimal tab you defined at 2" on the ruler.

6. Highlight all the lines, then drag the tab marker to the right one inch.

   That moves the tab so that it is set at 3" rather than 2".

7. Click on the decimal tab marker on the ruler and drag it from the bottom of the ruler.

   The decimal tab disappears and is replaced by default left tabs at every half-inch.

8. Place the cursor at the end of the last line and press `Enter` twice. Click on the Tab Alignment button to select a left tab. Click on the bottom edge of the ruler directly below the 1" mark. Click on the Tab Alignment button twice to select a right tab, and place a right tab below the 5" mark.

9. Press `Tab` to position the cursor at the first tab marker. Enter the text `Chapter One`. Press `Tab` to position the cursor at the second tab marker. Type `1`.

   You now have the first line of a table of contents. Chapter One begins on page 1.

10. Press `Enter` and press `Tab`. Type `Chapter Two`. Press `Tab` and type `23`.

11. Enter chapters three through five. Invent your own page numbers for the chapters.

   No matter what number you make the page numbers, they will align on their right-hand sides because they are lined up on a right tab.

   The table of contents looks good, but it could look better. It is difficult to tell which chapter name goes with each page number when there is so much white space between the names and the numbers. To avoid this, you can attach a *leader* to the second tab. A leader is a character, typically a dot or a dash, that leads the eye by filling the white space from the point where the cursor was located when you pressed the `Tab` key to the left-most character in the text (often a page number) lined up at the tab. Leaders cannot be added from the ruler. They are defined from the Format/Tabs dialog box.

12. Highlight all of the lines in the table of contents. Select Format/Tabs to display the dialog box shown in Figure 7.7.

   You may reach the same dialog box by selecting Format/Paragraph and clicking on the Tabs button. This box can be used to set tabs if you prefer not to use the ruler. You could enter a new position, select the alignment, and click on Set to set the tab. However, you have already set up the tabs you need. You just need to modify one.

13. In the Tab Stop Position box, click on 5" to highlight it.

   The option button (circle) next to Right in the Alignment box is filled in because the tab is a right tab.

14. Click on the circle next to 2 in the Leader box to set the dot leader. Click on OK.

FIGURE 7.7
*The Format
Tabs dialog box*

```
┌─────────────────────────────────────────────────────────┐
│ ─                        Tabs                            │
├─────────────────────────────────────────────────────────┤
│ Tab Stop Position:   Default Tab Stops: [0.5"   ] ⭤        [   OK    ] │
│ [              ]                                          │
│                    ┌─Alignment─┐ ┌─Leader──┐    [  Cancel  ] │
│              ↑     │ ◉ Left    │ │ ◉ 1 None│                │
│                    │ ○ Center  │ │ ○ 2 ....│    [   Set    ] │
│                    │ ○ Right   │ │ ○ 3 ----│                │
│                    │ ○ Decimal │ │ ○ 4 ____│    [  Clear   ] │
│              ↓     │ ○ Bar     │ └─────────┘                │
│                    └───────────┘              [ Clear All  ] │
│ Tab Stops to Be Cleared:                                 │
│                                               [   Help    ] │
└─────────────────────────────────────────────────────────┘
```

The dots lead from the chapter name to the page number, the white space between the two columns having been replaced by dot leaders.

A final element available in the Format/Tabs dialog box is the spacing of default tabs. When Word is first installed, there is a default left tab located every half-inch from the left to the right margins. These default tabs show up as small dots at the bottom edge of the ruler. You can change the spacing between the default tabs in your document by selecting a different value in the Default Tab Stops section of the Format/Tabs dialog box.

Paragraph Indents

Individual paragraphs can be indented from the left or right margins of the document, or both. You may *indent* the entire paragraph, only the first line, or all lines except for the first. Indentation is controlled by the ruler and the Format/Paragraph command.

The triangular markers on the left and right sides of the ruler, shown in Figure 7.8, are used to set the indent amounts for each paragraph. To indent the right side of a paragraph, click on the right paragraph indent marker at the right side of the ruler and drag it to the position where you want the new right side to be. The ruler is calibrated in inches by default, so it should be easy for you to indent a specific amount. Word will figure the new places for word wrap for each line and will then redisplay the paragraph. The marker that represents the left paragraph indent, located at the left edge of the ruler, consists of two parts. The upper triangle is the indent amount for the first line of the paragraph. The lower triangle is the indent amount for all lines but the first. The small square below the lower triangle on the left moves both the upper and lower triangles together.

To indent the first line of every paragraph in a document, you could press the [Tab] key at the beginning, then type the paragraph. Instead, Word allows you to indent

FIGURE 7.8
The ruler

First line
Subsequent lines
Left indent
Right indent

the first line automatically by setting the indentation from the ruler. To indent only the first line of the paragraph one-half inch, you would drag the upper triangle to the right to the tick mark halfway between the 0 and the 1. The lower triangle stays in place; therefore, the second and subsequent lines of the paragraph are not indented.

Like all paragraph format commands, paragraph indents only affect the paragraph containing the cursor or any paragraphs partially or completely highlighted. All other paragraphs will be unaffected. Paragraph indents will only affect the entire document if it is completely highlighted first.

Word also includes a way to quickly indent (or unindent) the left edge of a paragraph to the next (or previous) tab stop. To indent a paragraph to the next tab stop, press the Increase Indent button on the toolbar. All of the lines in the paragraph will be indented to the next tab stop to the right. If no tab stops are set, the indent will be set to the default tab stop. The Reduce Indent button shifts the paragraph indent one tab to the left. The shortcut keys for these operations are [Ctrl][M] to increase indent, and [Ctrl][Shift][M] to reduce indent.

Sometimes the first line of a paragraph is not indented, but the remaining lines are. For example, a numbered list has the number at the left margin, but the rest of the paragraph is indented, as in the Guided Activities in this book. To set this type of indentation, move the lower triangle on the left indent marker, but leave the upper triangle at the margin. This is termed a *hanging indent* because the first line is left hanging. Word automates this operation with the shortcut key [Ctrl][T], which indents the lower triangle to the first tab stop or default tab, if none is set. The shortcut key [Ctrl][Shift][T] removes the hanging indent. The shortcut keys used in formatting paragraphs are shown in Table 7.1.

TABLE 7.1	SHORTCUT KEY	FORMAT
Paragraph formatting shortcut keys	[Ctrl][1]*	Single space
	[Ctrl][2]*	Double space
	[Ctrl][5]*	Space-and-a-half
	[Ctrl][0] (zero)*	Add and remove blank line preceding paragraph
	[Ctrl][E]	Center
	[Ctrl][J]	Justify
	[Ctrl][L]	Left-align
	[Ctrl][R]	Right-align
	[Ctrl][M]	Increase indent
	[Ctrl][Shift][M]	Decrease indent
	[Ctrl][T]	Hanging indent
	[Ctrl][Shift][T]	Reduce hanging indent
	[Ctrl][Q]	Remove all paragraph formatting

*Use the numbers along the top row of the keyboard.

Indenting Paragraphs

1. If you closed the original document in this unit, open A:7_A.DOC. If not, select the command Window/A:7_A.DOC to return to the document you created in this unit.

2. Position the cursor in the first paragraph. Drag the right indent triangle one inch to the left. If the right side of the ruler does not appear on the screen, click on the horizontal scroll bar at the bottom of the screen until it comes into view.

   The right side of the paragraph should move to the left one inch.

3. Click the Increase Indent button on the Toolbar *twice*.

   The left side of the paragraph moves to the one-inch mark on the ruler, if you are using the default tabs.

4. Click the Reduce Indent button on the Toolbar.

   The left edge of the paragraph moves back under the half-inch mark on the ruler.

5. Drag the square on the left indent marker to the right one-half inch.

   The paragraph is again indented one inch on both sides. This format may be used with long quotations from another source.

6. Click anywhere in the second paragraph to position the cursor there. Drag the lower triangle on the left indent marker one-half inch to the right.

   The first line of the paragraph is not indented, but the rest of the paragraph is.

7. Position the cursor in the third paragraph. Select Format/Paragraph.

   It is not mandatory to use the ruler to set the indent amounts.

8. Use the up arrows next to the Left box to enter 0.5". Select First Line in the Special box under Indentation and 1" in the By box, as shown in Figure 7.9. A sample of this indentation format shows in the preview area of the dialog box. Click on OK to execute the command.

   Either method of paragraph indenting will work. Using the ruler allows you to see the text as you position the indent markers, but the dialog box allows you to specify the measurements more accurately.

Text Flow

Word gives the user control over how the text flows between pages, from the Text Flow tab of the Paragraph dialog box, shown in Figure 7.10. For instance, you may occasionally create a paragraph that you do not want separated at the end of a page. You may elect to keep a paragraph intact by checking the Keep Lines Together check box. Rather than breaking your paragraph at the end of a page, Word will move the entire paragraph to the top of the next page.

FIGURE 7.9
*The Paragraph
dialog box
showing
indentation
settings*

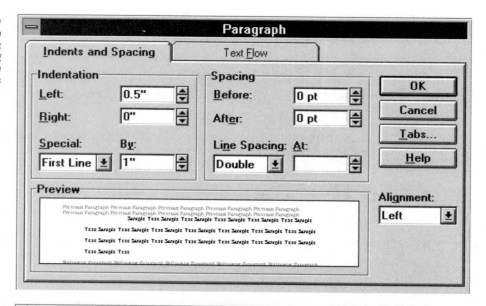

FIGURE 7.10
*The Text Flow
tab of the
Paragraph
dialog box*

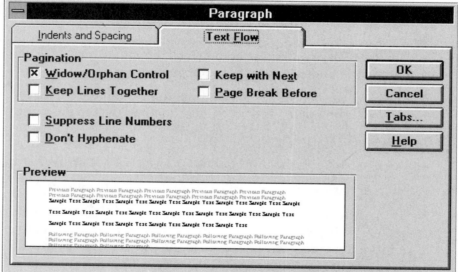

A second option is to keep a paragraph together with the next paragraph. This is extremely useful to avoid having headings appear alone at the bottom of a page, or separating a graph from an explanatory caption or paragraph. To prevent these kinds of occurrences, check Keep with Next. The Page Break Before option may be used with headings that must always begin at the top of a page, regardless of the amount of text before them. Widow/Orphan control prevents a single line of a paragraph from appearing on a page separate from the rest of the paragraph.

Borders and Shading

Another useful paragraph attribute is the ability to have a line above, beside, or under a paragraph or any other object like a picture or graphic, or to set apart a portion of text with shading. Like other paragraph formatting, *borders* and *shading* affect paragraphs that are partially or completely highlighted, or the paragraph where the cursor is located. The Borders button on the Formatting toolbar causes a new toolbar to be displayed on the screen. The Borders toolbar, shown in Figure 7.11, contains buttons for adding a border to the top, bottom, left, or right side of a paragraph, as well as to the inside (if several paragraphs are highlighted) or outside of a paragraph or paragraphs. The No Border button, toward the right side of the toolbar, removes any borders that have been applied. The drop-down box on the left of the toolbar gives choices for the line style of the border, from thin to thick, and single, double, dotted, or dashed. The drop-down list box on the right sets the shading behind the paragraph. Shading may be very light (5%) through very dark (90%) or even patterned. Not all these effects are available on dot-matrix printers. To remove shading, select the choice Clear, which is the default. When you are through formatting the borders and shading, you may remove this toolbar from the screen by clicking again on the Borders button.

FIGURE 7.11
The Borders toolbar with Line style choices

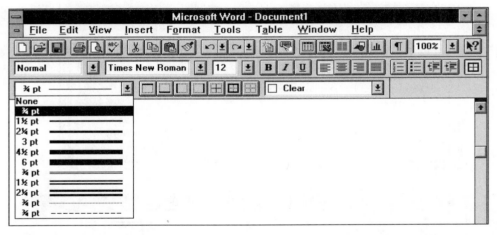

The only way to add color to the borders and shading is through the dialog box, accessed with the command Format/Borders and Shading.

Placing Numbers and Bullets on Paragraphs

Placing bullets or numbering paragraphs with a word processor is an easy process. Word makes it even easier with two buttons on the Formatting toolbar, plus the Bullets and Numbering command found on both the Format menu and the shortcut menu.

To place numbers automatically on lines or paragraphs, highlight the paragraphs in the document that are to be numbered and click on the Numbering button. A number appears at the beginning of each of the selected paragraphs. This is much easier than typing in numbers by hand. You may choose to insert a number before every paragraph in the document or only before certain highlighted paragraphs.

Clicking the Numbering button turns on numbering, and as you press Enter⏎, each paragraph is automatically numbered and formatted with a hanging indent of .25 inches. If the paragraphs are later rearranged, the paragraphs are automatically renumbered. The user can specify the numbering scheme through the Bullets and Numbering dialog box. The Numbered tab is shown in Figure 7.12. The Modify button opens a dialog box where the starting number and the size of the hanging indent may be changed, as shown in Figure 7.13. To remove numbers, highlight the paragraphs and click on the Numbering button again.

A ***bullet*** is a small symbol generally placed at the left of several lines to catch the eye and visually separate and emphasize each line. Placing bullets at the left edge of

FIGURE 7.12
The Numbered tab of the Bullets and Numbering dialog box

FIGURE 7.13
The Modify Numbered List dialog box

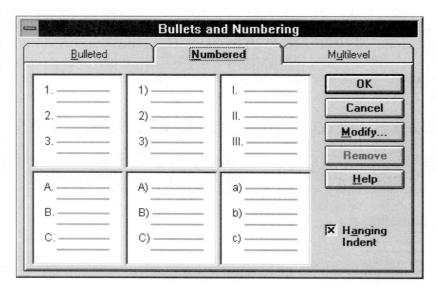

a paragraph is similar to placing numbers. It is accomplished by clicking on the Bullets button on the Formatting toolbar. A small round symbol appears at the left margin, and the paragraphs are given a hanging indent format.

The Bulleted tab portion of the Bullets and Numbering dialog box, shown in Figure 7.14, also contains a Modify button. This button reveals a dialog box, shown in Figure 7.15, with several additional options for modifying bulleted paragraphs. It is a simple matter to choose a color, to specify a different style of bullet (such as diamond, arrow, or asterisk), or to change the size of the available bullets by increasing or decreasing the point size. Sometimes there is a need for a special symbol to be used as a bullet, such as a check mark or a check box. To get other choices for bullets, click the Bullet button. The Symbol dialog box appears (the same one that appears when you select Insert/Symbol), in which you may change the font to find new bullet choices. The TrueType font Wingdings is a set of small symbols—some quite

FIGURE 7.14
The Bulleted tab of the Bullets and Numbering dialog box

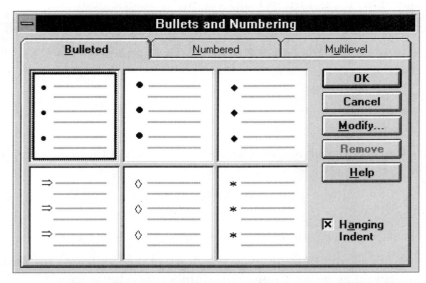

FIGURE 7.15
The Modify Bulleted List dialog box

More bullet symbols

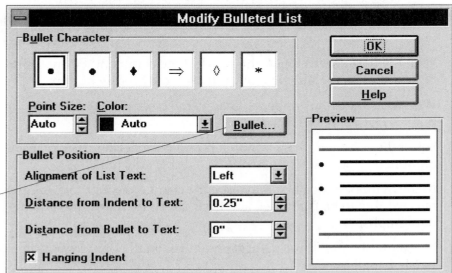

decorative—suitable for use as bullets. Selecting one of the symbols, numbers, or images from the fonts available and clicking OK causes the new symbol to replace the bullet that was highlighted when the Bullet button was pressed.

GUIDED ACTIVITY 7.5

Adding Borders, Numbers, and Bullets to Paragraphs

1. Create a new document. Enter the following text.

   ```
   Paragraph One
   Paragraph Two
   Paragraph Three
   ```

2. Highlight the three lines and click on the Numbering button.

   The paragraphs are immediately numbered, and the text is indented .25 inch.

3. Place the cursor at the end of Paragraph Three and press ⏎Enter. Add the following text.

   ```
   Paragraph Four
   Paragraph Five
   Paragraph Six
   ```

   Since the Numbering format was turned on, each of these paragraphs is numbered immediately.

4. Using cut-and-paste or drag-and-drop, move Paragraph Four above Paragraph Three.

   The paragraphs are automatically renumbered.

5. Highlight all six paragraphs. Use the shortcut menu to open the Bullets and Numbering dialog box. Change the numbering scheme to ABC, and click OK.

6. Highlight the last three paragraphs and change the numbers to bullets by clicking on the Bullets button.

7. With the paragraphs highlighted, select the command Format/Bullets and Numbering, choose the Bulleted tab, and click the Modify button.

8. When the dialog box appears, change the color of the bullets and increase the point size, then click OK.

9. Select the command Format/Bullets and Numbering, click on Modify, then click on Bullets.

10. In the Symbol dialog box that appears, change the font to Wingdings. Select a new symbol to be the bullet, and click OK twice to see the changes to the paragraphs.

11. Highlight the first three paragraphs. Click on the Borders button to reveal the Borders toolbar.

12. Press the Outside Borders button to place a box around all three paragraphs.

13. With the first three paragraphs highlighted, change the line style of the border to double lines, and click the Outside Borders button again.

14. Access the command Format/Borders and Shading. Choose the Shading tab, then change the color of the Foreground to blue and the Shading to 20%. Click OK.

15. Highlight Paragraph Two. Remove the shading by changing back to Clear on the Borders toolbar.

16. Remove the border from Paragraph Two by clicking on the Top, Bottom, Left, and Right buttons on the Borders toolbar. Remove the toolbar from sight by clicking on the Borders button.

Checking and Copying Formats

Paragraphs may have several formats, such as indents, tabs, alignment, and borders, which have taken several steps to apply. You may wish to reveal all the formatting that has been applied to a section of text. To do this, simply click on the Help button, then click on the text where you wish to see the formatting. A window appears describing the paragraph and font formatting for that segment of text.

Word stores the formatting in the ¶ symbol at the end of each paragraph, which denotes when the Enter key was pressed. Sometimes the Enter character is invisible on the screen, and it is never printed: it is meant to separate paragraphs and terminate lines, not to actually be seen. However, you may see the exact location of the Enter symbol in Word by clicking on the Show/Hide ¶ button on the toolbar. This button displays or hides special characters in the work area that are normally hidden. These characters include spaces, Enter characters, and tabs. With this feature turned on, a paragraph symbol (¶) will appear at each location the Enter key was pressed. Even though the special characters are displayed in the work area, they will never print. To make the special characters invisible on the screen again, click on the paragraph button once more.

To copy the paragraph format from one paragraph to another, simply click the Show/Hide ¶ button to reveal the nonprinting characters. Copy the ¶ symbol at the end of the correctly formatted paragraph and paste at the end of the paragraph that needs to be formatted.

Style

The Style feature in Word can save you a tremendous amount of time and ensure that paragraphs are formatted consistently. When you get a paragraph formatted the way you want it (indents, tabs, alignment, spacing, and so on), you may discover that you need other paragraphs in your document formatted exactly the same way. You could execute all of the necessary format commands, one by one, each time to get the desired effect, or you could carefully copy ¶ symbols; however, Word allows you to save the format attributes under a new style name that you select, enabling you to use it many times in a document. Several styles are predefined and listed in the drop-down box on the Formatting toolbar, as shown in Figure 7.16.

FIGURE 7.16

Formatting Toolbar showing Styles

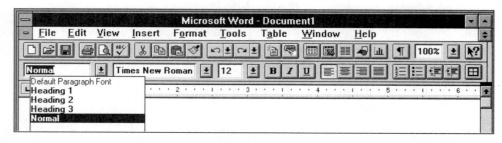

GUIDED ACTIVITY 7.6

Defining Styles

1. Position the cursor in the first paragraph of your document. Double-click the Style box at the left-most edge of the Formatting toolbar. The word Normal will be highlighted. Type the word New and press [Enter].

2. Position the cursor in the fifth paragraph. Click on the down arrow to the right of the Style box on the toolbar.

3. Select New from the list by clicking on it.

   All of the format attributes from the first paragraph are applied to the fifth paragraph. You can position the cursor in any paragraph and select the New style to immediately apply the format attributes from the first paragraph. The paragraph containing the cursor and any completely or partially highlighted paragraphs will be formatted with the attributes defined for the style. To apply the style to the entire document, you must highlight the document before selecting the style.

   Styles can also be defined from the menus by selecting Format/Style.

   Styles are saved as part of the template. Word provides many preformatted styles that you may view by selecting Format/Style Gallery. The Style feature can save you time and aggravation while ensuring consistency when you have many paragraphs in the same document that require the identical paragraph format attributes.

Summary

Paragraph format commands affect the paragraph where the cursor is located or any paragraph that is completely or partially included in a highlighted segment of text.

Many paragraph format commands are available from the toolbar, including alignment, indentation, bullets, numbering, borders, and shading. The ruler can be used to change indents and tabs. These functions can also be performed from the Format/Paragraph, Format/Bullets and Numbering, and Format/Borders and Shading dialog boxes. The dialog boxes offer more options for commands than are available from the ruler or the toolbar. Paragraph formatting may be copied by copying the ¶

paragraph symbol at the end of the paragraph, or by creating a new style and applying the style elsewhere.

Exercises

1. Write a paragraph comparing the paragraph formatting found in a textbook and the paragraph formatting in a magazine or newspaper. Make three additional copies of the paragraph in the same document. Make the first, second, third, and fourth paragraphs left-aligned, right-aligned, centered, and justified, respectively. Print the result. Save the file as A:EX7_1.

2. Continue with the file from Exercise 1. Change the spacing of the second paragraph to 1.5 lines, the third paragraph to double-spacing, and the fourth to triple-spacing. Print the result and save the document.

3. Enter the following table into a new document. Use left tabs to align the columns at one inch and four inches. Save the file as A:EX7_3. Print the result.

```
Jeff          772-1551
Andrew        776-8528
Caroline      751-1611
Stephanie     799-4044
```

4. Continue with the document from Exercise 3. Change the tab at four inches to a tab at five inches. Change the tab to have an underline leader. Print the result.

5. Create a new document. List six elements on the ruler and explain how each may be used to change the format of a paragraph. Format the first two items with a hanging indent. Format the second two items with bullets. Number the last two items. Execute each format command once by highlighting the segment before changing the format. Save as A:EX7_5. Print the result.

6. Open the file A:EX7_1. Justify the entire document. Change the indent so that only the first line of each paragraph is indented one-half inch. All other lines in the document should be against the left margin. Indent the right side of the second and third paragraphs one inch. Print the result. Save the changes.

7. Open the file A:EX7_5. Place borders around the second, third, and fourth paragraphs. The second paragraph border should be a single line outline, the third a double outline, and the fourth a dashed outline with light shading. Print the result.

8. Open A:EX7_1. Format the first paragraph to 1.5-line spacing, one-half inch hanging left indent, one-half inch right indent, a right tab at two inches, and full justification. Create a style based on this paragraph called STYLE7.

Format the fourth paragraph to the style STYLE7. Print the result.

Review Questions

*1.   What determines which paragraphs will be formatted when a paragraph format command is executed?

2.   Which methods may be used to apply paragraph formatting?

*3.   What are the four paragraph-alignment methods available in Word? What is each one used for?

4.   What is leading? Why does Word include leading by default? How is leading modified?

*5.   What is a tab? How are tabs set? How do the four different types of tabs work? What is the purpose of a leader? What kinds of leaders are available?

6.   Explain the functions of the triangular markers at the right and left edges of the ruler. How are the same functions performed using the Format/Paragraph dialog box?

*7.   What is the purpose of the Keep Lines Together and Keep With Next commands?

8.   What are bullets? How are they applied? What choices in bullets are available? Which paragraph indent is automatically applied?

*9.   Which new toolbar appears when you click a button on the Formatting toolbar? Which formats may be applied or removed from the new toolbar?

10.   How can you view the formatting of a certain segment of a document? How can paragraph formatting be copied?

*11.   What is a style? How are styles defined?

Key Terms

Alignment	Indent	Shading
Border	Justified	Style
Bullet	Leader	Tab
Default tab	Leading	
Hanging indent	Line spacing	

Documentation Research

1.   What styles are available through Word?

2.   What is the multilevel list format used for?

8 Formatting Documents

This unit describes the use of document format commands, the third and most general level of formatting. These commands will not change the actual appearance of the text or individual paragraphs but *will* change the way the pages as a whole look by allowing you to select the paper size, text margins, and other items affecting the entire document or sections of the document.

A document may be viewed in several ways. You may view a page in closeup to see details, or far away to get the overall appearance of the page. You may wish to view the entire page to see how the text fits within the margins. The various views Word provides are useful for seeing formatting at the document, or page, level.

Learning Objectives

At the completion of this unit you should know

1. how to format the layout of a page,

2. several ways to view a document,

3. how some typical documents are formatted.

Important Commands

File/Page Setup

Insert/Break

Insert/Page Numbers

Tools/Word Count

View/Full Screen

View/Page Layout

View/Zoom

Formatting Documents

Document format commands may be used to change the look of a page or an entire document. You may have a document with an attractive font style and size, the paragraphs with the correct indent and line spacing, but to finish the formatting you need to establish the layout of the pages. The document may be printed on standard 8½"×11" paper or on another size, such as legal size paper (8½"×14"). The text may be printed sideways on a page rather than vertically, and on only one side of the page, or on both the front and back. The document may or may not be bound. Page numbers will be needed for documents over two pages long. Word provides several simple procedures to establish document formatting.

Margins

The margins are the distance between the edge of the paper and the printed text. They are independent of the size of the paper and any format attributes of the text on the page. Margins are set in two ways: with the ruler, and from a dialog box in the Margins tab of the File/Page Setup.

This command gives you the choice of displaying four different dialog boxes. To see the Margins section, click on the Margins tab. As you can see in Figure 8.1, the default margins are 1 inch at the top and bottom of the page and 1.25 inches at the left and right edges. You may change any of the margins by clicking the up or down arrows next to the Top, Bottom, Left, or Right box until the desired number appears.

FIGURE 8.1
The Margins tab of the File/Page Setup dialog box

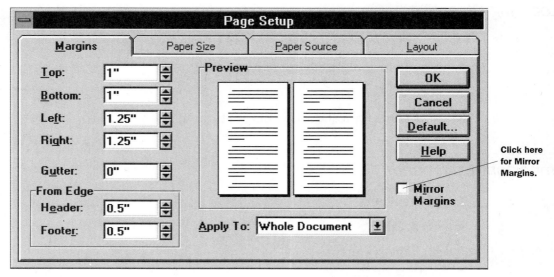

Click here for Mirror Margins.

If a document is to be bound, you need to leave extra space along the edge of the paper where the binding will go so that the text will not be hidden by the binding. Word provides a specific setting, the *gutter*, that is used to allow extra space along the side of the page for binding. When binding a document that is printed on the front of the page only, the gutter makes the left margin a specific distance wider than normal to allow for the binding. However, when binding a document that will be printed on both sides of the page, some document pages will be bound on the left and others on the right.

Word allows you to set up different margins for even-numbered (left-hand) and odd-numbered pages (right-hand) in a document by using the *Mirror Margins* feature. This allows you to specify margins for documents printed on both sides of the page. In the File/Page Setup dialog box, click in the box next to Mirror Margins. The words Left and Right are replaced by Inside and Outside. You may now set the inside and outside margins for each page. The inside margin is the margin that will be against the binding, while the outside margin is the one at the outer edge of the document.

In the Guided Activity below, you will set up the page to have asymmetrical margins, then add a gutter to leave room for the binding. Both odd and even pages will print correctly, with extra space left along the right or left margin, whichever is against the binding for each page.

GUIDED ACTIVITY 8.1

Setting Margins Using Page Setup

1. Type two short paragraphs, each at least four lines long, or open A:4_A (from Unit 4).

2. Position the cursor in the first paragraph. Change the left paragraph indent by moving the square at the left side of the ruler and dragging it one inch to the right (or click the Increase Indent button twice). Select File/Print Preview.

   The left edge of the first paragraph is indented one inch farther than the second. Paragraph indentation is different from margins in that indentation only affects the highlighted paragraph, while margins affect the entire document.

3. Select File/Page Setup. Change the left margin to 1.5 by clicking 3 times on the up arrow next to the Left box. Press OK.

   The new margin you selected increases the space between the edge of the paper and the closest text to 1.5 inches. The left edge of the first and second paragraphs are one-fourth inch farther to the left than previously. However, the first paragraph is still indented on its left edge 1 inch farther than the second. It is indented 1 inch from the left margin, regardless of the margin setting.

4. Select File/Page Setup. Double-click in the Left box of the Margins section of the dialog box. Type 2.25 and press Enter.

Wherever the left margin is placed, the first paragraph will appear 1 inch farther to the right than the second.

5. Close the preview screen. Select the entire document by triple-clicking on the left edge of the work area. Select Edit/Copy.

6. Position the cursor at the end of the document. Select Insert/Break and click on the OK button.

    A dotted line labeled Page Break stretches across the page, and the cursor is now located at the beginning of page 2. By selecting Insert/Break you inserted a page break at the location of the cursor.

7. Select Edit/Paste.

    A copy of the first page appears on the second page.

8. Repeat steps 6 and 7 to create a third page and paste the text on it.

9. Select File/Page Setup and click in the box next to Mirror Margins to place an X in the box, as shown in Figure 8.2.

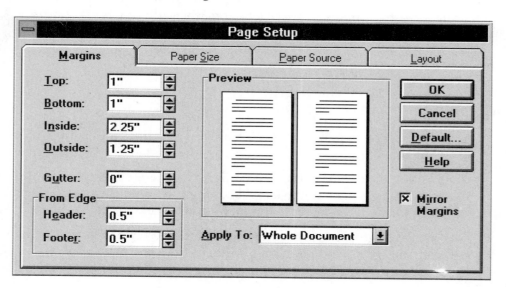

With Mirror Margins selected, the words Left and Right change to Inside and Outside. This feature is used to set the margins for a document that will be printed on both sides of the page and be bound.

10. Use the up arrow to increase the value in the Gutter box to .5. The gutter appears in the Preview section of the dialog box as a shaded area on the inside margin. Click OK.

11. Position the cursor at the top of page 1. Click on the Print Preview button. Click-and-drag on the Multiple Pages button to view two pages at once on the preview screen.

    The first page is displayed on the right-hand side of the screen.

12. Click on the Next Page button in the lower-right corner to view pages 2 and 3.

In a bound document, page 2 would be on the left and page 3 on the right. The right margin for page 2 and the left margin for page 3 are wider than the outside margins to allow extra room for the binding. The gutter is added to the inside margin to allow room for the binding. You can see the difference in size between the two margins in Print Preview, but the gutter appears only as part of the inside margin.

13. Click on Close to exit the preview screen. Save the document as A:8_A.

Paper Size

Word offers complete flexibility when selecting a size of paper. The Paper Size tab on the Page Setup dialog box allows you to enter any height and width, as shown in Figure 8.3.

FIGURE 8.3
*The Paper
Size tab*

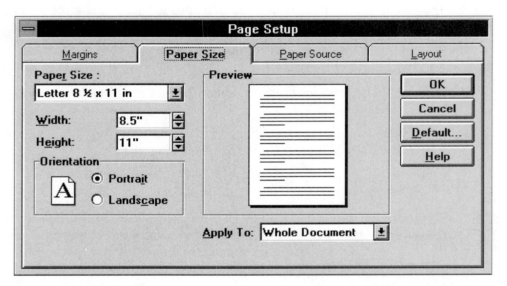

The default values are 8.5" wide by 11" high, the dimensions of a standard sheet of typing paper. You may pick one of the standard paper sizes by selecting from the Paper Size list or enter any values by double-clicking in either the height or width box and typing in a new number.

While the word processor may allow you to change these settings to any value, your printer may require certain paper sizes. Pin-feed paper used by some printers only comes in certain sizes. Laser printers often will only accept paper of specific sizes. Check your printer manual for more details.

You may also select the print *orientation* of the document from this section of the dialog box. Orientation refers to the direction of the sheet of paper with the text right side up. If the paper is taller than it is wide, that is termed *portrait* orientation, just as a portrait of a person is generally taller than it is wide. If the paper is wide rather than tall when the text is right side up, this is termed *landscape* orientation, just as landscape paintings are most often horizontal. Wide tables of information may fit better on a page in landscape orientation. In Word for Windows 6.0, the orientation is stored along with the document, not as a printer setting. This allows you to work with both portrait and landscape documents at the same time—or in both orientations within one document—without having to worry about changing the printer setting.

GUIDED ACTIVITY 8.2

Changing Paper Size and Orientation

1. Use the document from the previous guided activity. Click on the Print Preview button to view a picture of the standard-size page. Click the One Page button.

2. Select File/Page Setup and select the Paper Size tab. Select `Legal 8½ x 14 in` from the list of paper sizes. Click on the OK button.

    The picture of the page is now three inches longer than before you changed the page size.

3. Select File/Page Setup, and change the paper size back to 8½ by 11 inches. Select Landscape and click OK.

    Now the page is wider than it is long. The text automatically wraps to fit the wider page.

4. Select File/Page Setup, and change the orientation back to Portrait. Click OK. Click on the Close button to exit the preview screen.

Paper Source

Another section of the Page Setup dialog box allows you to select the paper source for your document. Many printers have more than one paper source. This is particularly useful for documents like letters where the first page would print on letterhead and the rest on plain paper. Students in computer labs desiring to print on letterhead stationery may wish to manually feed the special paper into the printer. Word allows you to take advantage of the capability of printers to feed different kinds of paper from different sources. To change the paper source, select File/Page Setup and select the Paper Source tab to see the result shown in Figure 8.4.

The different paper sources available for your printer will be displayed in both the First Page and Other Pages boxes. Select the paper source for the first and other pages in your document and click OK. Make sure the proper paper types are in the bins you selected before printing.

Numbering Pages

Documents that are more than one or two pages long will most likely require page numbers. Word automatically numbers pages when you issue the command Insert/Page Numbers. The dialog box that appears is shown in Figure 8.5. The user must specify the position and alignment of the page numbers on the page.

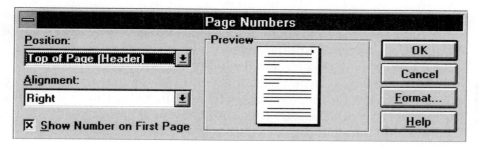

FIGURE 8.4
The Paper Source tab

FIGURE 8.5
The Page Numbers dialog box

Page numbers may be placed within either the top margin or the bottom margin of every page. Once that position is specified, the alignment must be chosen. Page numbers may be at the left side, the center, or the right side of the page. If Mirror Margins is checked in Page Setup, then the page numbers may also be placed on the inside or outside of the page. The Format button on the dialog box allows you to specify the starting page number, in cases where the document does not start on page 1, as well as the numbering sequence, such as arabic or roman numerals or alphabetic letters.

GUIDED ACTIVITY 8.3

Numbering Pages

1. Use the three-page document from the previous guided activity. Select the command Insert/Page Numbers.

2. Select Top of Page (Header) from the Position drop-down box.

3. Select Right under Alignment and Click OK.

4. Use Print Preview to see the page numbers on each page.

They are really too small to appear as anything more than dots.

5. Click on the Magnifier tool, place the mouse pointer over the page number, and click. Now you can see the page number clearly.

6. Press ⌊PgDn⌋ or click the Next Page arrow on the scroll bar to view the page numbers on pages 2 and 3.

Click Close to exit Print Preview.

Page numbers may also be inserted and modified as headers and footers.

Working in Other Views

Word provides more than one way to accomplish many tasks. Some tasks of document formatting can be performed more easily if you change to a different view. Until now, you have been working in Normal view, which shows a many-paged document as a seamless flow of text broken only by dotted lines showing where pages break. To see the actual pages, you use Print Preview. Buttons on the Print Preview toolbar allow you to zoom in for a close-up view of the page, to zoom out again, or even to view multiple pages at a time.

A hybrid of Normal view and Print Preview is Page Layout view. Page Layout view is accessed by selecting from the menu View/Page Layout or by clicking the Page Layout view button, which is in the middle of the three view buttons in the lower-left corner of the screen. To return to Normal view, click the button on the left. The button on the right displays the document in Outline view, which you will learn about in Unit 14.

Like Print Preview, Page Layout view shows the page exactly as it will appear when printed, including the margins and page numbers. Like Print Preview, Page Layout view displays a vertical ruler and the two arrow buttons on the vertical scroll bar that allow you to jump quickly to the next or previous page. (If the vertical ruler does not appear, select Tools/Options, choose the View tab, and click in the check box next to Vertical Ruler.)

Like Normal view, the Standard and Formatting toolbars appear in their usual place. Unlike Normal view, Page Layout view allows you to see the entire width and length of every page, so that the bottom margin of the first page is followed by the top margin of the next page against a darker desktop. The new features of Page Layout view, shown in Figure 8.6, make it easier to apply document formatting and quickly see the effects.

Page Layout view allows you to change the margins of a document by dragging the margin settings on the ruler. The part of the document between the margins shows on the ruler in white; the shaded part of the ruler is the margin area. On the vertical ruler, the top of the document is set at the zero mark on the ruler. When you place the mouse at the top of the vertical ruler on the line between the white and shaded part, the mouse pointer changes to a two-headed arrow. As you drag on the boundary to change the top margin, the rulers reflect the new measurement. The horizontal ruler changes the left and right margins. Place the mouse pointer on the left edge of the horizontal ruler just between the upper and lower triangles in order

FIGURE 8.6
Page Layout view

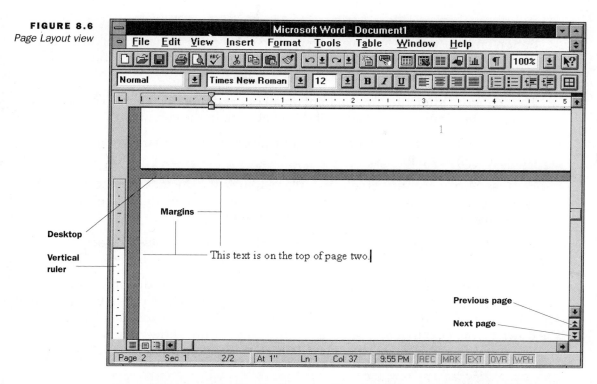

to turn it into a two-headed arrow. To view the measurement of the margins in numbers, rather than ruler markings, hold down the [Alt] key.

GUIDED ACTIVITY 8.4

Changing the Margins with the Ruler

1. Using the document from the previous guided activity, press [Ctrl][Home] to place the cursor at the top of the first page.

2. Click on the Page Layout View button on the horizontal scroll bar, or select View/Page Layout.

   You may need to move to the left to see the left margin. If so, click on the left side of the horizontal scroll bar. If you move to the right you may see the page numbers in gray within the top margin.

3. Place the mouse pointer at the top margin on the vertical ruler. Drag the margin down until the top margin is set to 1.5 inches. Look at the marks on the ruler, or hold down the [Alt] key while dragging, to see the measurement in numbers.

4. Change the left margin to 1.25 inches. Carefully place the mouse pointer on the left side of the ruler between the triangular indent markers. When it changes to a two-headed arrow, drag to the right until the margin displays 1.25".

5. Changing the margins from the ruler may also be done in Print Preview.

Click on the Preview button. If the rulers are not showing, click the View Ruler button on the Preview toolbar. Drag the top side of the vertical ruler down until the top margin is set at 4". Click on the Next Page button at the bottom of the scrollbar.

The change is immediately apparent on all pages of the document. The rulers disappear when you view a page that does not contain the cursor.

6. Go back to the first page. Drag the right side of the horizontal ruler to set the right margin at 1.5 inches.

Because Mirror Margins is selected, Word adjusts the document to keep the left page symmetrical to the right page. That is, changes to the right margin of right pages are mirrored on the left margin of the left pages.

7. Click Close to exit Print Preview. Change back to Normal view and save the document.

Word has several other views that enable the user to see the document in different ways. At the right side of the Standard toolbar is the Zoom Control box, shown in Figure 8.7. You may type a percentage to shrink or enlarge the document, or click on the down arrow next to it and select a setting. This feature allows you to *zoom* in to

FIGURE 8.7
Zoom Control box

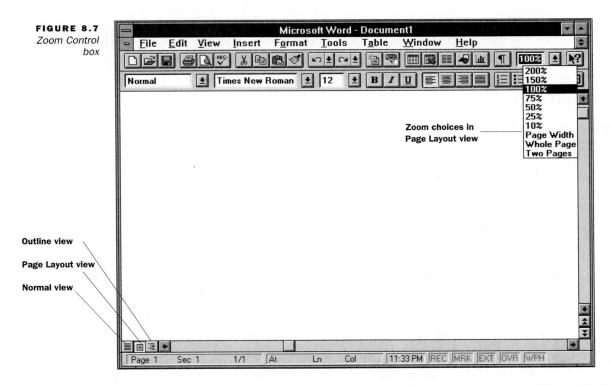

see detail or zoom out to see the entire page. The menu command View/Full Screen allows the maximum space for editing and entering text. In full screen view, the title bar, menu, toolbars, ruler, status bar, and scroll bars are all removed from the screen.

To restore them, click on the Full Screen button, the only thing remaining on the screen besides the text.

GUIDED ACTIVITY 8.5

Using Other Views of a Document

1. Use the document from the previous guided activity. Select from the menu View/Full Screen.

    The usual elements of the Word screen disappear, allowing the maximum amount of space for entering and editing text. The only new feature is the Full Screen button.

 2. Click on the Full Screen button to restore the usual elements of the Word screen.

3. Click on the down arrow next to the Zoom Control box. Select 200%.

    The fonts appear twice their normal size. This feature allows you to see even the smallest font clearly.

4. Click on the down arrow next to the Zoom Control box. Select Page Width.

    In Normal view, zooming to Page Width does not display the margin area, but the document is reduced to a certain percent to allow you to see both the right and left edges of the ruler. In documents with narrow margins, the text may extend beyond the right side of the screen. Using this view allows you to see all the text within the window.

5. Change the Zoom back to 100%. This is the default setting for Word documents.

6. Change to Page Layout view by clicking on the Page Layout View button.

7. Zoom to Page Width.

    In Page Layout view, the document is reduced to a percent that allows you to see not only the text area of the page, but also the entire left and right margins against a dark desktop. This view gives you a good idea of how the proportions, spacing, and margins of the document will appear when printed.

8. While still in Page Layout view, click on the down arrow by the Zoom Control box and select Two Pages.

    This option is only available in Page Layout view. Compare this view to Print Preview.

9. Click on the Print Preview button. Click-and-drag on the Multiple Pages button to view two pages at once.

    Note that the two pages and the rulers look nearly the same. The difference is that the Print Preview toolbar appears, and the other toolbars disappear.

10. Click Close to exit Print Preview. Select from the menu View/Zoom. Select 100% and click OK.

Using the dialog box has the same result as using the Zoom Control box on the toolbar.

11. Select from the menu the command View/Normal. This has the same effect as pressing the Normal View button.

Counting Words

As you create a document and change the formatting of the text, the paragraphs, and the page as a whole, you are probably wondering how long the document has become. Since the number of pages a document fills depends on the style and size of the font, the spacing of the paragraphs, and the width of the margins, the best measure for the length of a document is the number of words it contains. The formatting of the document has no effect on this statistic. Rather than counting the words yourself one by one, issue the command Tools/Word Count. Pages, words, characters, paragraphs, and lines are counted automatically. This tool is very useful for those times when you are asked to write an article of so many words for a newsletter or a term paper.

Summary

Document format commands affect the entire document. They are the most general of format commands. The File/Page Setup command is used to access the Page Setup dialog box. All document format commands are located in this dialog box. Since they are used only once when creating each document, these format commands are not located in a prominent location like the toolbar or the ruler.

The commands in the Page Setup dialog box affect the entire document (unless you select Apply to This Point Forward). The Margins tab allows you to set the margins and gutters for the document. The margins are the distance between the edge of the paper and the printed text. The Paper Size tab allows you to enter the paper size and print orientation for the document. Another tab allows you to select the paper source used when your document is printed. You may select a different source for the first page and for the remaining pages of the document.

Word provides several views to help you to accomplish your formatting and editing tasks.

- Normal view lets you see the font and paragraphs the way they will appear on paper.

- Page Layout view lets you see the formatting of the entire page as it will appear on paper.

- Full Screen view lets you enter and edit text with the maximum amount of space in the work area.

- Zoom view lets you move closer in to see details and farther out to see the overall effect.

- Print Preview lets you view multiple pages on screen at one time, and displays a different toolbar.

You can instruct Word to automatically number pages within the top or bottom margins of long documents, and even to count the number of words in a document to determine how long it is.

Exercises

1. Enter into a new document a paragraph at least four sentences long explaining two methods for changing margins. Format the paragraph to double-spacing. Paste copies of the paragraph to the end of the document until you have two full pages. Change the left margin to 1 inch and the right margin to 2 inches. Save the document as A:EX8_2. Print the document.

2. Use the document from Exercise 1. Assume that the document will be printed on both sides of the page and bound. Format the document with an inside margin of 2 inches and an outside margin of 1 inch. Add a half-inch gutter to allow for the binding. Print the result. (You will not actually print on both sides of the page. Pages 1 and 2 will appear on separate pages on your printout. You can hold them back to front against the light, lining up the page numbers, to see how the margins are different.)

3. You are creating name tags for yourself and a celebrity who will be speakers at a conference. These name tags must be visible across a large room. Your idea is to type the names in a very large font (70 to 90 points) sideways on the page, so that the page can be folded in a triangle to stand on the table. Increase the top margin so that the names are more or less in the middle of the page to allow for a fold above and below the name. Change the side margins and point size so that the names fit without wrapping to the next line. If you are able to obtain paper in a unique color for the name tags, use manual feed. Print both names and fold.

4. Write an essay of at least 150 words comparing and contrasting the various ways to view a document in Word. Double-space and copy and paste the paragraph until at least three pages are filled. Add a title and your byline ("By Jennifer Genius"), along with the word count of the first paragraph, centered at the top of the first page. Format the pages so that they may be copied on both sides and bound. Add page numbers to the outside edge of the top margin. Save the document as A:VIEWS and print. Staple down the left side to bind the pages.

Review Questions

*1. Why are the format document commands intended for the most general level of formatting?

2. Why are the format document commands not located in a prominent place in the work area?

*3. What is the limitation when setting the paper size in the File/Page Setup dialog box? What is the default paper size?

4. What are the margins? What are two methods for changing margins?

*5. How are margins different from paragraph indents? How do margins affect paragraph indents?

6. When is the Mirror Margins option used? What changes when Mirror Margins are selected?

*7. What is a gutter? When is a gutter used? How does the effect of the gutter differ when Mirror Margins are on or off?

8. What different ways can a document be viewed?

*9. What features appear in Page Layout view that are not visible in Normal view?

Key Terms

Gutter	Mirror margins	Portrait
Landscape	Orientation	Zoom

Documentation Research

1. How do you center a one-page document vertically on the page?

2. How do you specify whether the page numbers are printed on or omitted from the first page of a document?

3. How do you print one part of a document in portrait mode, and another part in landscape?

Using the Format Commands to Create the Right Impression

The three levels of formatting may be used to enhance the meaning of a document. Giving a document a pleasant and professional appearance not only makes the message easier to read, it also makes a more favorable impression on the recipient. Of course, while there is no substitute for good content, the presentation on paper is important for communicating your good ideas.

In this case, you are a faculty or staff member of your college or university. You have an idea for a project that might improve academic or campus life. Write a memo to the appropriate administrator, dean, or faculty member to present your idea. Use the standard memorandum form: centered at the top of the page in a larger font, all caps, and expanded spacing, is the word MEMORANDUM. Below that are the heading lines with Date: To: From: and Subject: in bold, double-spaced. Set a tab so that the text that follows each of these is aligned. These heading lines are followed by a single line (a border) across the page. A sample of the heading appears at the end of this application (Figure B.1). You may select a problem other than on-campus parking.

The next several paragraphs should be single-spaced, with the first line indented, and with a blank line between the paragraphs. The first paragraph should outline the problem at your school. Use tactful wording that does not lay blame, or you will alienate your audience before they read your proposed solution. The last paragraph or two should outline your proposed solution, and finish with a closing paragraph expressing goodwill, a common interest, and a desire to look to the future. Place all or part of your solution in a series of three or four bulleted or numbered points in order to increase the readers' comprehension.

Adjust the margins so that the memorandum fits on one page. If it is short enough, a 2" top margin is most attractive. Print the memo, and initial next to your name. Save as A:MEMO.

FIGURE B.1
*Sample
memorandum*

MEMORANDUM

Date: January 31, 1995

To: President Jay Kesler

From: Emily Ketcham

Subject: On-campus parking

Advanced Word Processing Techniques III

■ **PART THREE** of this manual gives you techniques that are used to make complex tasks simple. Many features in Word are as complete as those in desktop publishing software, such as those that place text into columns or tables and insert graphic objects. Word greatly reduces the effort required to produce headers and footers, which are required on many documents. The advanced functions automate the process of mail merge to create customized form letters, envelopes, and mailing labels. The outline feature organizes the creation of long documents. Word simplifies footnoting reference material and preparing a table of contents and an index. Word may be fully customized to your liking, including creating your own selections on the menus and toolbar.

The advanced word processing features are not necessary to produce useful documents, but they can save you a great deal of time by taking the difficult work out of your hands and letting the microcomputer do it for you.

Tables 9

This unit presents the creation and formatting of tables, used to store text and pictures in row-and-column or side-by-side format. The purpose of a table is to allow fast and easy access to information that fits into two categories. The reader can follow a row and column, representing two categories, to their intersection to quickly find an individual piece of information.

Word allows you to easily create, maneuver through, and modify tables. Existing text can be placed into a table, as can portions of spreadsheets, pictures, and any other item that can be cut and pasted. The dimensions of the rows and columns can be changed to allow for the most effective presentation of the information in the table. Items in a table can be formatted, like any other selection of text, with bold, italics, small caps, and any other attribute. Predefined borders and styles may be added with the AutoFormat command.

Learning Objectives

At the completion of this unit you should know

1. what a table is,

2. what kind of information fits best in a table,

3. how to create and enter information into a table,

4. how to modify and format a table,

5. how to sort and calculate information in a table.

Important Commands

Edit/Copy

Edit/Paste Cells

Format/Borders and Shading

Table/Cell Height and Width

Table/Convert

Table/Delete

Table/Formula

Table/Gridlines

Table/Insert

Table/Merge Cells

Table/Select

Table/Sort

Table/Split Cells

Table/Split Table

Table/Table AutoFormat

Purpose of Tables

A *table* is a rectangular text structure that holds information in rows and columns. Tables are used to allow readers to look up pieces of information that fall into two intersecting categories. In a catalog, you might look up a type of product and a price range to decide which brand to buy. The two categories, type and price, allow you to narrow your choices. Using the table method, you can find individual items from a large set of information.

The table in Figure 9.1 allows you to look up quickly the average temperature of regions of the country by one of two seasons, summer and winter. If you know two pieces of information, the region and the season, you can quickly find the average temperature.

Tables are also useful for aligning any information that is most effectively presented side by side. While setting tabs may also achieve this for a small amount of text or numbers, tables can align paragraphs, graphics, or any amount of text with flexibility and ease of handling.

FIGURE 9.1
A table used for finding temperatures

	North	South	East	West
Summer	75	95	80	80
Winter	20	40	30	50

The table structure is very flexible. The table in Figure 9.2 shows the way Word can align even longer amounts of text in rows and columns. Any set of information that needs to be arranged side by side will fit into a table.

Textbooks	*Understanding and Using Microsoft Excel 5* by Ross & Hutson *Understanding and Using Microsoft Word 6* by Ketcham
Grade	Consists of the following elements 　　　Tests　　　　　　　　　80% 　　　Comprehensive final　　10% 　　　Assignments　　　　　10%

Tables have several other uses. Any portion of a spreadsheet that is inserted into a Word document will automatically become a table. Tables are also used during print merge operations for holding names and addresses and for creating mailing labels.

Creating Tables

There are two ways to create a table. One method requires that you create the table and enter information yourself. The other allows you to select existing text or numbers and create a table that will fit the items.

Creating an Empty Table

To create a table from scratch, position the cursor where the table is to be placed, then click on the Table button on the toolbar. On the Table button grid, drag the mouse to select the number of rows and columns you want in the new table, as shown in Figure 9.3.

Another option is to select from the menu Table/Insert Table. The dialog box that appears allows you to select the Table Wizard or to specify the number of columns and rows, as shown in Figure 9.4. The Table Wizard is a great time-saver for creating and formatting standard tables containing dates and numeric data. Many of the features incorporated into the wizard will be explained in this unit.

When creating a table using the dialog box, you need to enter only the number of columns you require in this table. Entering the number of rows is optional, since the

FIGURE 9.4
The Insert Table
dialog box

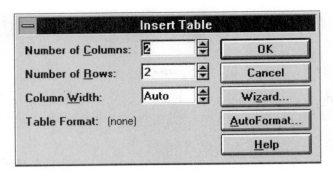

FIGURE 9.4
The Insert Table
dialog box

table will automatically add new rows to the bottom of the table as you type. The default value for the column width is Auto. This value will cause Word to make the width of each column equal to the total distance between the left and right margins divided by the number of columns specified. Each column will be the same width, and the table will fill the space between the margins. If the columns must all be a specific width, enter that value in the Column Width box before continuing. If not, accept the Auto default and continue, since the column width can be changed later.

GUIDED ACTIVITY 9.1

Creating Tables

1. Start Word and create a new document.

2. Click the Table button on the toolbar and drag to create a 1×3 table.

   Another method is to select the command Table/Insert Table.

3. Click Undo. This time use the command Table/Insert Table.

   The default values for the number of columns and rows are 2 and 2.

4. Change the value in the Number of Columns box to 3. Click on the OK button.

   The empty table structure appears at the point where the cursor was located before executing the command. The lines in the table are called *gridlines*. (If the gridlines do not appear, select Table/Gridlines to turn on this option.) The grid-lines will display in the work area but will not print. They are displayed only to make working with the table easier. Gridlines define the edges of the *cell*, the intersection of a row and column. Cells can contain text, pictures, or any other item that can be cut and pasted in Windows. If you press the Show/Hide ¶ button, the *cell marks* appear within each cell and at the end of each row, as shown in Figure 9.5.

FIGURE 9.5
An empty table

At this point the table is ready for you to input values into each cell. The cursor is in the top-left cell of the table, the point from which you would normally add data.

GUIDED ACTIVITY 9.2

Entering Text into a Table

1. Type your first and last name in the first cell.

    If your name is long enough to cause the cursor to reach the right-hand edge of the cell, a second line will appear in the cell to hold the extra text, as shown in Figure 9.6.

FIGURE 9.6
Word wrapping when text is wider than the cell

Entering text into a cell is much like entering items directly into the work area. As you moved the cursor to the edge of the cell, word wrap moved the long second word to the beginning of the next line. You could enter several paragraphs into the same cell, and Word will continue to increase the cell's height to hold them.

The Tab key ([Tab]) is used to advance the cursor to the next cell in a table.

2. Press [Tab].

    The cursor moves to the second cell in the top row.

3. Enter your street address and press [Enter].

    You can move the cursor to a second line inside a single cell by pressing [Enter].

4. Type your city, state, and zip code. Press [Enter]. Enter U.S.A.

    You can continue to make the cell taller by pressing [Enter] at the end of the last line in the cell.

5. Press [Tab] to advance to the last cell in the first row. Enter your phone number. If you press [Enter], you will receive another paragraph within that cell. To move to the beginning of the next row, press [Tab] again.

    When you press [Tab] from the last cell in a row, the cursor is moved to the beginning of the next row. If you are in the bottom-right corner of a table and press [Tab], a new row appears in your table. Although you originally created a table with only two rows, rows will be added as you enter information into the table. Each time you press [Tab] from the last cell in the table, a new row will be added, and the cursor will move to the left cell of the new row. This means you need not know beforehand how many rows will be in a table. You can always add rows to any existing table in this fashion.

6. Enter the name, address, and telephone number of a friend in the three cells on the second row. Remember to use [Tab] to advance the cursor to the next cell and row.

7. Enter the name, address, and phone number of a third person on the new row.

You may edit text in a table just as though it were outside the table and in the work area. Simply move the cursor to the location of the text to be edited and perform the function necessary to edit the text.

8. Move the cursor to the second cell of the first row. If you are using the mouse, click with the mouse pointer at the desired location. If you are using the keyboard, press [Shift][Tab] to back the cursor up one cell at a time.

9. Highlight the name of the city where you live. Type Anytown.

The original city name is replaced by Anytown. This is the same procedure you would use if you were editing text outside the table.

Text can also be formatted inside the table.

10. Move the cursor to the last cell of the second row. If using the mouse, highlight the entire cell by clicking-and-dragging. With the keyboard, use [Tab] to get the cursor to the appropriate cell. The text is automatically highlighted. Make the text bold by clicking on the Bold button on the toolbar or by using the Format/Font command.

Any character format attribute can be given to selected text in a table. Paragraph format commands also work.

11. Center the phone number in the cell by clicking on the Center button on the toolbar or by using the Format/Paragraph command.

The phone number is centered, but not between the page margins. It is centered between the left-hand and right-hand edges of the cell.

When the previous Guided Activity is complete, you should have a table that looks like the one in Figure 9.7.

FIGURE 9.7
Results of Guided Activity 9.2

Alexander Riemenschneider	5501 Main Street Anytown, NY 11111 U.S.A.	976-2345
Jonathan Donaldson	P.O. Box 98146 Waco, TX 76798	**769-7395**
Steven Andrews	7451 Broadway Denver, CO 62948	847-6382

Creating a Table from Text

The second way to create a table is to use an existing segment of text and convert it into a table. If you already have text typed with tabs, you will find that formatting and aligning are much easier if you convert the text into a table.

When typing text to be converted into a table, you must define what text will appear in each cell. The character used to separate the contents of the cells is called a *delimiter*. The delimiter may be an Enter character (¶), a comma, or a tab. A delimiter is placed after the text that will be in each cell to separate it from the next.

GUIDED ACTIVITY 9.3

Creating a Table from Text

1. Select File/New to create a new file. Type the following text into the document:

   Product, Quantity, Price

   Apples, 1500, $1.20

   Oranges, 900, $1.00

   Mangoes, 150, $1.75

   The delimiter you used was the comma. The contents of each row is in a paragraph by itself, separated by commas. The commas separate the columns, and each row is a separate paragraph.

2. Highlight all of the text you just entered. Select Table/Insert Table or click the Table button on the toolbar. You could also use the command Table/Convert Text to Table.

   Word inspects the information you entered, senses the delimiters, counts the number of lines and columns, and places the text within a table sized to fit the current margins.

   You can also take text out of a table.

3. Select Table/Convert Table To Text from the menu. Since a table is highlighted, the Convert menu selection changes.

   You could place any of the three delimiters between the contents of each cell by clicking in the option button next to that selection, as shown in Figure 9.8.

FIGURE 9.8
The Table/Convert Table to Text dialog box

4. Click on the OK button to execute the command.

   The text is back in paragraph format with columns separated by tabs.

5. Save the file as A:9_A.

Modifying Tables

Word provides several commands to modify tables. It is simple to add, delete, rearrange, and format rows and columns. These features allow you to quickly modify a table so that it is presented most effectively.

The Table/Insert and Table/Delete commands are used to add and delete cells, rows, and columns from a table. The command changes, depending on whether a row, a column, or a cell is highlighted before the command is selected.

Adding and Deleting Rows and Columns

In Guided Activity 9.2, you added a row to the end of the table by pressing Tab with the cursor in the last cell of the last row. If you want to add a row in the middle of the table, place the cursor at the desired location of the new row and select the Table/Insert Rows command. When the mouse pointer is positioned within a table, you can click the right mouse button to access this command on the shortcut menu, shown in Figure 9.9. The row containing the cursor moves down to make room for the new row.

To insert new cells or new columns, you must select either a cell or a column first. To select a cell, place the mouse pointer at the left edge of a cell until it changes from the I-beam into an arrow pointing up and to the right, then click. To select a column, move the mouse pointer over the top border of the column until it changes into a small down-pointing arrow, then click. The entire column is highlighted.

After highlighting, new cells or columns are added by selecting the Table/Insert Cells or Table/ Insert Columns command from the menu. This command changes, depending on what is highlighted. New cells or columns are added above or to the left of the highlighted items.

Rows and columns are deleted in the same manner from the Table menu. Select the cell, column, or row to be deleted, then issue the Table/Delete command. The cell, row, or column where the cursor is located will be deleted. Rearranging rows and columns may be done by simply using the Edit/Cut or Edit/Copy and Edit/Paste commands. Cells may also be moved by the drag-and-drop method.

FIGURE 9.9
The shortcut menu when the pointer is on a table

Cut
Copy
Paste Cells
Insert Rows
Delete Cells...
Table AutoFormat...
Font...
Paragraph...
Bullets and Numbering...

GUIDED ACTIVITY 9.4

Adding and Deleting Rows and Columns

1. Using the table created in Guided Activity 9.3, highlight the fruit data. Select Table/Insert Table, or click on the Table button in the toolbar to put the data back into table form.

2. Position the cursor anywhere in the row that contains the data on Oranges.

    The new row will be added above the location of the cursor. Placing the cursor here will cause a new row to be inserted between the existing second and third rows.

3. Select Table/Insert Rows.

    A new row appears above where you positioned the cursor, as shown in Figure 9.10. The rest of the table moves down.

FIGURE 9.10
Table with new
row inserted

Product	Quantity	Price
Apples	1500	$1.20
Oranges	900	$1.00
Mangoes	150	$1.75

4. Type the following data into the blank cells, pressing [Tab] to move to the next cell.

    Bananas   800 $1.10

5. You can delete cells using a process similar to inserting. Highlight the entire Bananas row by clicking at the far left side of the row outside of the gridlines.

6. Select the command Table/Delete Rows. The new row has now been deleted.

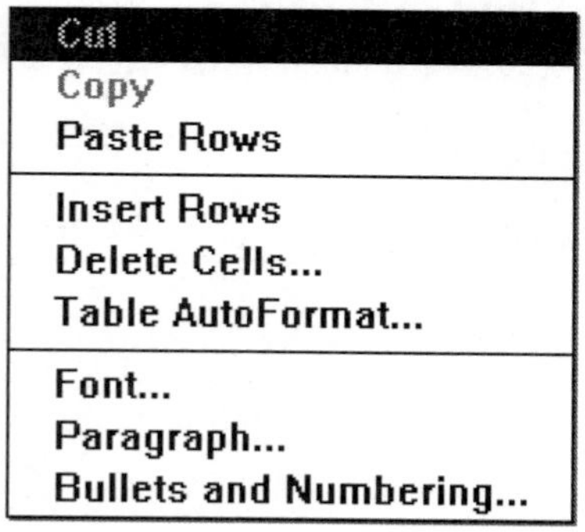

FIGURE 9.11
The shortcut
menu with
Paste Rows
command

Cut
Copy
Paste Rows

Insert Rows
Delete Cells...
Table AutoFormat...

Font...
Paragraph...
Bullets and Numbering...

Information is copied from one cell, row, or column to another by using the Edit/Copy and Edit/Paste Cells, Edit/Paste Rows, or Edit/Paste Columns commands. These last commands do not appear on the Edit or shortcut menus unless the cursor and mouse pointer are located in a table, in which case they replace the Paste command, as shown in Figure 9.11.

To highlight a row with the mouse, move the mouse pointer to the far left side of the row and click, or position the cursor in the row you want to highlight and select the command Table/Select Row.

7. Highlight the row that contains the Mangoes information. Select Edit/Copy.

8. Position the cursor in front of Oranges. Select Edit/Paste Rows.

The information from the Mangoes row is copied into a new row, moving the Oranges row down. You now have two rows containing the Mangoes information.

9. Highlight the entire second Mangoes row. Press ⌊Del⌋.

The Mangoes information disappears, but the row is still there. The only way to remove the empty row is with the Table/Delete command.

10. Click Undo to get the information back. With the row highlighted, select Table/Delete Rows.

The original Mangoes information is deleted along with the row that contained it.

You can also insert more than one row or column at a time by highlighting the areas where you want the new rows inserted. To highlight more than one row using the mouse, position the mouse pointer to the left of the first row, then drag down to the last row to be highlighted. Using the keyboard, position the cursor within the first row, select Table/Select Row, then press and hold ⌊Shift⌋ and press ⌊↓⌋ to highlight another row below the first.

11. Highlight the two rows below the Apples information and select Table/Insert Rows or press the Table button on the toolbar.

Two new rows appear at the highlighted location. The Mangoes and Oranges rows move down to make room for the new rows, as shown in Figure 9.12.

FIGURE 9.12
Table with two new rows inserted

Product	Quantity	Price
Apples	1500	$1.20
Mangoes	150	$1.75
Oranges	900	$1.00

12. Add the following information to the appropriate cells in the new rows.

```
Watermelons   100   $3.25
Cantaloupes   250   $2.25
```

Columns can also be added to an existing table. To add a column, highlight the column at the desired new location and use the Table/Insert Columns command.

13. Carefully place the mouse pointer over the top of the Quantity column until the pointer turns into the small down-arrow then click. You may also select a column by positioning the cursor within the column and using the command Table/Select Column. Click the Table button on the toolbar and a column of blank cells appears to the left of the Quantity column.

14. Add the following text to the blank cells in the new column. Use the ⏎ key to move to the next cell in the column.

Reorder Quantity

1250

130

300

1300

200

The table is now too wide to fit in the work area or on the page. Each of the original columns took up one-third of the width of the page. The new column is the same width as the others, therefore the last column extends beyond the right margin. This needs to be adjusted.

Formatting Tables

Once the rows and columns in a table are positioned where you want them, you can change the width, height, borders and shading, and alignment of the cells in the table.

Column Width

The width of the columns is set when the table is first created. However, the table may need to be modified so that it better fits the information, the page, or the document. The table you created in Guided Activity 9.4 extends beyond the right margin by one column. It is therefore necessary to change the column width after modifying the table.

As soon as a table is inserted in a document, the ruler changes to display column markers to denote the edges of the columns, as shown in Figure 9.13. The width of a column may be changed with the mouse by dragging the column markers on the ruler or dragging directly on the column's right-hand gridline.

FIGURE 9.13
*The ruler
showing column
markers*

More precise measurements may be obtained by using the Cell Height and Width dialog box. Highlight the column to be changed and select Table/Cell Height and Width, and view the Column tab. Type the desired column width into the Width box, as shown in Figure 9.14, and press Enter.

Once in the dialog box, you may change widths of other columns in the table by clicking on the Next Column button or on the Previous Column button. Using this method, you can format the width of all the columns in the table without having to exit the dialog box for each one.

Word provides a handy way to make cells fit the contents of the cell—wider for long text, narrow for short. AutoFit may be applied from the dialog box by clicking on the AutoFit button on the Column tab, as in Figure 9.14.

FIGURE 9.14
The Cell Height and Width dialog box, Column tab

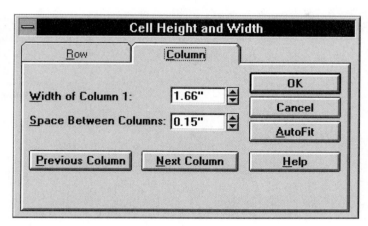

When you change the width of a column by dragging either the gridlines or the column markers on the ruler, all the columns to the right are changed in size to accommodate the change in width, so that the table overall retains its size. When you hold down the Shift key and drag the column, the single column just to the right of the changed column adjusts to be wider or narrower to accommodate the change, and the overall table size remains unchanged. The only way to change the size of the overall table is to hold down both the Shift and Ctrl keys while dragging, or to drag the right-most gridline.

GUIDED ACTIVITY 9.5

Changing Column Widths

1. The table in Guided Activity 9.4 is wider than what will fit between the margins, since we added a column. Highlight the entire table by selecting Table/Select Table from the menu. Remember that the cursor must be positioned within a table for this choice to be available.

2. Select Table/Cell Height and Width and click on the Column tab. Click on the AutoFit button.

   This makes the columns just wide enough to display the contents of the cell without wrapping, as shown in Figure 9.15. AutoFit adjusts the column widths to the different length of the headings, and the result is not very attractive in this case.

3. Place the mouse over the gridline just to the right of the Reorder Quantity column. When it changes to a double line with two arrows, drag the gridline to the left to narrow the Reorder Quantity column.

   Note that the table as a whole remains the same size, but both the Quantity and Price columns become wider to accommodate the change, as in Figure 9.16.

FIGURE 9.15
*The column
widths after
using AutoFit*

Product	Reorder Quantity	Quantity	Price
Apples	1250	1500	$1.20
Watermelons	130	100	$3.25
Cantaloupes	300	250	$2.25
Mangoes	1300	150	$1.75
Oranges	200	900	$1.00

FIGURE 9.16
*Changing one
column width
changes the
width of all the
columns to
the right.*

Product	Reorder Quantity	Quantity	Price
Apples	1250	1500	$1.20
Watermelons	130	100	$3.25
Cantaloupes	300	250	$2.25
Mangoes	1300	150	$1.75
Oranges	200	900	$1.00

**These column
widths changed**

4.   Undo the last action. This time hold down [Shift] while narrowing the Reorder Quantity column. This time, just the Quantity column is changed, while the table as a whole is not changed, as in Figure 9.17.

FIGURE 9.17
*Effect of holding
down the* [Shift]
*key when
changing
column width*

Product	Reorder Quantity	Quantity	Price
Apples	1250	1500	$1.20
Watermelons	130	100	$3.25
Cantaloupes	300	250	$2.25
Mangoes	1300	150	$1.75
Oranges	200	900	$1.00

**Only this column
width changed**

5.   Highlight the three columns with the numbers. To make these columns all the same width, use the command from the menu.

6.   Select Table/Cell Height and Width, and click on the Column tab. Set the column width at 1.5" and click OK. The columns should be all the same width and wide enough to accommodate the long heading.

7.   Save the table again and leave the document open.

Column Alignment and Tabs Within a Table

By default, the contents of a table are left-aligned within each column. Some-times, such as in the case of numbers, it is more appropriate to right-align (or in the case of titles to center-align) the text within the column. This formatting is done the same way as formatting ordinary text, by simply clicking the Left, Center, and Right alignment buttons on the toolbar, or by using the Format/Paragraph command. Likewise, indentation applied to the paragraphs affects the indentation of the text within the column itself. The indentation of text within a column may be changed by dragging the indent markers on the ruler. In addition, it is possible to set tabs within a table in order to align text in columns within a table. Specifically, adding a decimal tab to a column causes numbers to automatically align at the decimal point. Tabs other than decimal tabs within a column must be accessed by pressing [Ctrl][Tab], since pressing [Tab] alone will jump the cursor to the next cell.

GUIDED ACTIVITY 9.6

Changing Column Alignment

1. Select the columns for Quantity and Price.

2. Change the alignment to right alignment. With the mouse, click on the Right-align button on the toolbar. The contents of the cells move to the far right side of the column. Now the numbers are properly aligned, but the titles are not, as in Figure 9.18.

FIGURE 9.18
Effect of changing alignment

Product	Reorder Quantity	Quantity	Price
Apples	1250	1500	$1.20
Watermelons	130	100	$3.25
Cantaloupes	300	250	$2.25
Mangoes	1300	150	$1.75
Oranges	200	900	$1.00

3. Highlight the Price column only and change the alignment to Center. This alignment works for this column since the numbers are all the same length.

   Set the alignment of the numbers in the Reorder Quantity column using a decimal tab.

4. Highlight the column by clicking on the top border or by selecting Table/Select Column. Click 3 times on the Tab Alignment button on the far left side of the ruler until a decimal tab is displayed. Click on the ruler to set the tab slightly to the right of the center of the column, as in Figure 9.19.

5. Highlight the Quantity column and change it back to left alignment. Set a decimal tab in this column as you did in the previous step.

6. Center the headings only in the Reorder Quantity and Quantity columns. Highlight these two cells only, and center by clicking on the Center-align button on the toolbar.

   The centering of the headings is thrown off by the decimal tab.

Set
tab
about
here

Product	Reorder Quantity	Quantity	Price
Apples	1250	1500	$1.20
Watermelons	130	100	$3.25
Cantaloupes	300	250	$2.25
Mangoes	1300	150	$1.75
Oranges	200	900	$1.00

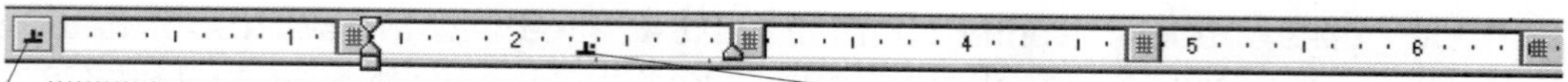

7. Highlight the cell containing the word Quantity and delete the decimal tab by dragging it down and off the ruler. Repeat for the cell containing Reorder Quantity.

8. Change the appearance of the column headings by formatting them to bold. Select the top row by clicking on the far left side of the row or by using the command Table/Select Row. Apply the bold formatting by clicking on the Bold button on the toolbar. The results of this application should look something like Figure 9.20.

Product	**Reorder Quantity**	**Quantity**	**Price**
Apples	1250	1500	$1.20
Watermelons	130	100	$3.25
Cantaloupes	300	250	$2.25
Mangoes	1300	150	$1.75
Oranges	200	900	$1.00

Row Height and Alignment

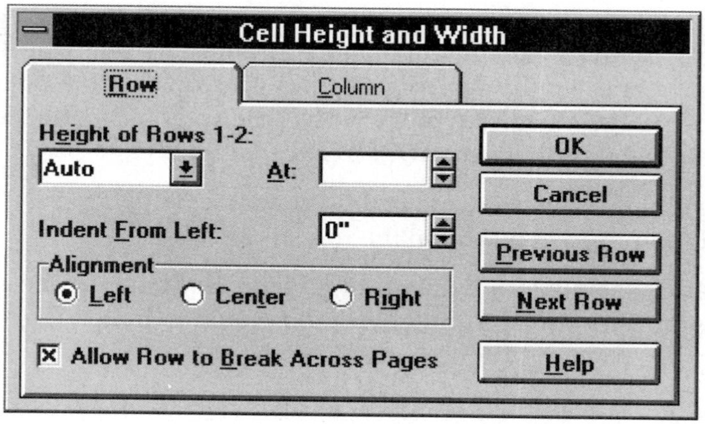

Ordinarily, the row height is set to the minimum value needed to contain everything in the row. You can override this default through the Row tab in the Table/Cell Height and Width dialog box, shown in Figure 9.21, or by dragging the settings on the vertical ruler in Page Layout view. You can select any of three options: Auto (the default), At Least, or Exactly. The At Least option sets a minimum value for each row, but allows the cell to expand if the contents of a cell exceed the minimum height. The Exactly option sets the row height to a fixed amount, and if the cell's contents exceed this amount it may appear cropped (trimmed) on the screen and when printed.

The Row tab of the Cell Height and Width dialog box is also used to set the indentation and alignment of the entire row of cells. Any regular paragraph formatting applied to text within a table has the effect of formatting the alignment or indentation within the cell *only*. To indent or to center the entire row of cells between the margins on a page, you must change the indent or alignment within this dialog box.

GUIDED ACTIVITY 9.7

Setting Row Height and Alignment

1. Use the table created in Guided Activity 9.6. To create more space in the heading of the table, change the row height from the default Auto setting. Select the top row by clicking the mouse pointer on the far left side of the row or by placing the cursor within the top row and issuing the command Table/Select Row.

2. The only way to change the automatic row height is to access the dialog box. Select Table/Cell Height and Width and click on the Row tab.

3. Select the Height of Row 1 option and change it to At Least.

4. Set the minimum height of the row by clicking on the At option and changing it to 24 points. Click OK.

   Change the alignment of the entire table so that it is centered between the margins rather than left-aligned. This will not affect the text within the columns.

5. Highlight the table with the command Table/Select Table, then issue the command Table/Cell Height and Width. Click on the option for Center under Alignment, then click OK. The table is centered between the two margins, the way you would want it to be if it were presented in a paper or report.

6. Save the table.

Borders, Shading, and AutoFormat

The dotted gridlines that surround the cells in a table are there to show you the edges of the cell. They will not appear on paper when the document is printed. However, some tables are easier to read if the cells are separated by some type of line. You may add borders as well as shading to the cells in a table by using the Format/ Borders and Shading command or the Borders toolbar, just as you apply borders and shading to paragraphs of normal text. Borders and shading may be added to individual cells in the table as well as to the entire table.

It is not difficult to format the borders and shading, but Word makes it even easier by providing 34 predefined formats to choose from. These are applied with the command Table/Table AutoFormat. This command may be used to apply several types of formatting, including borders, shading, font, color, and AutoFit, as shown in Figure 9.22.

FIGURE 9.22
*The Table/Table
AutoFormat
dialog box*

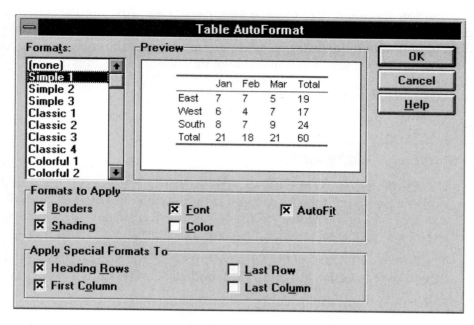

GUIDED ACTIVITY 9.8

Using Cell Borders

1. Select the command Table/Gridlines to remove the checkmark so that the non-printing gridlines disappear from the screen.

2. Highlight the entire table by selecting Table/Select Table or by using the mouse.

3. Create a border that will print gridlines between all the cells of the table by issuing the command Format/Borders and Shading and then selecting Grid under Presets, and click OK.

   This places a heavier border around the outside of the table and thinner gridlines inside the table. Check Print Preview to see that these gridlines will print. Close Print Preview. These borders may be enough to complete the table. Using Auto-Format will replace these borders with new ones.

4. Select the command Table/Table AutoFormat. Click on each choice in the list of formats to see the effect of each on the sample table. Do not press OK yet.

   Click the Color check box to show the color formatting of several of the choices. The colors are only useful for on-screen viewing or printing in color. Adding color to a table that you plan to print on a black-and-white laser printer will generally make the table too dark and hard to read. Click Color again to remove the X.

5. Click next to AutoFit to remove the X from the box. You previously went to a great deal of trouble fixing the column widths when AutoFit did not give attractive results in this case.

6. Click in the Heading Rows and First Column choices to see the effect on the sample. When you have made all your choices, click OK to see the results on the fruit table.

7. If you like the results, save the table again. Otherwise click Undo and try again.

Sorting and Calculating

Tables often hold numeric or financial data that need to be totaled or averaged. You could use a hand-held calculator to tally the numbers or switch to the Calculator accessory in Program Manager, but both operations would require typing in the same numbers over again. Word allows you to perform simple calculations such as these with the command Table/Formula.

The Table/Formula dialog box, shown in Figure 9.23, gives several simple formulas for use with data in tables, including SUM and AVERAGE.

After typing the data in a table, you may find that you would like to have the data sorted. It would be rather time- consuming to drag-and-drop to get everything in order. The Table/Sort command sorts a table automatically, in either ascending (A–Z, 1–10) or descending (Z–A, 10–1) order, on one or more columns in the table.

In the table with the fruit information, the types of fruit are not listed in alphabetical order. With a small table like this one, it would be simple to use drag-and-drop to rearrange the data, but let's try the sorting function on this data anyway.

FIGURE 9.23
The Table/ Formula dialog box

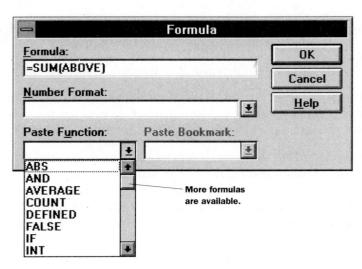

GUIDED ACTIVITY 9.9

Sorting and Calculating

1. Issue the command Table/Sort. The dialog box in Figure 9.24 appears.

    Word guesses the title of the left-most column as the item you wish to sort on. The default sort order is Ascending, which is A-to-Z order.

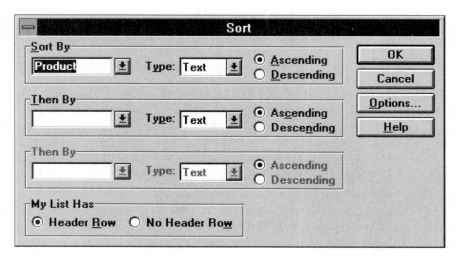

FIGURE 9.24
The Table/Sort dialog box

2. Make sure that Header Row is selected. This prevents the title Product from being alphabetized in with the names of the fruit. Click OK to sort the data.

    The formatting of borders and shading may get mixed up as a result of sorting. For this reason, it's a good idea to sort before applying the formats to a table.

3. Place the cursor in the bottom-right cell of the table and press ⟦Tab⟧ to add a new row at the bottom of the table.

4. Enter Total in the first cell, then press ⟦Tab⟧ to get to the next column.

5. Issue the command Table/Formula. Word guesses that you wish to total, or sum, the numbers above it within the column. Click OK, and the total Reorder Quantity appears in the cell. Save the table.

    The number representing the total Reorder Quantity is not just typed digits. It is actually a field code showing the results of the formula. When you select it, the number turns gray (dimmed). If you want to view the formula behind this number, point the mouse at the shaded area and click the right mouse button to access the Toggle Field Codes from the shortcut menu. You may also press ⟦Alt⟧⟦F9⟧.

    The table is now complete. It was created with Table/Insert Table, where you set up the original dimensions and entered information into the table. You used Table/Insert and Table/Delete to add, delete, and move rows and columns in the table. The Table/Cell Height and Width command allowed you to change the height of rows and the width of columns, as well as to align the table in the center of the page. Format/Borders and Shading and Table/Table AutoFormat put on the finishing touches. Table/Formula and Table/Sort simplified the process of alphabetizing and totaling the data. Table 9.1 contains tips to help you with hard-to-remember techniques for tables.

TABLE 9.1
*Techniques for
tables*

ACTION	RESULT
[Tab]	Moves cursor forward to the next cell or down to a new row.
[Shift][Tab]	Moves cursor backward and upward to the previous row.
[Ctrl][Tab]	Moves cursor to a tab set within a cell.
Drag column width	Changes the current column, affects all columns to the right. Entire table remains the same size overall.
[Shift] and drag column width	Changes the current column, affects also the adjacent column to the right. Entire table remains the same size overall.
[Ctrl][Shift] and drag column width	Changes only the current column. Overall size of the table is affected.

Merging Cells in a Table

Another table feature allows you to merge cells on the same row into one cell. The new cell contains the contents of the original cells and is as wide as the original cells combined.

To merge cells in a table, highlight the cells and select Table/Merge Cells. If cells contain text, such as the cells containing 5 and 6 in Figure 9.25, the result of merging is a single cell twice as tall, with the contents of the original cells in separate paragraphs. Empty cells that are merged, on the other hand, become a single, wide cell without the extra height. To split a cell into two, highlight the cell and issue the command Table/Split Cells.

FIGURE 9.25
*When merged,
two cells
become one cell
two lines tall.*

Before   After

GUIDED ACTIVITY 9.10

Merging Cells

1. Create a new document. On the top line of the document, insert a table with four columns and four rows. Turn on the gridlines if they are not showing. Type in the information from Figure 9.26.

2. Highlight the two empty cells in the lower-right corner of the table. Select Table/Merge Cells. The result is a single cell two columns wide.

FIGURE 9.26
New table

	Eastern	Central	Western
Sales	$100,000	$175,000	$225,000
Expenses	70%	65%	80%
Returns	5%		

3. Type data not available. Center the text in the last cell.

The merged cell represents information valid for both the Central and Western areas. By centering the text across both columns you make this more apparent.

It would be nice to have a title appear above the table, but there is no empty line to type it on. Use the Table/Split Table command to insert a regular paragraph above a table or to break a table in two.

4. Place the cursor at the top-left corner of the table. Issue the command Table/Split Table.

5. On the blank line that appears, type the title, Profit by Sales Region. Center and bold the title. Close the file, and save as A:9_A2. The result should resemble Figure 9.27.

FIGURE 9.27
*Sample table
with merged
cells*

Profit by Sales Region

	Eastern	Central	Western
Sales	$100,000	$175,000	$225,000
Expenses	70%	65%	80%
Returns	5%	data not available	

Summary

Tables are rectangular text structures used to contain information that can be presented effectively in a two-dimensional format. Tables are created and placed into documents with the Table button on the toolbar or the Table/Insert Table command. They may be created from scratch or from information that already exists in a document. You may maneuver the cursor through a table with the [Tab] key, with arrow keys, or with the mouse. The intersection of a row and a column in a table is a cell. Text in cells may be formatted like any other text by using the buttons on the toolbar or the Format/Font command.

The Table/Insert and Table/Delete commands are used to add and delete cells, rows, and columns. Rows and columns can be added or deleted one at a time or several at once, depending on what is highlighted before the command is executed.

Once a table contains the desired information, you may change the column width, row height, and alignment, with the Table/Cell Height and Width command. The functions are used only to alter the appearance of the table and do not affect the information in the cells themselves. Cells may be merged to span two or more columns. The appearance of a table may be enhanced by the use of borders and shading, or with a preset AutoFormat. Data in tables may be sorted and totals and averages calculated automatically.

Exercises

1. Create a new document with an empty table consisting of three columns and one row. Turn on borders that will print a grid on the table. Print the result.

2. Continue with the table from Exercise 1. Create a schedule of events for a convention. Place the day of the week in the first column, the event in the second column, and the time of day in the third column. Put several events on each day, and have the convention last at least two days. Apply any appropriate character formatting. You may use the information in the sample, Figure 9.28, or create your own. Save the document as A:EX9_2. Be sure to proofread for errors. Print the result.

FIGURE 9.28
The completed schedule of events

Iota Beta Mu National Convention
San Antonio, Texas
June 23 - 27, 1994

Iota Beta Mu National Convention Schedule of Events

Day	Event	Time
Thursday	Registration	1:00 p.m.
	Convention Welcome	3:00
	Crown Chapter Dinner	5:30
	Development Video	7:30
Friday	Fraternity Insurance Group	9:00 a.m.
	Alumnae Recruitment Project	11:00
	Collegiate Rush	2:00 p.m.
	Crown Chapter Dinner	5:30
Saturday	Ritual Services	9:00 a.m.
	Brunch	11:00
	State of the Fraternity Address	2:00 p.m.
	National Council Election	4:00
	Recognition Banquet	7:30

3. Widen the event column so that the text is displayed without wrapping, if possible. You may need to resize other column widths to make it fit correctly on the page. Save. Print the result.

4. Apply a decimal tab in the time column so that the times are aligned at the colons, then save. Print the result.

5. Add a new row to the top of the table. Add the title Convention Schedule. Merge the cells of the top row so that the cell with the title Convention Schedule extends over all three columns. Format the title to a larger font and boldface it. Center the title and delete extra lines. Save and print the result.

6. Place text on normal paragraphs above the table with the name, dates, and location of the convention. Customize the border for the best appearance. Save and print the final result.

Review Questions

*1. For what kind of information is a table best suited?

2. What is a cell? What kind of information can be stored in a cell?

*3. How is a table created from scratch? What kind of information must you supply when creating a table?

4. What is the default value for column widths when creating a table?

*5. What happens when the text typed into a cell is too wide to fit in the cell?

6. How is the cursor moved forward and backward through a table using the keyboard?

*7. How is a new row added to the bottom of a table?

8. How are characters in a cell formatted?

*9. How is a table created from existing text?

10. What is a delimiter? What kinds of delimiters are available when creating a table from existing text?

*11. What command is used to change a table back to text? When is this command available?

12. How are rows and columns added to a table? What is the procedure used to move a row or column?

*13. What is the difference in procedure for adding a single row or column as opposed to adding multiple rows and columns at once?

14. What elements are found on the ruler when the cursor is within a table?

*15. How are cells in a table merged? When is it appropriate to merge cells in a table? What criteria must cells meet before they can be merged?

16. How are the row height and column width changed using the mouse? Using the keyboard? What is the default row height?

*17. How do cell borders differ from gridlines? How are they activated? What formatting does AutoFormat do?

18. Why is the Alignment section of the Table/Cell Height and Width dialog box necessary? Aren't these functions already available?

*19. What are tabs used for within a table? Which keys must be pressed to move the cursor to a tab setting in a table?

20. What calculations may be performed on numeric data in a table?

Key Terms

Cell	Delimiter	Table
Cell mark	Gridline	

Documentation Research

1. How do you get the headings of a long table to appear above the data on a second page?

2. How do you automatically number cells in a table?

APPLICATION C

Using Tables to Create a Résumé

Create a résumé by inserting a table into an empty document. Use merged cells to create the wide cells (like the one containing the Objective) and the cells to the right of Education, Work Experience, Honors and Awards, and Computer Skills. In the sample résumé in Figure C.1, the borders have been turned on to show you how the cells are formatted. Do not include the borders in your résumé. You may wish to use a bulleted list as subpoints within the right column. Be sure to carefully proofread your document. Absolutely no mistakes are tolerated on a résumé.

FIGURE C.1
Sample résumé

FIRST AND LAST NAME
Street address either here or below
City, State Zip
Phone number

Present address		Permanent address
Street		Street
City, State Zip		City, State Zip
Phone number		Phone number

Objective: To obtain a full-time position working in the field in which you are trained with XXX company	
EDUCATION	
WORK EXPERIENCE	
HONORS AND AWARDS	
COMPUTER SKILLS	

Pictures and Graphics

An advantage of a graphical environment such as Windows is the ability to display pictures and graphics. Windows also makes it simple to share pictures among programs. Many applications are good sources for pictures and graphics, some of which run in Windows and therefore allow you to copy images to any other Windows application. Anything that you see on the screen can be pasted into the work area of a document.

Word allows you to insert pictures and graphics directly into documents. There they may be selected, resized, and cropped to fit the space available on the page. Pictures may be placed anywhere on the page, and text may flow around them. Word has several features that allow you to create pictures. You can use the tools on the Drawing toolbar to create illustrations. WordArt is a miniapplication that allows you to create artistic effects with text. This unit covers the way images are inserted into Word and then moved, cropped, sized, and positioned on the page.

Learning Objectives

At the completion of this unit you should know

1. several sources for graphics and pictures,

2. how to place graphic images into a document,

3. how to manipulate and position pictures and graphics in a document,

4. how to create your own graphic image using MS WordArt and drawing tools.

Important Commands

Format/Drop Cap

Format/Frame

Format/Picture

Insert/Frame

Insert/Object

Insert/Picture

Tools/Options/View

Pictures and Graphics

Pictures, which include icons, graphs, charts, drawings, images, lines, shapes, or anything that isn't a character, can greatly enhance the presentation of information in a document. Because Word exists in a graphical environment, it is extremely flexible in the way it handles graphic images. The word processor allows you to insert pictures into a document and then resize and crop them. Pictures can even be placed in a specific position on the page and have text flow around them.

One process of inserting pictures is familiar to you. You already know that items that are cut or copied from the Edit menu are placed in the Clipboard. The contents of the Clipboard can then be pasted to the location of the cursor in your document. Therefore, any picture viewed on screen that can be copied to the Clipboard can also be pasted into Word. This paste procedure has been demonstrated in several Guided Activities that you have completed in previous units.

Another method for inserting pictures is to import them with the Insert/Picture command. There are several sources for pictures that can be imported into a document. First, if the images are fairly simple, you may create your own drawings in the Paintbrush accessory in Windows or with the drawing tools included with Word. For more complex art, Word provides over a hundred selections of *clip art*, professionally drawn pictures that may be used in any Windows software. Clip art also comes from many other manufacturers and in various file formats. In addition, anything on a printed page can be placed on a device called a *scanner*, scanned into the computer, and reproduced electronically on the screen.

Pictures in a document can be resized (scaled) or cropped. After a picture has been inserted and formatted to look the way it is supposed to, it can be moved freely just like the text around it or be positioned at a certain place on the page. If a picture is fixed on a page at a certain location, any text will flow around the picture (this is called *run-around* text). This is an extremely effective presentation style because the text that describes the picture surrounds the picture rather than being above or below it. However, text should not flow around both sides of a picture unless the text is formatted into two columns; otherwise, the reader may become confused about how to read the text on each side of the picture.

With all of the advantages, pictures in a document have a disadvantage. Because of the memory they consume, they make the document scroll very slowly. When you scroll through a document that does not contain pictures, text in the work area scrolls smoothly. Even if you are working in Page Layout view, the delay is short. When a picture is inserted into a document, however, the computer has to work hard to keep the image updated on the screen so that it will look right. When you scroll through a document, there is a noticeable pause while the computer refreshes the picture that is being displayed. To avoid this problem, once a picture looks the way you want it to, select Tools/Options/View and check the box next to Picture Placeholders. A box the size of the picture will be displayed in the document, but the contents of the picture will not. The document will scroll much more smoothly. Although an empty box rather than the picture is displayed, the picture is still in the document and will print correctly. To view the picture, select Print Preview or select Tools/Options/View to turn Picture Placeholders off.

Inserting Word Clip Art

Word provides nearly 100 professionally drawn clip art images stored in separate files in the \CLIPART subdirectory. Do not use the command File/Open to access a clip art file; rather, use the command Insert/Picture to import the picture into a Word document.

The Insert/Picture dialog box, shown in Figure 10.1, closely resembles the File/Open dialog box in that file names, drives, and directories are listed. One difference is that the files listed have various extensions, rather than the .DOC extension. The extensions of files let you know what kinds of files they are or where they were created. The clip art pictures packaged with Word have the extension .WMF, which stands for Windows Metafiles. This type of graphic may be used in every Windows software application. Another type of file is a bitmap, which has the extension .BMP. Bitmaps may be created in Paintbrush, a Windows accessory. Scanners produce

FIGURE 10.1
The Insert/Picture dialog box

Click here to select .bmp, .tif, or other types of graphics files

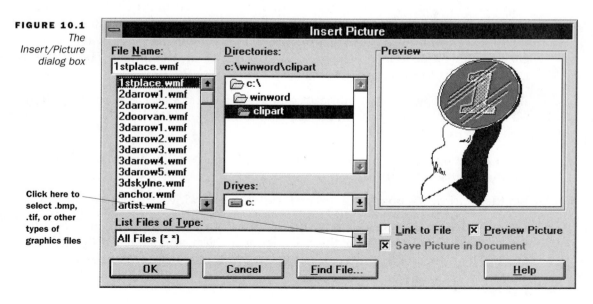

"TIFF" files, so called for their extension, .TIF, which stands for "tagged image file format." To see only files with a certain extension, change the selection under List Files of Type.

During installation, Word creates a subdirectory named \CLIPART where it stores the picture files. You may need to switch drives to find the directory where Word and its \CLIPART subdirectory are located. Once you have the correct subdirectory on screen, you see an alphabetical list of clip art files, beginning with 1STPLACE.WMF. Word makes it convenient to preview the graphics before they are actually inserted into the document. Highlight the name of the desired file and then click the Preview Picture box to display a thumbnail image of the picture.

GUIDED ACTIVITY 10.1

Inserting Clip Art

1. Start Word. Create a new document.

2. Type a paragraph several lines long on the subject of using graphic images in documents. At the end of the paragraph, press ⏎Enter twice. Make sure your cursor is on the last line of the document.

3. From the menu select Insert/Picture.

4. A dialog box that looks much like the one used to open documents is displayed. This box allows you to navigate through the subdirectories and drives available to you to find graphics files. The Word clip art files should be stored in the \WINWORD\CLIPART subdirectory. If you cannot find this subdirectory, your teacher will instruct you.

5. Select one of the clip art files by highlighting it. Check the Preview button to display a thumbnail in the Picture Preview box. Scroll down in the list of files and select another picture to preview. The image in the Picture Preview box changes to display the second picture. Select the file DIVIDER1.WMF and click OK to exit the dialog box and insert the picture into the document. You may also double-click the file name to insert the picture directly into the document. The picture is inserted at the location of the cursor.

    Another type of graphic, a bitmap, comes with Windows 3.1. You may recall the pictures that you can place on the desktop in Program Manager. These files are located in the \WINDOWS subdirectory.

6. Press ⏎Enter once or twice and insert another picture into the document. Issue the command Insert/Picture.

7. On the drop-down box, List Files of Type, select Windows Bitmaps.

8. Double-click on the root directory under Directories. The root directory is at the top of the list, and consists of the drive letter, a colon, and a backslash, such as C:\ or H:\. A new list of directories appears. You may need to change drives to find the \WINDOWS subdirectory.

9. Scroll down and double-click on the \WINDOWS subdirectory. A list of files beginning with 256COLOR.BMP appears in the Files box.

10. Select ARGYLE.BMP and click OK to insert the picture into the document.

Modifying Pictures

When pictures are first placed into a document, they become part of the text. The line spacing of the paragraph containing the picture expands to fit the picture. If the paragraph is centered, the picture within it is also centered. If text is inserted above or to the left of the picture, the picture moves down or to the right.

FIGURE 10.2
A selected picture has sizing handles.

Selecting the picture is done by clicking on it with the mouse, or using the [Shift] and arrow keys. You can distinguish text in a document that is highlighted because the color of the text is different from the color of the text that is not highlighted. When a picture is highlighted, however, Word draws a non-printing border around it and displays eight *sizing handles*, one at each corner and one in the middle of each edge of the picture, as in Figure 10.2. Besides helping you see if the picture is highlighted, these handles are used to change its size and which parts are displayed. If you drag a sizing handle that is in the middle of an edge, only that edge will move. Dragging a sizing handle at a corner of the picture allows you to move both the intersecting edges at the same time.

Once a picture is selected, you may *scale* (resize) or crop it. Both functions can be performed using either the mouse or the Format/Picture dialog box, shown in Figure 10.3.

Scaling a picture changes the size of the image. To scale a picture with the mouse, drag a sizing handle to a new location. If you drag only one edge of the picture, you will distort the image. If you are scaling an abstract object, such distortion may be acceptable. If you are sizing a realistic image, such as a picture of someone's face, however, you probably want to keep the picture proportional. A good idea when scaling is to drag only the corner sizing handles to keep the picture proportional.

Pictures may also be scaled to exact percentage from the dialog box. Make sure the picture is highlighted, select Format/Picture, and enter the desired scaling percentage. Scaling percentages smaller than 100% will decrease the image size; percentages larger than 100% will increase it.

FIGURE 10.3
The Format/Picture dialog box

Picture

Crop From
Left: 0"
Right: 0"
Top: 0"
Bottom: 0"

Scaling
Width: 100%
Height: 100%

Size
Width: 1.78"
Height: 1.67"

Original Size
Width: 1.78"   Height: 1.67"

OK
Cancel
Reset
Frame...
Help

To *crop* a picture means to remove unwanted parts of it by changing its dimensions without changing the image size. A picture is cropped when you want only a portion of the entire image to appear in the document. You may crop a picture by hand with the mouse or use a dialog box to enter the exact dimensions to be removed.

To crop a picture with the mouse, hold [Shift] and drag the sizing handle of the edge to be cropped to increase or decrease that edge. If you drag the edge toward the picture, part of the picture will be hidden. If you drag the edge away from the picture, the area you add to the picture will be filled with white space.

Pictures can also be cropped using the Format/Picture dialog box. While not as visual as using the mouse, it may be a more precise method. Select Format/Picture, and enter the measurements to crop from each edge of the picture. Although the picture is inserted within the flow of the text in a document, pressing [Backspace] will not remove it. Rather, you must first select the picture, then delete it.

GUIDED ACTIVITY 10.2

Scaling, Cropping, and Deleting

1. Highlight the divider picture. A border appears around the picture, along with the eight sizing handles. The handles are small squares at each corner and at the middle of each edge.

2. Drag the sizing handle at the bottom-right corner down and out until the picture is about twice its original height. As you drag, the status bar displays the scaling percent. (Double is 200%.)

   The picture stays in proportion because you sized it from a corner rather than from an edge.

3. Select the argyle design and drag the corner sizing handle until it has approximately tripled in size.

   Bitmaps are made of tiny "bits" of color. You can see that these squares are enlarged, and the design has lost its sharpness and has become jagged. Because of this, bitmaps are best used at their original size or smaller.

4. Drag the sizing handle in the middle of the right edge to the right margin of the text. This causes the picture to be stretched out of proportion horizontally. The small squares of color are each stretched into rectangles.

5. Select the divider picture and repeat the stretch. As you drag, notice that the status bar reflects the change in proportion. The diamond in the design is elongated, which is an interesting shape. Using the edge sizing handles to size a realistic picture, however, is generally not a good idea.

6. Select Format/Picture.

Notice that, under Scaling, the Height is around 200% but the Width is about 300% of the original size, as in Figure 10.4. When a picture is in proportion, these values will be identical.

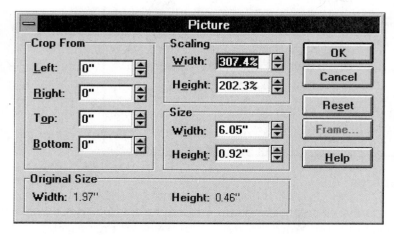

7. Enter 150 in both the Scaling Height and Width boxes and click on the OK button. (You need not enter the % sign.)

    The picture is exactly one-and-one-half times its original height and width.

    When cropping a picture with the mouse, the mouse pointer shows a new shape, and the status bar at the bottom of the screen displays the amount of the picture being removed in inches.

8. While holding down [Shift], drag the sizing handle on the center of the right edge of the picture to the left to remove the line on the design. As you drag, the status bar shows the measurement being cropped. The right 0.85 inch of the picture is now obscured. The line on the right will not be displayed when the picture is printed with the document.

9. While holding down [Shift], drag the sizing handle in the center of the left edge to crop the other line.

    The Format/Picture dialog box reflects the amount of cropping, as shown in Figure 10.5. For more specific measurements, you may enter the amount of cropping directly into the dialog box.

10. To restore the picture to its original, uncropped and unscaled size, select Format/Picture and click on the Reset button and then OK. The size is placed back to 100% of original, and crop values are set to zero.

11. To place a border on the picture that will print, select the picture, then select Format/Borders and Shading and click on Box under the Presets options, or click on the Borders button to display the Borders toolbar, then apply an outside border.

12. Select the argyle picture and press [Del]. The picture is removed from the document.

FIGURE 10.5
Cropping displayed on the Format/Picture dialog box

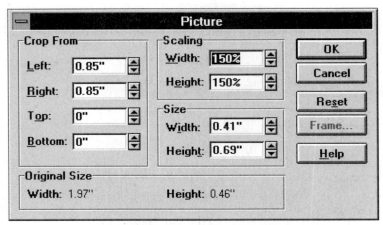

Editing Graphics

Original art may be created and clip art images may be edited using the drawing program that is built into Word. To create your own art images, click on the Drawing button on the toolbar, which has a drawing of a circle, square, and triangle. To edit a clip art image, double-click on the image.

As soon as you click on the Drawing button or double-click on a picture, the Drawing toolbar, shown in Figure 10.6, appears at the bottom of the screen between the scroll bar and the status bar. At this point, objects may be added using the various drawing tools, and line and fill colors may be specified. An image may be flipped vertically or horizontally or rotated clockwise, and the parts of an image may be grouped or ungrouped to work on them together or separately.

FIGURE 10.6
The Drawing toolbar found at the bottom of the screen

GUIDED ACTIVITY 10.3

Editing Clip Art

1. At the end of the document, press ⌷Enter once or twice. Select Insert/Picture and choose SPORTS.WMF from the \CLIPART subdirectory, and click OK.

2. Click on the sports picture so that the sizing handles appear. Notice the message in the status bar that says, "Double-click to edit."

3. Double-click on the picture.

   Immediately, as Figure 10.7 shows, the picture is placed into a square in a document with the name Picture in Document1. The document appears in Page Layout view, even if you were previously working in Normal view. The Drawing toolbar is displayed at the bottom of the screen, and a very short toolbar with only two buttons appears on top of the document, the Picture toolbar.

FIGURE 10.7
Editing a picture changes the Word screen.

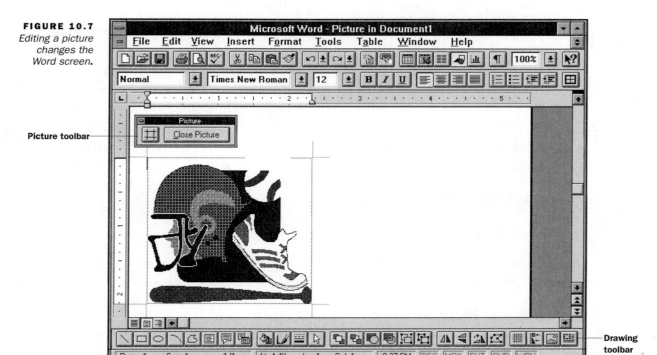

Picture toolbar

Drawing toolbar

4. Click on the picture of the baseball bat so that sizing handles appear.

5. Click on the Fill button on the Drawing toolbar at the bottom of the screen. On the palette that appears, select the color tan.

The baseball bat is now colored like a wooden bat, but it seems a little bland.

6. Add a black outline to the bat by clicking on the Line Color button, and selecting black.

7. Elongate the baseball bat by dragging on the sizing handle on the right or left edge.

Bring to   Send to
Front   Back

8. This picture is composed of elements in several layers. You can control in what order the layers appear. Click on the black square in the background. Click on the Bring to Front button to change the order of the picture's layers. Click on the Send to Back button to put it in the background again.

9. Use the Select Drawing Objects button and drag a large dashed rectangle enclosing the entire graphic image, in order to select all the elements in the picture. When you release the mouse button, sizing handles for each item appear all over the picture.

10. Click on the Group button to assemble these elements into a single graphic image. This prevents you from moving one out of place, but also keeps you from changing colors or attributes of an individual part of the picture.

11. Suppose you want the person facing right. You can reorient the picture by clicking on the Flip Horizontal, the Flip Vertical, or the Rotate button. Experiment with these buttons until the picture looks best.

Since you have elongated the bat, it is no longer enclosed in the boundary square on the edit screen. Only what is within the boundary square appears in the document after you finish editing.

12. Click the Reset Picture Boundary button on the Picture toolbar, shown in Figure 10.8.

FIGURE 10.8
*The Picture
toolbar*

Reset Picture Boundary button

13. To return to the regular document and update the picture in the document to reflect the changes you made, click the Close Picture button on the Picture toolbar.

Positioning Pictures

When a picture has been inserted into a document, it is treated like a single character within the text. The picture causes automatic line spacing to enlarge to accommodate the height of the picture. Text on the same line appears very small next to the picture or is placed above or below the picture. How do we get the text to appear at the side of the picture?

One way is to place the picture into a table, then put the text into the cell next to the picture. This works well with small amounts of text such as a caption that would always be located next to the picture (as in this book). To get the text to flow around the picture, however, you must use another method.

Often, to be effective, a picture must be positioned at a specific location on a page. This includes logos and letterheads on letters as well as pictures on personalized stationary. To position pictures at any location on the page, or to have the text flow around a picture, you first enclose it within a boundary called a *frame*. This may be done by selecting the command Insert/Frame or by clicking the mouse on the Frame button on the Drawing toolbar, if it is displayed.

To use the frame effectively, you must work in Page Layout view. If you are working in Normal view when you apply a frame to a selected picture, the program prompts you to switch to Page Layout view. When the frame is applied and the view changed to Page Layout view, the picture is surrounded by a crosshatched border, and text immediately flows around it. This crosshatched border does not print, but as the mouse pointer points at the crosshatching it turns into a four-headed arrow. This reminds you that in Page Layout view, a framed picture may be simply dragged with the mouse to any location on the page—even into the margins. If the framed picture is moved on top of text, the text will flow around it. If you change back to Normal view, the text will no longer flow around the framed picture.

Although it is simple to move a picture around the page by dragging it, the frame may be more precisely positioned on a page by specifying its horizontal and vertical positions in the Format/Frame dialog box, as shown in Figure 10.9.

FIGURE 10.9
The Format Frame dialog box

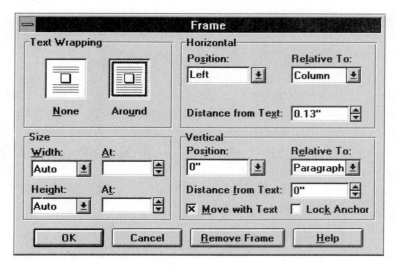

In the Horizontal position box, you may select Left, Center, or Right (and Inside or Outside for Mirror Margins) or may enter a measurement in inches. To see the actual horizontal position, you need to combine the contents of this box with the information immediately beside it. In the dialog box shown in Figure 10.9, the picture is positioned at the left side of the column that contains it. It could be positioned at the left, center, right, inside, or outside relative to the margins, page, or column.

The Vertical Position box allows you to select Top, Bottom, or Center. Again, the picture may be positioned relative to the Paragraph, Margin, or Page. The default, 0", does not actually position the picture at all but keeps it in the same place it was inserted.

You can specify the distance the picture appears from the text that flows around it by entering a value in the Distance from Text boxes in the Format/Frame dialog box. Very small distances may distort or crowd the framed item. Large distances may leave too much space and diminish the effect you are trying to achieve by wrapping text around the picture.

GUIDED ACTIVITY 10.4

Positioning Pictures

1. Highlight the clip art picture. Place it into a frame by selecting Insert/Frame or by clicking on the Drawing button to display the Drawing toolbar and then clicking the Frame button on the toolbar. When the program prompts you to switch to Page Layout view, choose Yes.

2. Drag the framed picture to the center top of the page. Notice how text flows out of the way.

3. Use the dialog box to set the picture in the exact center of the page. Select Format/Frame and change the horizontal and vertical settings to Center and click OK.

4. Change the view back to Normal view. The picture is not shown centered, although Print Preview and Page Layout view show that it will print centered.

5. Click on the Page Layout view button at the bottom of the screen, then choose Whole Page from the Zoom Control box at the top right. Now you are able to see and edit the whole page at once in Page Layout view.

6. Drag the framed picture to the bottom-right corner of the page. With the keyboard, select Format/Frame and set Horizontal Position to Right and Relative To to Page, then set Vertical Position to Bottom and Relative To to Page. Click OK. A framed picture may appear anywhere on the page, even within the margins.

7. Return your document to the normal size by selecting 100% from the Zoom Control box. Save the document as A:10_A.

Creating Text Pictures

Another source for graphic images is to create a picture out of text. Word can automatically format a paragraph to have the first letter or word appear as a **drop cap** (dropped capital) with the command Format/Drop Cap, as shown in the dialog box in Figure 10.10. To create this effect, Word changes the size of the first letter or word in a paragraph, then sets it into a frame by itself. The framed letter or word may be positioned either within the paragraph (dropped) or out in the margin.

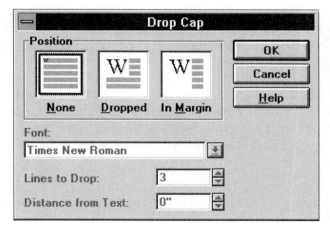

FIGURE 10.10
The Format/ Drop Cap dialog box

Word also can create special effects with text using the built-in program Microsoft WordArt. This program is accessed through the command Insert/Object. The screen changes to display the menus and toolbars for this new program, as shown in Figure 10.11, rather than the usual Word menus and toolbars, although you still see your Word document on screen.

After typing your text into the small window, you may change several attributes, including the font, the shape of the text, and the color. Word allows you to see the results of your work as a graphic image in a crosshatched border (a frame) within the document. To return to the usual Word screen, click anywhere in the document. WordArt images may later be edited by double-clicking on the image.

FIGURE 10.11
*The WordArt
screen*

New
menu and
toolbar

Using WordArt and Drop Caps

1. Place the cursor within the paragraph of text. Issue the command Format/
   Drop Cap.

2. Click on the Dropped selection. Change the font to Arial for contrast. Click OK.

   Word prompts you to change to Page Layout view if you are not already working
   in it. The dropped capital appears in a frame with a crosshatched border, and the
   rest of the paragraph flows around the frame. If you want to remove the dropped
   capital letter, issue the command Format/Drop Cap and click on None.

3. Place the cursor in a new paragraph. Open the WordArt program by issuing the
   command Insert/Object, and select Microsoft WordArt 2.0 from the list.

4. Type in the phrase New and Improved! replacing Your Text Here. Click
   the Update Display button to display the new words in the document.

5. Click on the arrow next to the font box in the toolbar at the top of the screen to
   display the drop-down list box of fonts. The fonts are listed in alphabetical order.
   Use the up and down arrow keys to preview the look of each font. Select the one
   that best communicates the message.

6. Drop down the list box containing "Plain Text" by clicking on the down arrow.
   The choices for the shape of the text are shown in Figure 10.12. Click on the second selection, an upward slanting line. Try several other selections to see the
   effect.

7. Click on the other buttons on the WordArt toolbar to see the effects each has on
   the WordArt image.

8. To exit WordArt and return to the document, click anywhere in the text of the
   document.

   The WordArt menus and toolbar disappear, and the usual Word screen returns.
   Back in the document, the WordArt image may be sized, cropped, and framed
   just like any other picture.

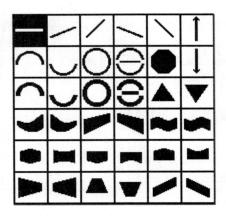

FIGURE 10.12
The choices of text shapes for WordArt

Summary

Word allows you to insert pictures into documents. These pictures can be graphic images from various publishers, scanned images, or art prepared in WordArt. Scanned images and clip art are inserted with the Insert/Picture command. WordArt objects are inserted via Insert/Object.

Pictures in a document may be cropped or scaled using either the mouse or the Format/Picture command. The mouse allows you to visually crop or scale a picture and is easier to use, whereas the Format/Picture dialog box allows more precise measurements.

To edit a picture, simply double-click on the image. The Drawing toolbar appears, giving you the ability to change the color and line style, group and ungroup separate elements of the picture, and flip or rotate the picture to change its orientation.

A picture can be framed with the Insert/Frame command so that text will flow around it. In Page Layout view a framed picture may be dragged anywhere on the page, or it may be positioned precisely using the Format/Frame command. This dialog box allows you to set the horizontal and vertical position of the frame on the page. If there is text at the location of the framed picture, the text will wrap around the picture.

Exercises

1. Create a new document. Insert a clip art image from the \WINWORD\CLIPART subdirectory. Print the result.

2. Create a new document. Type several paragraphs of text comparing books or magazines with pictures to those without, and explaining to your colleagues at your company how pictures enhance the message of a document. Press Enter to move the cursor to a new blank paragraph. Open WordArt and type the text, Enhancing The Company Image. Change the font if you desire. Change the style from Plain Text to the Bottom to Top style, denoted by a long upward-pointing arrow. Print the result.

3. Continue with the document from Exercise 2. Place the WordArt picture into a frame and position it on the top-left side of the page so that the text flows on the right side of the picture. Print the result.

4. Continue with the document from Exercise 3. Change to view the whole page and scale the picture proportionally so that it is nearly as long as the entire page. Print the result.

5. Continue with the document from Exercise 4. Crop the bottom portion of the picture so that only the words The Company Image appear. Scale the picture again so that it runs the length of the page. Place a border on the right side of the image and print the result. The final page should look something like Figure 10.13.

FIGURE 10.13
The result of Exercises 2 through 5

Review Questions

*1. What advantage does Word's graphical environment give when one is using pictures and graphics?

2. What are three types of graphics files mentioned in this unit? What are the file extensions and sources for each type?

*3. What is the disadvantage of having pictures in a document? How is it overcome?

4. What are sizing handles? When do they appear? What significance does the location of a sizing handle have?

*5. What is the difference between cropping and scaling? How are cropping and scaling performed? How is each measured?

6. As a rule, what should you be careful of when sizing images that contain pictures of real things (such as people's faces)?

*7. What do you do to edit a picture? What new features appear on screen while you are editing a picture?

8. What are some functions of the buttons on the Drawing toolbar?

*9. How may pictures be positioned in any location on the page? What view must be in effect to see the picture in position?

10. What effect does a positioned picture have on text that is already on the page?

*11. What is the difference between a frame and a border on a picture?

12. What are two ways to create a graphic out of text?

Key Terms

Clip art	Frame	Scale
Crop	Picture	Scanner
Drop cap	Run-around	Sizing handle

Documentation Research

1. How is a caption added to a framed picture?

2. How can you create a watermark?

3. How do you create a composite picture containing both an imported graphic and objects created with the Drawing toolbar?

4. How does a text box differ from a frame?

Using Pictures to Enhance Text

Any document can be enhanced by adding pictures to support the text. For this application, preview the clip art included in Word and select several pictures of items that are typical of other countries. Type in three paragraphs describing three different regions of the world. For each paragraph, insert the clip art image illustrating the region. For example, you might pick the golf picture to depict St. Andrews in Scotland, or, more symbolically, you might use the bear to represent Russia. Scale each image so that it is one inch wide. Place a border around the picture. Position the picture against the right margin at the top of the paragraph that describes it, so that the text in the paragraph wraps around it.

At the top of your document, below the title, place a picture of the map of the world. Use the drawing tools to place a spot or arrow on the map to highlight each location discussed. If all your locations are in one hemisphere, you may wish to crop the map of the world to display only the relevant part. Be sure to proofread your document. Save the file as APPD and print it.

Columns

Word provides two methods for producing text in several columns. Tables provide the capability of printing parallel, or side-by-side columns, of information. Some types of documents such as newspapers and newsletters require you to enter text into "snaking" columns on a page, where the text flows from the top to bottom of one column, then from top to bottom in the next column. Traditionally, this required physically cutting and pasting up documents that were printed in a single, long, narrow column. Because the text had to be perfect before being pasted up, this method led to a great deal of inaccuracy and much unnecessary revision.

Word allows you to create documents in newspaper-style columns and gives you control over the number of columns and the space between the columns. Text can be entered directly into multiple-column format and will automatically scroll from one column to the next. If changes need to be made in the text, the word processor reorganizes the columns to reflect the changes in much the same way it moves text from one page to another when lines are added or deleted. This unit covers the procedures provided by Word for the creation and use of columns. The Newsletter Wizard incorporates many of the elements explained in this unit.

Learning Objectives

At the completion of this unit you should know

1. how to place a document into newspaper-style columns,

2. how to place part of a document into several columns when the rest is regular single-column text,

3. how to balance and manipulate the format of the columns.

Important Commands

File/Page Setup

Format/Columns

Insert/Break

View/Normal

View/Page Layout

Columns

Columns are used in documents for several reasons. In newspapers and magazines, it is much easier to align articles and advertisements in multiple-column format. This particular style gives greater flexibility when laying out pages, and lets more headlines fit on a single page. Also, the reader's eye can scan narrow columns more quickly than the width of a full page. This means that more text can be read in the same amount of time if it is printed in multiple-column format. However, when columns are less than two inches wide, the text in them begins to look choppy because of loss of continuity in sentences and paragraphs. There is an optimum range of widths that provides the easiest and fastest reading, usually 30 to 65 letters across (about 5 to 10 words).

A graphic positioned between two columns of text describing the picture is a very efficient method of conveying information. The combination of text and graphics helps the reader remember the point of the document.

For these reasons, many publications use multiple-column format exclusively. Word allows you to create a document in multiple-column format or change existing documents to multiple-column format.

Creating Columns

You may enter text directly into columns or take existing text and change it into multiple-column format. Word provides a button on the Toolbar to quickly format the document into several columns. Click on the Column button and drag to highlight the number of columns desired, as shown in Figure 11.1. By default, the entire document is placed into columns.

The width of the columns is determined by the distance between the margins divided by the number of columns and allowing for a space of one-half inch (as a default) between the columns. The ruler displays column markers for each column.

FIGURE 11.1
*Column button
on the toolbar*

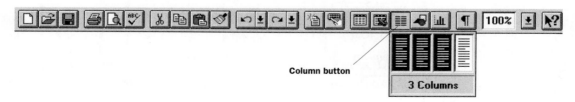

Column button

3 Columns

After text is placed into several columns, Normal view displays it in a single, long, narrow column on the left of the work area. While Normal view shows accurate column widths and is easy to use for text entry and editing, it does not display the columns as they will print.

Page Layout view, on the other hand, displays the columns side by side along with any framed graphics in correct position. Because text flows from the bottom of one column to the top of the next, Page Layout view may be awkward for text entry and editing, but it is excellent for final viewing to see the format of the columns on the page.

Changing Column Widths

Because the widths of columns are determined by the margins, the number of columns, and the amount of space between, changing any of these three elements affects the column width. The ruler, shown in Figure 11.2, displays markers that may be dragged to change all of these settings for the document. Dragging these markers left or right affects either the left and right margins of the document, or the width of the columns and therefore the space between the columns.

FIGURE 11.2
Ruler with equal column markers

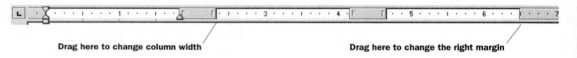

Drag here to change column width   Drag here to change the right margin

Columns may also be formatted to unequal column widths through the Format/Columns dialog box, shown in Figure 11.3. This dialog box allows you to specify the exact widths of the columns and the space between them. Clicking the Line Between check box places vertical lines between the columns. To see the columns and vertical lines as they will appear when printed, select Page Layout view or Print Preview. To

FIGURE 11.3
The Format Columns dialog box

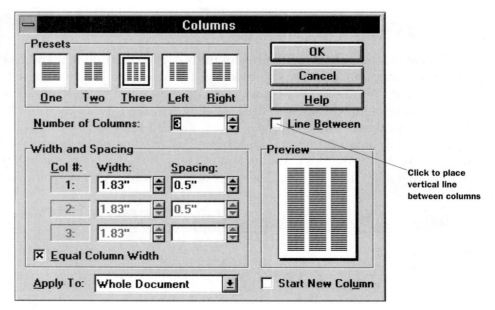

remove the multiple-column formatting, click the Column button and drag to high-light only one column.

GUIDED ACTIVITY 11.1

Creating Columns

1. Start Word and open SAMPLE3.DOC in the \WINWORD\WORDCBT directory that comes with Word, or open any rather long document if that is not available. Erase the text that appears in the document before the word Venus.

2. Click on the Column button and drag the highlight across two columns. Press PgDn a few times to see the long, single column.

   The ruler shows the width of the two columns with column markers.

3. Click on the Page Layout View button at the bottom of the screen or select View/Page Layout to see the two columns side by side. Press PgDn a few times to view the bottom of the first column. Nothing happens when you press PgDn again to see the next part of the text. Because of the way it shows the flow of the text, Page Layout view is best for seeing the format of the column, but it is awkward for editing text.

4. Click on the Column button and drag the highlight across three columns. Notice the change in the width of the columns, both in the text and on the ruler.

5. These columns are really too narrow, and the paragraphs are too choppy to read easily. By changing the margins we can make the columns wider.

6. Click once on the ruler, then carefully place the mouse pointer at the left edge of the ruler between the indentation markers. When you see the two-headed arrow, drag to make the margin 1" wide. Repeat for the right margin. The width of the columns adjusts to use the space available.

   If you drag the indentation markers on the ruler by mistake, the paragraphs in the column will be indented, which may also affect the width of the text within the column.

7. Drag the right side of a column marker to make the space between the columns narrower.

   Because the columns are equal widths, any adjustment you make to one column is automatically done to the other.

8. Select Format/Columns. In the dialog box, click on Left to change to unequal col-umn widths. Click on the box next to Line Between to place lines between the columns. Click OK.

   There are now two columns, the left one narrower than the right, with a vertical line drawn between them.

9. Change to Normal view. The vertical line disappears, and the text is displayed in one long column. The column width of the text does not reflect the width of either the narrower left column or the wider right column. The ruler still reflects the actual column width, however, as shown in Figure 11.4.

FIGURE 11.4
Ruler with unequal column markers

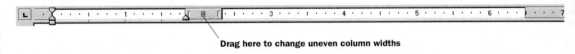

Drag here to change uneven column widths

10. Change back to Page Layout view to see the unequal columns just as they will print. Drag the crosshatched area on the column marker to the right so that the left column is twice as wide as the right. This changes the unequal column widths so that the left column is wider and the right column is narrower.

11. Save the document as A:11_A.

Separating Sections

Usually, an entire document does not appear in multiple-column format. For example, most documents have a title that appears centered above the text: the title does not appear in multiple-column format, even when the text does. Such a title on a newspaper or newsletter is termed a *masthead* (from sailors' practice of raising their flag to the top of the mast).

To have several column formats within a single document, it is necessary to break the document into several sections. Each section, separated by a *section break*, may be formatted to have a different number of columns, different margin settings, or a different orientation.

Changing the Columns in One Section

To change only a section of a document to a different number of columns, you must first highlight the section. Click on the Columns button and select the desired number of columns, and the column formatting is applied immediately to the highlighted portion of the text, without affecting the rest of the document.

Behind the scenes, Word has placed a section break above and below the highlighted area. These section breaks appear in Normal view as double lines across the text labeled End of Section, or may be viewed in Page Layout view by clicking the Show/Hide ¶ button.

A section break is inserted to separate those portions of the document that have one column or page format from those that have another. Section breaks may be manually inserted in a document by selecting Insert/Break. Section breaks may be used to break to a new page, break to a new column, or begin a new section that continues on the same page.

To insert a section break, click on the option button next to Continuous and then on the OK button. In the Normal view, you will see a double dotted line labeled End of Section across the page to indicate the section break. Each section may be formatted separately, without affecting other sections. Sections are formatted with settings in the File/Page Setup dialog box as well as with Format/Columns.

Word makes it simple to create a masthead in one section of a document and continue with several columns of text in another section on the same page. If you begin with the multiple-column text, as in Guided Activity 11.1, you can later highlight the text for the masthead and format it to a single column, and Word will insert a section break for you. If you are starting a document from scratch, you may first create the masthead, then select the Format/Columns dialog box and specify the number of columns, changing the Apply To setting from Whole Document to This Point Forward. Word automatically inserts a section break and formats the following section for the desired number of columns.

Using Section Breaks to Balance Columns

A common problem with multiple columns is that they end unevenly on the last page of a document or section. When a multiple-column format document ends in the middle of a page, the two columns on that page should ordinarily be the same length. This is known as ending with a balanced page. To balance a page, position the cursor after the last text on the page and insert a section break. (You may also have to add or delete a few words of text or rebreak one paragraph into two, to create an equal number of lines in each column.)

GUIDED ACTIVITY 11.2

Creating a Newsletter with a Masthead

1. Continue with the document from the previous Guided Activity. Place the cursor at the beginning of the document. Type The Solar System and press ⌈Enter⌋.

2. Highlight the headline. Click on the Column button and drag across one column only.

3. Change to Normal view to see the section break that Word has applied. Change back to Page Layout view.

4. With the masthead The Solar System still highlighted, format to 48 points and centered. Apply a border above and below the line.

5. See the results of your work in Print Preview, then Close to return to the document.

   It is also simple to begin with the masthead, then create the multiple-column text.

6. Create a new document. Select View/Normal.

7. Enter the title Creating Columns. Center the title at the top of the page. Press ⌈Enter⌋ twice. After pressing ⌈Enter⌋, left-align the current paragraph by pressing ⌈Ctrl⌋⌈L⌋ or by clicking on the left-align button on the toolbar.

8. Change the top margin to 2 inches.

9. Select the command Format/Columns and select 2 for the number of columns. Change the setting next to Apply To from Whole Document to This Point Forward and click OK. A section break appears across the document.

10. Enter the following excerpt from the Microsoft Word Help.

Column balancing means making columns equal in length. In a section having multiple text columns, uneven columns may occur at the end of a partially full page or on the last page of the section of document.

By inserting a continuous section immediately after the columns, you can have Word divide the text and graphics on the page equally between the columns.

Place the insertion point at the end of the columns you want balanced. If necessary, insert an extra paragraph mark, and then place the insertion point in the empty paragraph. Do not place the insertion point in a paragraph containing text or graphics. Choose Insert Break. Select Continuous and choose OK.

11. Select Page Layout view to see the columns as they will print.

The text appears in a single column on the left side of the page. These columns are out of balance. To solve this problem, insert a section break at the end of the document.

12. Position the cursor at the end of the document. Press [Enter] to place the cursor in an empty paragraph. Select Insert/Break, fill in the option button next to Continuous, and click OK.

The columns are now balanced on the page. If you add or delete text, the column lengths will adjust to remain approximately equal.

Many newspapers and newsletters use pictures or a bit of text to add contrast and attract interest to the page. A sentence or phrase pulled out of the text and set apart with a different format is called a *pull quote*. Pictures and pull quotes (often set in a larger and contrasting font) may be placed into a frame and positioned within a column or between two columns, and the rest of the text will run around the frame.

13. Use the Window menu selection to return to the first document, A:11_A. Place the cursor to the left of the word Geology.

14. Issue the command Insert/Frame, then drag a rectangle about 2 inches square on top of the text in the center of the page, something like Figure 11.5.

The frame appears with a crosshatched border, and the text flows around it. The cursor is blinking inside the frame. Enter the following sentence.

> Although scientists postulate the existence of other solar systems around the myriad of stars in the universe, no other planets have ever been discovered.

15. Format the text in the frame to Arial font, 14-point, bold but not italic.

16. Resize the frame to fit the text. To do this, click on the frame to reveal the sizing handles. Place the mouse pointer over the handles until the pointer turns into a two-headed arrow, then drag the appropriate handles until the frame is the right size.

17. View the whole page by selecting Whole Page from the Zoom Control box. To position the pull quote on the page, move the mouse pointer over the cross-hatched border until it turns into a four-headed arrow, then drag into position just to the left of the line between the columns, and even with the top edge of the paragraph on geology.

FIGURE 11.5
A frame ready for a pull quote

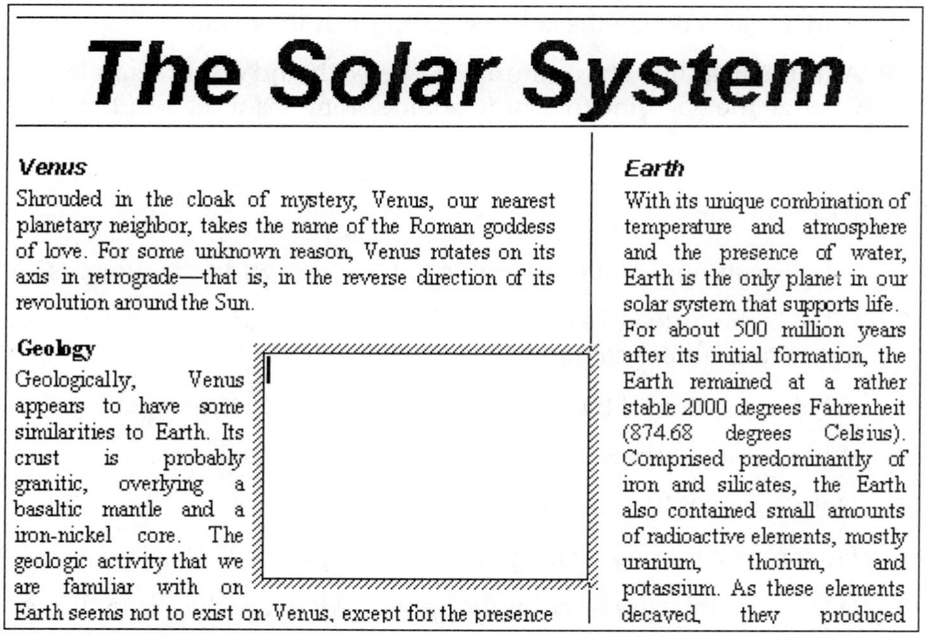

The Solar System

Venus

Shrouded in the cloak of mystery, Venus, our nearest planetary neighbor, takes the name of the Roman goddess of love. For some unknown reason, Venus rotates on its axis in retrograde—that is, in the reverse direction of its revolution around the Sun.

Geology

Geologically, Venus appears to have some similarities to Earth. Its crust is probably granitic, overlying a basaltic mantle and a iron-nickel core. The geologic activity that we are familiar with on Earth seems not to exist on Venus, except for the presence

Earth

With its unique combination of temperature and atmosphere and the presence of water, Earth is the only planet in our solar system that supports life. For about 500 million years after its initial formation, the Earth remained at a rather stable 2000 degrees Fahrenheit (874.68 degrees Celsius). Comprised predominantly of iron and silicates, the Earth also contained small amounts of radioactive elements, mostly uranium, thorium, and potassium. As these elements decayed, they produced

Summary

Some documents and many publications require a multiple-column format. Column format is preferable to full-page-width for several reasons. It permits pages to be laid out more readily, is easier to read, and allows text and pictures to be combined more effectively.

Word allows you to create documents in multiple-column format by separating the portion of the document with section breaks and using the Format/Columns command. This dialog box allows you to specify the number of columns, the width of the columns, and the space between columns. Documents may have more than one section, each with a different number of columns. These sections are separated with section breaks. A typical problem with multiple columns is that they become uneven on the last page of the section or document. Columns can be balanced by inserting another section break at the end of the text on the page or in the section. This will force the columns on the last page to be approximately the same length.

Exercises

1. Find a newspaper article at least three paragraphs long, with a minimum of three sentences in each paragraph. Enter the text of the article into a new document. Separate the second paragraph only into two columns, and print the result.

2. Change the second paragraph to three columns, and print the result.

3. Remove the section breaks by placing the cursor on the line and pressing [Del]. Make the whole article two balanced columns, then print the result.

4. Add a line between the columns, and print the result.

5. Add the headline above the article. Select it and apply a single-column format. Change the headline to a larger, bolder font. Print the results.

Review Questions

*1. Why is column layout preferable to full-page-width documents?

2. What is the difference between Normal view and Page Layout view when working with multiple columns?

*3. What is required if the entire document is not to be placed in multiple columns?

4. What column attributes are controllable from the Format/Columns dialog box?

*5. How is the width of columns changed?

6. How may columns of unequal width be specified?

*7. Where do unbalanced columns appear? How are they remedied?

Key Terms

Masthead   Pull quote   Section break

Documentation Research

1. How can you control where columns and pages break?

2. How can you specify where a frame will appear relative to the columns in a multiple-column document?

Using Columns to Create a Newsletter

The columns feature allows you to create attractive newsletters without complicated (and expensive) page layout software. This project entails the use of several dvanced word processing techniques covered in the preceding units.

In a new document, set the margins to .5" on all sides. On the top line, create a masthead using at least a 48-point font for the name of the newsletter. Leave a few blank lines at the bottom of the document and move the cursor up to just under the masthead. Insert a table three columns by one row. In the left cell place the date published, in the center cell the motto or theme of the newsletter, and in the right cell the price or volume number. Use a small font for this information. Place bold borders on the top and bottom of this small table.

Below the table, place the cursor in an empty paragraph, use the command Format/Columns, and specify that text should flow in three columns from this point forward. Begin typing the text of the newsletter below the section break. Format headlines in a large, bold, sans-serif font, and format the body text in a 10-point serif font. Format all paragraphs of text so that a space one-half line high is placed before each paragraph and the first line of each paragraph is indented .2".

Enter the text in Normal view, but switch to Page Layout view to see the columns as they will print. Place a line between the columns if you desire. Balance the columns by adding a final section break.

Create a pull quote to attract the reader's interest. Use a bold, italic, 18-point font. Position the frame within the center column. Make sure that text flows around it. Use View/Zoom Whole Page to examine the newsletter. Be sure to examine your newsletter to catch any errors. Save as A:APPE.DOC and print.

12
Headers and Footers

Headers and footers appear at the top or bottom of every page of a document to give the reader pertinent information about the text on the page. They appear on many different kinds of documents. Most publications have at least one or the other to help the reader keep track of the organization of the text.

Headers and footers could be added manually to the top and bottom of each page in a document, by simply typing text on the top and bottom line. This would require a great deal of work, and any modifications to the body of the document would force you to reposition the headers or footers on subsequent pages.

Word allows you to create the header or footer one time, then it automatically inserts it in the correct place on every page. You can make numerous additions and deletions to the body of the document, and the word processor will take those into account and keep the headers and footers at the top or bottom of the page. This unit covers how to create and edit headers and footers for various categories of pages.

Learning Objectives

At the completion of this unit you should know

1. what headers and footers are,

2. how to add headers and footers to different categories of pages,

3. how to insert special fields into headers and footers,

4. how to edit headers and footers.

Important Commands

File/Page Setup

Insert/Break

Toggle Field Codes

View/Header and Footer

Headers and Footers

Headers are lines of text that appear at the top of every page, separate from the body of the document, to give information about the text. They may contain chapter titles, page numbers, the author's name, or any other information pertinent to the text. *Footers* function exactly like headers except that they appear at the bottom of the page. They are added to a document using the View/Header and Footer command.

Most documents do not have headers and footers on every page. The top and bottom of the first page in a report or letter are usually blank. The page number and organizational titles that appear in the header or footer usually appear only on the second and subsequent pages. You may wish to create a header and a footer for the first page different from those on other pages or, if you leave them blank, no header or footer will appear on the first page. The regular header and footer will appear only on the second and subsequent pages.

Previously, you learned how to set margins for documents that were to be printed on both sides of the page and bound at one edge. You used Mirror Margins to make the inside margin larger than the outside margin for every page, regardless of whether it was an even-numbered (left-hand) or an odd-numbered (right-hand) page. The header and footer are usually placed against the outside margin in this situation; if they were against the inside margin, the binding might make them difficult to read. Placing them against the outside margin ensures that the reader will be able to read the text. However, this does require a different header or footer alignment for even-numbered and odd-numbered pages.

If a page number is included in a header or footer, the number needs to be different for every page. Instead of typing a real number, you may place a page-number *field code* in the header or footer. Word automatically keeps track of the page numbers of every page in the document. The word processor will substitute the actual page number for the field code when you print or view the document.

In addition to automatic page numbers, Word also offers field codes for the system date and time. Most computers maintain the current date and time in memory. Word can look up these values and substitute them for field codes. Because field codes can be inserted anywhere in a document, including the header or footer, when you execute a certain command the date and time will be recorded in the document. This feature can be very useful if you are keeping track of different versions of a document or are working on a document with several people and need to organize each one's work.

When you are creating a document, at times you will want to see the field codes themselves rather than their results. To see field codes, select Toggle Field Codes from the shortcut menu. All field codes in the document will be displayed. You may switch back and forth between viewing field codes or viewing their results with the shortcut menu selection, or with the shortcut key [Alt][F9].

Inserting Simple Headers and Footers

A simple header or footer appears on every page of the document within the top or bottom margin. The page numbers inserted with the command Insert/Page Numbers are simple headers or footers that you have already created. Headers and footers consisting of other text (with or without page numbers) can be created or edited from any page by using the View/Header and Footer command.

As soon as you issue the View/Header and Footer command, the screen changes. The text of the document is dimmed, and Word displays the Header and Footer toolbar, shown in Figure 12.1.

FIGURE 12.1
*The Header/
Footer toolbar*

The cursor will be positioned within the top margin area of the page in the header area that is enclosed by a nonprinting dashed rectangle and labeled Header or Odd Page Header, as shown in Figure 12.2. A document may be set up with different headers and footers for odd and even pages. To turn this feature off, click on the Page Setup button on the Header and Footer toolbar, and clear the check box specifying Different Odd and Even.

FIGURE 12.2
*The header area
of the page*

Instead of the regular default tab settings, only two tabs are set in the header or footer area of the page. If the ruler is displayed, you will see these tabs. A center tab is set at the 3" mark on the ruler and a right tab at the 6" mark. Most of the information in a header or footer is typed at the left or right margin or centered on the page, so the word processor places correct tabs at these locations, assuming that you will use them.

To jump the cursor to the footer instead of the header, click on the Switch Between Header and Footer button. To create the header or footer, type the desired text and apply formatting just as you would in a regular document. For instance, if you wish to have a black line printed at the top of every page, apply a border to a blank paragraph within the header area.

Three buttons on the Header and Footer toolbar insert field codes. The button with the number sign places a field code that automatically numbers pages. To the right of that button are the buttons for the current date and the current time.

You may type as many lines of text in the header or footer as you wish, and the margin of the document will increase to hold the entire header or footer. However, if the header is more than three lines long, you may want to put a return as the last line to separate it from the document body. Similarly, for long footers you may want to start the footer with a return to separate the footer from the last line of text on the page. As a rule, though, headers and footers should be brief.

While you are editing the header or footer, you may view the main part of the document in gray or hide it completely by clicking on the Show/Hide Document Text button on the Header and Footer toolbar. When you have finished the header or footer, click the Close button to return to the main part of the document.

In Page Layout view, you can see the contents of the header and footer in gray when you view the top or bottom margin of the page. From other views, you will not see the header or footer again unless you preview the document or select the View/Header and Footer command.

GUIDED ACTIVITY 12.1

Creating and Deleting Headers from the Normal View

1. Start Word and create a new document. Make sure you are in Normal view.

2. Type Page One. Press [Enter]. Select Insert/Break. Page Break is already high-lighted in the dialog box, so press [Enter]. A shortcut to insert a page break is to hold down [Ctrl] and press [Enter].

3. Type Page Two. Press [Enter]. Insert another page break.

4. Type Page Three.

   There are now three pages in your document. Each page break you inserted is represented in the work area by a horizontal dotted line across the page.

5. Select View/Header and Footer. The cursor appears in a dashed rectangle in the top margin of the document and the rest of the text is grayed (dimmed).

6. If the header is labeled Odd Page Header, you will need to change settings in the Page Setup dialog box, the Layout tab.

   Click on the Page Setup button that looks like an open book. Click in the box next to Different Odd and Even to clear that option. Make sure that Different First Page Only is also clear. Click OK to return to the header. It should now be labeled Header.

7. Type Chapter One.

8. Switch to the footer by clicking on the button on the left side of the Header and Footer toolbar. The cursor will be positioned within a dashed rectangle at the bottom of the page.

9. Type Section Five.

10. Click on the Close button on the toolbar to return to the main part of the document. Position the cursor on page 1. To verify the location of the cursor, read the status bar at the bottom of the window.

11. Select File/Print Preview.

    The header and the footer appear on all three pages. You may use PgUp and PgDn or use the scroll bars to see the header on each page.

12. Close the preview screen. Page Layout view also allows you to see the header within the top margin.

13. Change to Page Layout view. Each page appears separately, and the header and footer look gray (dimmed) within the top and bottom margin. Since the document is in the Page Layout view, Word shows you exactly how the page will look when it is printed.

14. Press the Next Page button at the bottom of the scroll bar to view the page numbers on page 2 and then on page 3.

    To delete the header and footer, delete the text in the header and footer. To be able to quickly edit the header and footer in Page Layout view, double-click the grayed header or footer.

15. Double-click the grayed header within the top margin.

    Immediately the header appears in dark letters, the main document appears grayed, and the Header and Footer toolbar reappears.

16. To delete the header, delete the text in the dashed rectangle. Click Close or double-click on the main part of the document.

Creating a Different Header and Footer for the First Page

Often, you will not want a header or footer to appear on the first page. Word allows you to suppress them by creating a different header or footer for the first page and leaving it blank. The regular header or footer contains information and appears only on the second and subsequent pages. The different first-page header or footer is created by checking the box next to Different First Page in the Page Setup dialog box.

The dashed rectangle is labeled First Page Header or Header, depending on the page where the cursor appeared before issuing the View/Header and Footer command. After you enter the text to appear in one header, you may use the Show Previous and Show Next buttons to move the cursor to the previous or next type of header or footer.

In the following Guided Activity you will modify your document to contain a different first-page header and footer.

GUIDED ACTIVITY 12.2

Creating Different First-Page Headers and Footers

1. Select File/Page Setup, and choose the Layout tab. Check the box next to Different First Page, as shown in Figure 12.3. Click OK.

FIGURE 12.3
Setting a unique header for the first page

Click here.

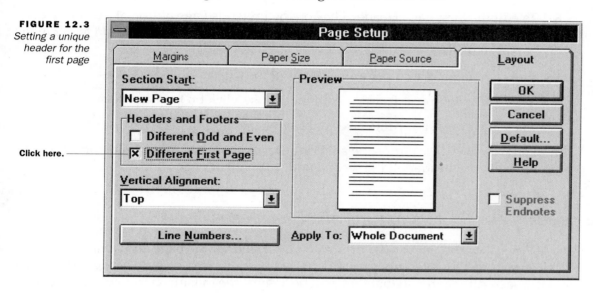

2. Select Print Preview. The footer that says `Section Five` does not appear on page 1, but only on pages 2 and 3. Selecting Different First Page creates a new, blank header and footer for the first page. The second-page and third-page footers are still the way you left them. Only the first-page header and footer have been changed.

3. Close Print Preview. Position the cursor on the second page. Select View/Header and Footer, so that the cursor is positioned within the header box.

4. With the cursor at the left margin, click on the Date button. Type two spaces with the [Spacebar] and click on the Time button.

5. Press [Tab]. The cursor moves to the center of the screen. This is the center tab that is set by default for headers and footers. Type your name.

6. Press [Tab]. The cursor moves to the right side of the screen. This is the right tab that is set by default for headers and footers. Type `Page` and press [Spacebar]. Click the Page Number button.

    Each of these buttons places field codes in the document. You can tell field codes when you click on them because they are shaded in gray. What is displayed is the result of the field code, and the result changes each time. The actual field code is quite different.

7. With the mouse pointing at the page number in the header, click on the right mouse button to reveal the shortcut menu. Select Toggle Field Codes.

The page number is replaced by {PAGE}. This is the field code for a page number. You may switch back and forth between displaying field codes and their results by selecting Toggle Field Codes. The shortcut key to accomplish this is [Alt] [F9]. Word substitutes the number of the current page for the page-number field code in the header for each page.

8. To edit the First Page Header, click on the Previous Page button at the bottom of the scroll bar. Click on the Switch Between Header and Footer button to move the cursor to the footer.

9. Press [Tab] to get the cursor to the center of the footer.

10. Type Page and press [Spacebar]. With the mouse, click on the Page Number button.

    The page number appears next to the cursor.

11. Click on the Close button. Select Print Preview to see the new footer on page 1, and the new header on the second and subsequent pages. Close Print Preview.

Creating Headers and Footers for Odd and Even Pages

When a document is to be printed on both sides of the page and bound, the headers and footers for even-numbered (left) and odd-numbered (right) pages are usually positioned differently, so that they will be against the outside margin of their respective pages. This means that the headers and footers for the even-numbered pages that usually appear on the left side of the book must be left-justified, and those for the odd-numbered pages that usually appear on the right must be right-justified.

Word allows you to create different headers and footers for odd and even pages by checking the Different Odd and Even box under Headers and Footers in the Page Setup dialog box.

To edit a different odd or even header or footer, you must first position the cursor on a page that contains the header or footer that you want to modify. To edit the odd-page header, you must position the cursor on an odd-numbered page.

In the Guided Activity below, both Different First Page and Different Odd and Even will be checked. This means that there will be three categories of headers and footers. Each category of page in the document will have its own header and footer. If the document is 20 pages long, all the even-numbered pages will have the same header and footer. Any modification to the header or footer on these pages will change them for all even-numbered pages. The first page has its own header and footer. Modifications to these will affect only the first page. All the odd-numbered pages after the first page will have the same header and footer. If you modify the header or footer while the cursor is on any of these pages, all the other pages in the same category will display the new header or footer.

GUIDED ACTIVITY 12.3

Creating Odd-Page and Even-Page Headers and Footers

1. Place the cursor on the second page. Select View/Header and Footer.

2. Click on the Page Setup button and check the box next to Different Odd and Even under Headers and Footers. Click OK.

    The dashed rectangle in the header area is now labeled Even Page Header, rather than just Header.

3. With the cursor positioned against the left margin, type Chapter One.

    Click on the Next Page button on the bottom of the scroll bar to view page 3.

4. Erase any text that appears in the Odd Page Header area, and press Tab twice to position the cursor against the right margin.

5. With the mouse, click on the Date button.

6. Click on the Close button or double-click on the main part of the document.

7. Change to Page Layout view and page through the document to see the headers.

8. The header for the first page is blank. The second page header contains the words Chapter One against the left margin. The header on the third page contains the page number against the right margin.

9. Move the cursor back to the first page. Select File/Print Preview.

    To get the proper effect of different headers and footers for odd and even pages, you should preview two pages at once.

10. Click and drag on the Multiple Pages button to view two pages.

    The first page is displayed on the right side of the preview screen. In almost all bound documents the first page and all odd-numbered pages are on the right side of the binding. The header for the first page is blank.

11. Click on the Next Page button or press PgDn.

    Pages 2 and 3 are displayed on the left and right sides of the preview screen, respectively. This is the way they will appear in a bound document. The header for page 2 is justified against its left margin and displays the name of the chapter. The third-page header is right-justified and contains the page number.

    This document displays the three kinds of headers and footers that are available from Word. These three categories cover the majority of applications and should allow you to create a wide variety of documents.

Summary

Headers and footers are lines of text that appear at the top and bottom of pages in a document, giving pertinent information about the text in the body of the document. They may contain any regular text and can be formatted with any of the commands on the toolbars or ruler.

Field codes may also be inserted into headers and footers. Field codes are markers in a document that cause Word to look up or calculate values. Some special field codes that can be easily and automatically inserted into headers and footers are the page number and current date and time.

The simplest headers and footers to create are those that will appear on every page in the document. These can be modified regardless of the position of the cursor in the document and the document view selected. However, most documents do not have the same header or footer on the first page as in the rest of the document.

The headers and footers may contain different text on even-numbered (left-hand) pages as opposed to odd-numbered (right-hand) pages. These headers and footers are used in documents that will be printed on both sides of the page and bound. Again, to modify a header or footer, the cursor must be on a page that fits into the category of the header or footer being edited.

Exercises

1. Open A:EX8_2. Create a header that will appear on both pages of the document. To do this, you may need to go to Page Setup and remove the check from Different Odd and Even. Type your name at the left side of the header and type `Exercise 12.1` at the right side. Print the result.

2. Continue with the document from Exercise 1. Create a footer for all pages. Type `Unit Twelve` at the left side and `Understanding and Using Word 6.0` at the right. Print the result.

3. Continue with the document from Exercise 2. Make sure that the document is formatted with inside and outside margins, using the File/Page Setup command, and selecting Mirror Margins on the Margins tab. Create different headers and footers for odd and even pages. The header should have the page number at the outside margin of even and odd pages. Create a footer with the date at the outside margin and the time at the inside margin. Print the result.

4. Continue with the document from Exercise 3. Change the document so that neither the header nor the footer appears on the first page. Print the result.

Review Questions

 *1. What are headers and footers used for?

  2. How much text can be placed in a header or footer? What must be considered when creating long headers and footers?

 *3. What kinds of pages can have different headers and footers? What is the purpose of each?

  4. How does the screen appear after you select View/Header and Footer?

 *5. What three buttons insert field codes into the document? How are the field codes viewed?

Key Terms

Field code   Footer   Header

Documentation Research

  1. How is the default header style changed?

  2. How do you adjust the amount of space between the document text and the header or footer?

  3. How may headers and footers be changed for different sections of a document?

Mail Merge

All of the features of Word allow you to create nicely formatted and letter-perfect documents. However, some documents need to be used repeatedly in slightly different forms. One alternative is to edit a document each time to meet your current needs. Another is to save a list of the changes to be made and to apply them automatically whenever necessary.

An example of this is a form letter that is to be sent to several people. While the body of each letter is identical, the address and salutation must be different for every person. Instead of creating a separate document for each person, Word allows you to create one document that is representative of the letter each person will receive. The form letter contains special markers in the places where the name and address would usually be located. A separate file contains a list of all the names and addresses of the intended recipients. The two files can be merged and printed to create personalized letters for every person on the list. The individual information for each person is substituted for the markers in the form letter before the letter is printed.

This unit covers the creation of a main document and a data source and the use of the Tools/Mail Merge command. You will also learn how to print mailing labels or envelopes for use with the form letters, and how to include only certain individuals from a large list of names.

Learning Objectives

At the completion of this unit you should know

1. what is required to execute a mail merge,

2. how to create a main document and the data source,

3. how to merge the two together,

4. how to select certain records for merging,

5. how to include conditional text,

6. how to create envelopes and mailing labels.

Important Commands

Insert/Date and Time

Toggle Field Codes (on shortcut menu)

Tools/Mail Merge

Requirements for Mail Merge

The Mail Merge command requires two files to execute correctly. One file, the **main document**, is the form letter that all the merged documents will resemble. This file can be created from scratch but is often a modification of an existing regular document, made when the user realizes that it will be used repeatedly.

The second required file is a **data source**. This document contains the information that will make each form letter unique. Each line in the data source contains all of the information required to print one merged copy of the main document. You may elect to print all of the lines or only selected lines in the data source when merging it with the form.

FIGURE 13.1
The Mail Merge Helper

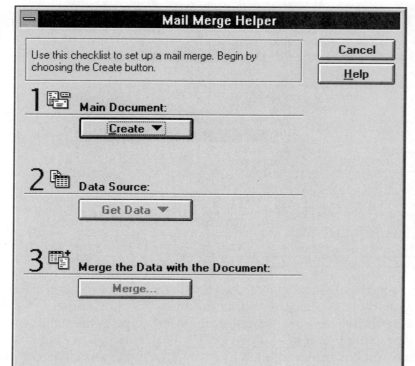

The Mail Merge Helper organizes the task of mail merge into several steps: creating the main document, creating the data source, and merging the two together.

To access the Mail Merge Helper, issue the command Tools/ Mail Merge. The dialog box shown in Figure 13.1 lists the steps in setting up a mail merge. One step is to create the main document, and it is the only option that is not grayed out and therefore inactive.

Clicking on the Create button gives the option to create form letters, envelopes, mailing labels, or a catalog. At this point you can choose to create a new document for a form letter, or use an existing letter with modifications.

Another step is to create the data source by clicking the Get Data button. If data already exists, either in a database or spreadsheet file or as a Word document, a dialog box resembling the File/Open dialog box allows you to specify which file contains data needed to create a link between the data source and the main document. If this is a new set of data, you can also create the data source from scratch.

The third step is to click Merge to combine the data with the document, and create a new document or send directly to the printer.

The Data Source Document

The data source is a table that contains the information that will be merged into a main document. The first row in this file, called the *header row*, contains the names of the *merge fields* that will be used to associate information on the subsequent lines with fields in the main document, much as a column heading explains the text below it. Word supplies several commonly used merge fields for the header row, including Title, FirstName, LastName, JobTitle, Company, Address1, Address2, City, State, PostalCode, HomePhone, and WorkPhone, as shown in Figure 13.2. These field names may not contain spaces, either within them or at the end. From this dialog box you may remove unneeded fields, add other necessary fields, and rearrange the order of the fields in the list of field names in the header row. After you save the file, you may either enter data into it or go back to modify the main document.

FIGURE 13.2
The Create Data Source dialog box

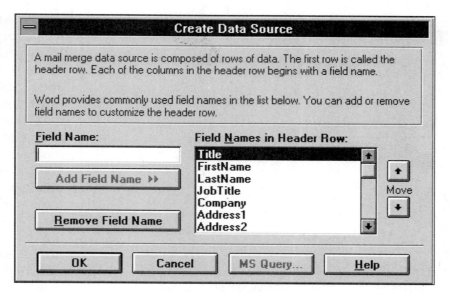

When you edit the data source, the Data Form box appears, as in Figure 13.3, allowing you to view the contents of one *data record* at one time. The field names you added to the header row are given on the left. Type in the data, going from item to item by pressing [Tab] or [Enter]. Press [Shift][Tab] or the arrow keys to move back up the form. When you have entered the information for one person (record), click Add

FIGURE 13.3
The Data Form

Data Form

Title:		OK
FirstName:		Add New
LastName:		Delete
JobTitle:		Restore
Company:		Find...
Address1:		View Source
Address2:		Help
City:		
State:		

Record: |◀ ◀ 1 ▶ ▶|

New to begin the next. Word automatically numbers the records. You may type the records in any order, since you may easily sort the data later. To see the actual data source rather than the data form, click on the View Source button.

The Data Source document running behind the data form is a table. The header row appears on the very first row in the document, and the fields in the header row may be in any order. The data on the lines following—that is, the data records—must be in the same order as the header row, and each line of data must have the same number of fields (columns) as there are fields in the header row. Each data record must be a separate row.

The Database toolbar at the top of the screen, shown in Figure 13.4, gives several common functions, including managing fields, adding and deleting records, sorting

FIGURE 13.4
*The Database
toolbar*

in ascending and descending order, finding records, and going quickly to either the data form or the mail merge main document.

In the following Guided Activity you will create a form letter from a magazine publisher encouraging people to subscribe by offering a large sum of money as a prize.

GUIDED ACTIVITY 13.1

Creating a Data Source

1. Start Word. Create a new document.

2. Issue the command Tools/Mail Merge. When the Mail Merge Helper appears, click Create under Main Document, and select Form Letters, then Active Document.

3. In the Mail Merge Helper, click Get Data, then select Create Data Source.

4. Scroll through the list of suggested field names. There are several that we can eliminate from this list for this document. Highlight JobTitle and click the

Remove Field Name button. Repeat to remove Company, Address1, Address2, Country, HomePhone, and WorkPhone from the list.

The suggested field names are changed for the current document. They will be available again the next time you create a data document.

5. To add the Street field name, click in the text box under Field Name and type `Street`. Click Add Field Name to add it to the list.

The new field is automatically placed at the bottom of the list. This would be awkward for typing in the names and addresses later.

6. To move the Street field to the line between LastName and City, click the up arrow button above Move 3 times. The field names are finished.

7. Click OK. When a dialog box appears, save the file under the name A:ADDRESS.

8. When the next dialog box appears, click on the Edit Data Source button.

9. Enter the following data into the data form, pressing `Tab` or `Enter` to proceed to the next field. Do not include the commas.

    `Mr., John, Smith, 1111 Adams Street, Mentor, Ohio, 44060`

10. Click the Add New button when you are finished and add the next two records, clicking Add New before each.

    `Mrs., Mary, Jones, 2222 Main Avenue, Austin, Texas, 78746`

    `Ms., Penelope, Peters, 3333 Oak Circle, Fort Worth, Texas, 76706`

11. Click View Source to see the data in table form.

The data is not in any particular order. It would be helpful to have the last names in alphabetical order.

12. Click in the LastName column, then click the Sort Ascending button.

To add more data records, you could go back to the data form by clicking the Data Form button, or you could type them directly into the table.

13. Click on the Add New Record button and type your name and address into the new row on the table.

This works fine with a small table, but if there were many records, the header row would not show on the screen with the bottom row. This is one reason to use the data form to enter data.

14. Save the finished data source file. Click on the Mail Merge Main Document button on the right side of the toolbar to continue the mail merge process.

The Main Document

The mail merge main document contains the text all of the printed documents will have in common, plus field codes in place of information that will be unique to each printout. The Mail Merge toolbar appears between the Formatting toolbar and ruler in the main document, as shown in Figure 13.5.

FIGURE 13.5
The Mail Merge toolbar

The next step for setting up mail merge is to enter the document text into the main document. When you reach a place where information is needed from the data source, insert a merge field by clicking on the Insert Merge Field button on the Mail Merge toolbar. The fields listed are the very ones that are in the header row of the attached data file. After a field is selected, the field name appears in the text surrounded by chevrons, for example, «name». This indicates that this is a merge field name and not merely typed characters. Merge fields may be inserted as many times as you want and in any order. Each merge field you enter will be replaced by information from the data source when the document is printed.

In the following Guided Activity, you will create a letter and merge it with the data source ADDRESS.

GUIDED ACTIVITY 13.2

Creating a Main Document

1. Continue with the mail merge main document from the previous Guided Activity. Use the File/Page Setup command to change the top margin to 2.25", typical for a letter printed on letterhead stationery.

2. The top line of the document should contain the date. Rather than typing the data, enter a field code that will cause the current date to print anytime the letter is printed. To do this, issue the command Insert/Date and Time. In the dialog box that appears, shown in Figure 13.6, select the correct format for the date. Click in the box to select Insert as Field then click OK.

FIGURE 13.6
Inserting the date as a field code

Date and Time

Available Formats:

1/22/95
Sunday, January 22, 199!
22 January, 1995
January 22, 1995
22-Jan-95
January, 95
Jan-95
01/22/95 7:37 PM
01/22/95 7:37:16 PM
7:37 PM
7:37:16 PM
19:37
19:37:16

OK
Cancel
Help

Click here.

☒ Insert as Field

When you click on it, the date field code shows up as a shaded area. Each day before you print the letter, update the field by pressing F9 or by pointing at the field and selecting Update Field from the shortcut menu. This field may be automatically updated every time you print if you select Update Fields from the Tools/Options/Print dialog box.

3. Place two blank lines after the date.

   The recipient's name and address usually appear after the date in a letter. This letter is going to four different people. Rather than change the letter each time before printing it, customize it by placing merge fields for the name and address.

4. Click on the Insert Merge Field button. Select `Title` from the list of merge fields.

5. The letter will print once for each line in the data source. For each printout, this field code will be replaced by the person's title at the beginning of each record: Mr., Mrs., and Ms.

6. Press `Spacebar`. Press the Insert Merge Field button and select `FirstName`.

   Each printed letter will contain the recipient's first name instead of this field code. Word maintains the exact punctuation and spacing that you place between merge fields in the form letter; thus, there must be space between the `Title` and `FirstName` merge fields.

7. Press `Spacebar`. Insert the merge field for the last name.

   The first address line will contain the recipient's title and first and last names. The second line contains the street address.

8. Press `Enter`. Insert a merge field for the `Street` merge field and press `Enter`.

9. Insert a merge field for `City` and insert a comma and a space.

10. Insert a merge field for `State`, leave two spaces, and insert another merge field for `PostalCode`. The result should look like the following:

    `«City», «State» «PostalCode»`

    The final line contains the city and state separated by a comma, two spaces, and the zip code. Now create the salutation.

11. Make sure the cursor is to the right of the zip field code. Press `Enter` twice.

12. Type `Dear` followed by a space. Insert a merge field for `Title`.

13. Leave a space after `Title` and insert a merge field for `LastName`, then place a colon after it, with a result as follows:

    `Dear «Title» «LastName»:`

14. Press `Enter` twice and insert the following text and field codes. Use `Tab` to indent the names and the `Sincerely` line at the end.

    ```
    You may have already won $10,000,000!!! Three of the four
    lucky people below have already won!!

         Robert Cranwell of California
         Lisa Mattheson of Maryland
         «FirstName» «LastName» of «State»
         Fred Lawson of Florida
    ```

If your number is selected, all you have to do is return the enclosed card to claim your prize!! Also, please take this opportunity to review our wide selection of publications and include your order with the prize claim card.

Imagine the excitement when we deliver your prize money to your doorstep in «City», «State». Return your claim card and order today!!

Sincerely,

15. Press [Enter] 4 times, then type your name. Save the file as A:FORMLET.

The use of the fields in the main document is independent of the order of the fields in the data source. This has been illustrated in this Guided Activity by the fact that several of the fields were used more than once.

 If you want to view the data source, it is a simple matter to click on the Edit Data Source button on the Mail Merge toolbar. This opens the file if it is not already open, and displays the data form.

Merging the Two Documents

 You can preview the merged documents together by clicking on the View Merged Data button on the Mail Merge toolbar. Clicking on this button replaces the merge fields with the data from the first record. Other buttons, shown in Figure 13.7, allow you to preview more records. Press the buttons on either side of the record number for the next or previous record, or type a specific record number in the box.

The buttons on either end go to the first and last records. To reveal the merge fields again, click on the View Merged Data button.

FIGURE 13.7
Record selection buttons on the Mail Merge toolbar

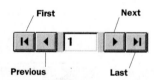

If you print the main document with the merge fields displayed, Word will print a single copy of the document with the merge fields in chevrons (« »). Once you view the merged data by clicking on the button, you will get a single copy of the main document merged with one of the records in the data source. Usually, however, you will print many copies of the main document, one for each record in the data source.

To merge the information in the data source with the main document, you may press one of the two buttons on the Mail Merge toolbar. The Merge to New Document button merges the two documents and stores the results in a single file, with each page separated by section breaks. This new file is called Form Letters1, rather than Document1, the name we are accustomed to seeing on new files. Merging to a document allows you to check for any errors.

 The Merge to Printer button merges and prints one copy of the main document for each line of data in the data source. Whether you merge to a new document or directly to the printer, the merge fields in the main document are replaced by the appropriate pieces of information from the data source.

One other way to merge the two documents is to click on the Mail Merge button. This reveals a dialog box that contains several options not available through the buttons, as shown in Figure 13.8.

FIGURE 13.8
The Merge dialog box

This message changes.

```
┌─────────────────────────────────────────────────────────────────┐
│ ▬                           Merge                                 │
├─────────────────────────────────────────────────────────────────┤
│ Merge To:                                          ┌───────────┐  │
│ ┌──────────────────────┐    ┌───────────┐          │   Merge   │  │
│ │ New Document      │▼│    │  Setup... │          └───────────┘  │
│ └──────────────────────┘    └───────────┘          ┌───────────┐  │
│ ┌─Records to Be Merged─────────────────────┐       │  Cancel   │  │
│ │ ◉ All   ○ From: │      │  To: │      │   │       └───────────┘  │
│ │                                           │       ┌───────────┐  │
│ └───────────────────────────────────────────┘       │Check Errors..│ │
│ ┌─When Merging Records──────────────────────┐       └───────────┘  │
│ │ ◉ Don't print blank lines when data fields are empty.│ ┌───────────┐│
│ │ ○ Print blank lines when data fields are empty.     │ │Query Options..│ │
│ └───────────────────────────────────────────┘       └───────────┘  │
│                                                      ┌───────────┐  │
│ No Query Options have been set.                      │   Help    │  │
│                                                      └───────────┘  │
└─────────────────────────────────────────────────────────────────┘
```

The first option allows you to specify whether you wish to merge to a new document or directly to the printer. Another option available only in the dialog box is to merge only certain records, say records 10 to 20, rather than the entire set of data records.

In certain circumstances you wish to merge only records meeting certain criteria. Asking for records matching certain criteria is called a *query*. Click the Query Options button to bring up yet another dialog box, shown in Figure 13.9. Here we can specify the *filter* to be used (criteria that must be matched) for the data to be merged. An example might be to merge only those records that have the merge field `State` equal to `Texas`, or those whose merge field `PostalCode` is less than `78700`. If any criteria are specified in this dialog box, the message on the bottom of the Merge dialog box changes from `No Query Options have been set` to `Query Options have been set`.

FIGURE 13.9
The Query Options dialog box

```
┌───────────────────────────────────────────────────────────────────────────┐
│ ▬                           Query Options                                   │
├───────────────────────────────────────────────────────────────────────────┤
│   ┌─Filter Records─┐   ┌──── Sort Records ────┐                             │
│                                                                             │
│        Field:           Comparison:            Compare To:                  │
│        ┌──────────────┐ ┌──────────────┐      ┌──────────────────────────┐  │
│        │State      │▼│ │Equal to   │▼│      │Texas                     │  │
│        └──────────────┘ └──────────────┘      └──────────────────────────┘  │
│ ┌────┐ ┌──────────────┐ ┌──────────────┐      ┌──────────────────────────┐  │
│ │And▼│ │           │▼│ │           │▼│      │                          │  │
│ └────┘ └──────────────┘ └──────────────┘      └──────────────────────────┘  │
│ ┌──┐   ┌──────────────┐ ┌──────────────┐      ┌──────────────────────────┐  │
│ │ ▼│   │           │▼│ │           │▼│      │                          │  │
│ └──┘   └──────────────┘ └──────────────┘      └──────────────────────────┘  │
│ ┌──┐   ┌──────────────┐ ┌──────────────┐      ┌──────────────────────────┐  │
│ │ ▼│   │           │▼│ │           │▼│      │                          │  │
│ └──┘   └──────────────┘ └──────────────┘      └──────────────────────────┘  │
│ ┌──┐   ┌──────────────┐ ┌──────────────┐      ┌──────────────────────────┐  │
│ │ ▼│   │           │▼│ │           │▼│      │                          │  │
│ └──┘   └──────────────┘ └──────────────┘      └──────────────────────────┘  │
│ ┌──┐   ┌──────────────┐ ┌──────────────┐      ┌──────────────────────────┐  │
│ │ ▼│   │           │▼│ │           │▼│      │                          │  │
│ └──┘   └──────────────┘ └──────────────┘      └──────────────────────────┘  │
│                                                                             │
│  ┌────────┐    ┌────────┐    ┌─────────┐    ┌────────┐                      │
│  │   OK   │    │ Cancel │    │Clear All│    │  Help  │                      │
│  └────────┘    └────────┘    └─────────┘    └────────┘                      │
└───────────────────────────────────────────────────────────────────────────┘
```

GUIDED ACTIVITY 13.3

Merging

1. Use the main document and data source created in the preceding Guided Activities. Check the main document carefully to be sure there are no errors.

2. Click on the View Merged Data button to see the data from record 1 in place of the merge fields.

3. Click on the Next Record button to view the results of each record. Click on the First Record button to return to record 1.

4. Click on the Merge to New Document button. Watch the status bar as the word processor merges the main document with the data source.

   A new document appears, containing four personalized copies of the main document separated by section breaks. Close this file, and do not save it, since it can be recreated anytime by merging the form and data documents.

   You may need to print letters for a range of people in the data source instead of every one. In this case, you don't want to send yourself a letter, so you want to eliminate record 4.

5. Click on the Mail Merge button to display the Merge dialog box and in the From box type 1. Press [Tab] to go to the To box and type 3.

6. Select Printer under the Merge To option and click Merge.

   Three documents are printed, one each for the first, second, and third persons listed in the data source. Suppose you wish to merge letters only for people who live in Ohio. In a large database, it would be very time-consuming to look through the entire data source to find each record number. You can automatically merge records that match certain criteria through Query Options.

7. Click on the Mail Merge button, then on Query Options.

8. In the Query Options dialog box that appears, click on the down arrow next to the top box under Field. Select State.

9. Click on the down arrow next to Comparison to display the comparisons available, shown in Figure 13.10. In this case, Equal To is the correct comparison.

10. Click in the box under Compare To and type Ohio. Press [Enter] or click OK. Click All under Records to Be Merged, and select New Document under Merge To. Click Merge to complete the merge to a new document.

    The result is a single letter to John Smith, the only record that matches the criteria. Close the Form Letters2 file and do not save it.

Using IF Fields with Conditional Text

Form letters sometimes need to have additional text printed only when certain conditions are met. For example, people who live within your state may have to pay

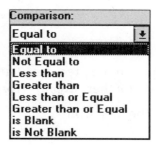

sales tax, whereas those from out of state may not. **IF *fields***
are a type of merge field that may be used to include text
but only under certain conditions. Word uses this logic:
examine an expression, make a comparison to another
expression, and give one result if the condition is true and
another if it is false.

To insert an IF field into the form letter, click the Insert
Word Field button. The list, shown in Figure 13.11, provides
several Word Fields, including one for If. . . Then. . .Else. . . .
When this field is selected, the dialog box in Figure 13.12 appears.

Each of the items in the IF dialog box must reflect the desired condition. Using
the sales tax example, the Field Name in the IF statement must be changed to `State`.
The choices of comparisons are like the one in Query Options. The text in the Compare To box must exactly match the data in the merge field in spelling and capitalization for the IF statement to be true.

The final step is to type the text that we would like printed if the comparison is
true or false. Type in the Insert this Text box `Be sure to add 6% for sales`
`tax.` for when the comparison is true. Type in the Otherwise Insert this Text box `No`
`sales tax is required.` for when the comparison is false.

GUIDED ACTIVITY 13.4

Using an IF Merge Field

1. Continue with the FORMLET document from Guided Activity 13.3. Click on the Edit Data Source button, and on the Data Form click on the View Source button to make ADDRESS.DOC the current document.

2. Click on the Manage Fields button.

    The dialog box that we used to design the original data source document appears.

3. Type in the new field name Subscriptions and click Add. Click OK.

4. Enter the following number in the right-most column of the table: 1, 2, 5, and 8, the number of subscriptions each person ordered in the past.

5. Click on the Mail Merge Main Document button on the right side of the toolbar to return to the FORMLET document, or use the Window menu selection.

6. The Query Options to select only Ohio is still in effect. Remove the query option by clicking on the Mail Merge button, clicking Query Options, and clicking Clear All. Click OK and click Close to return to the main document.

7. Place the cursor at the end of the second-to-last paragraph to add an IF statement that will urge recipients to subscribe if the number of the subscriptions in the Subscriptions field is fewer than 3.

8. Press [Spacebar] to add a space after the last sentence in the paragraph. Click Insert Word Field and select If. . .Then. . .Else. . . .

9. Click on the down arrow next to the first box and select Subscriptions to insert the merge field.

10. Click on the comparison operator to select Less than. Click in the Compare To box and type 3.

11. In the Insert this Text box type You need to subscribe to at least three magazines in order to win. Click OK.

12. Click the Merge to New Document button and examine the resulting form letters. The new text should appear only in the first two letters. These were the two letters that had subscriptions fewer than three in the data source.

Creating Mailing Labels and Envelopes

Merged letters are often used in mass mailings (also known affectionately as "junk mail"). Not only are the letters themselves merged, but the envelopes must be directed to each address in the data records. Because bulk mailings must contain at least 200 pieces to qualify for reduced postage rates, the process of addressing the envelopes must be automated.

Some companies print the addresses on adhesive labels that are later stuck onto envelopes. Even clear labels, though less noticeable than the standard white labels, warn the recipient not to waste much time with the letter. For a more professional appearance, the addresses may be printed directly onto the envelopes. To fool recipients into thinking they have received personal mail, the addresses may be printed in a font that resembles handwriting, but we can always tell from the bulk rate postage what it really is. Although individuals do not send letters bulk rate, it is convenient to use Word's Mail Merge tool to create mailing labels and to address envelopes for many recipients at once.

To begin the process of creating mailing labels, access the Mail Merge Helper from the button on the Mail Merge toolbar or with the command Tools/Mail Merge. Under Main Document, click Create, then select Mailing Labels. Attach the new main document to the existing data source by clicking Get Data and then selecting Open Data Source and choosing the correct file. When you choose Set Up Main Document, you must first select the type of labels you will be using from the Label Options dialog box that appears, shown in Figure 13.13.

FIGURE 13.13
Specifying the size and type of mailing labels

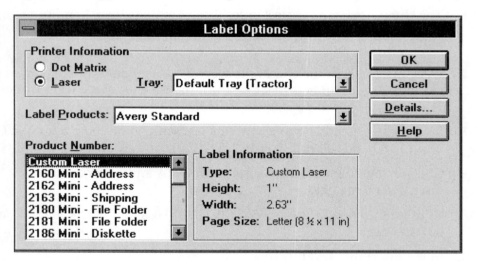

First, you must specify whether you wish to print the merged labels on a laser printer or a dot-matrix printer. These two kinds of printers handle the job in different ways. Laser printers only handle individual sheets. To print labels on laser printers, you must purchase adhesive labels that come in 8½"×11" sheets. Often these sheets contain two or three columns of labels, each label being an inch or two high. A dot-matrix printer, on the other hand, handles continuously-fed paper best. You may purchase labels for dot-matrix printers that come in long strips, sometimes 5,000 labels long, with tractor feed guides on each margin.

The next step is to specify what size labels you wish to print. There are many sizes and shapes of adhesive labels, according to their use. They come in sizes as small as file folder labels or as large as shipping labels, plus disk labels, videotape labels, and others. Even common mailing labels come in several sizes. A popular brand name of adhesive mailing labels is Avery. The product number of Avery labels is used in Word to specify the size of the labels.

FIGURE 13.14
*Creating the
sample mailing
label*

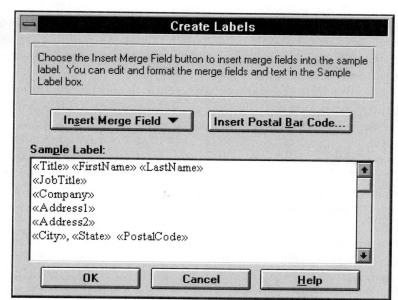

Once the size and type of labels is specified, pressing the OK button brings up the Create Labels dialog box, shown in Figure 13.14. In the Sample Label area you will insert the merge fields in the order you wish them to appear on the mailing label, pressing the ⌷Spacebar⌷ between fields and ⌷Enter⌷ at the end of each line. If you wish to print the Postal Bar Code above the address information, click the appropriate button. Pressing OK returns you to the Mail Merge Helper, which displays the type of main document, the name of the two files involved, and the merge options in effect. If you were to view the mailing labels document at this point, you would see a page-sized table with cells each containing the merge fields specified in the sample label.

Before you send your merged files to the printer, it is always a good idea to print a sample page or two to make sure the addresses fit the labels. Inside the box of labels you will often find a grid sheet that you can hold up to the light along with your printout to make sure that the labels are positioned correctly. You may need to adjust the margins a little, change the height or width of the cells in the table (which is what the mailing label main document is), or change the font size so that a long address (such as South Padre Island, TX 78987-4523) doesn't wrap to another line.

Creating envelopes is a similar process. From the Mail Merge Helper, create a main document for Envelopes. You will be asked to select the size of the envelope and you may set other envelope options. The Envelope Address dialog box is identical to the Create Labels dialog box. The process of merging envelopes and mailing labels is identical to that of merging main documents.

Summary

Some documents need to be used repeatedly with only minor modifications. In Word, you may create a data source with the pieces of information that will be unique for each printout. The main document contains the text that will be common to all printouts.

The first line in the data source is the header row. The header row consists of merge fields that are used to associate places in the main document with information in the data source. The second and subsequent lines in the data source contain the data records that will be merged into the main document.

The main document is a normal word processing document, with two exceptions. The Mail Merge toolbar appears between the Formatting toolbar and ruler. Within the document there are merge fields placed at each location that needs unique information from the data source.

The buttons on the Mail Merge toolbar perform several functions, editing the data source and viewing the data in place of the merge fields. The merged documents may be stored in a separate file for additional modification or sent to the printer through the use of the Merge to New Document or Merge to Printer buttons. By default, the command will print one copy of the merged main document for every line of data in the data source; however, you may elect to merge only information from selected records of the data source through the use of the Mail Merge button. IF statements may be used to include additional text only when certain criteria are met.

Word also provides an easy way to create mailing-label and envelope main documents for use in merging with name and address data. The user supplies the name of the data source, type of label or envelope, and the format of a sample label or envelope. Merging the resulting mailing-label document is identical to the process of merging form letters.

Exercises

1. Mail merge is used to notify departments of supplies used in your company. The data source will contain the following merge fields: department name, type of supplies, dollar amount of supplies, beginning date, and ending date. Remember that field names may not contain any spaces. Create the main document and a new data source. Enter the data lines shown below and print the data source file. Save the file as A:EX13_1.

    ```
    Manufacturing   staples       75    8/1/95   9/1/95
    Accounting      red pencils   90    7/2/95   8/1/95
    Management      aspirin       350   6/1/95   9/1/95
    Marketing       stamps        150   7/1/95   10/1/95
    ```

2. Sort the data source so that the departments are in alphabetical order. Print.

3. Edit the main document based on the memorandum below, which is written using the information from the data source created in Exercise 1, A:EX13_1. Replace the variable values with merge fields that refer to data in the data source. Use File/Print to print one copy of the main document with the merge fields showing. Save the main document as A:EX13_2.

    ```
                          MEMORANDUM

    TO:   Manufacturing
    FROM: Supplies
    DATE: October 9, 1995
    ```

Based on our records, your department used $75 in
staples from the period beginning 8/1/95 and ending
9/1/95.

Please check your records and verify this amount.

4. Use a button on the Mail Merge toolbar to merge A:EX13_1 and A:EX13_2 to the
   printer. The printed result will be four memos, one to each department.

5. Use the Mail Merge button to place memos only to the third and fourth departments (Manufacturing and Marketing) in a new document. Print the document.

6. Insert an IF field that checks to see whether the dollar amount of supplies
   exceeds 100. If it does, include text that notifies the departments of budget over-
   runs for their supplies. Merge and print.

7. Set Query Options that merge only those records for which the ending date is
   before (less than) September 15, 1995. Merge and print.

8. Create mailing labels using the data in the ADDRESS document created in the
   Guided Activities. Select the appropriate type of printer, and select Avery labels
   product number 5162 to create 1.25-inch-tall labels. Save the mailing labels main
   document as A:EX13_7 and print.

Review Questions

*1. What is the purpose of performing a mail merge?

2. What two types of files are required to execute a mail merge?

*3. What information is found on the first line of the data source? On subsequent
    lines?

4. What is the difference between using Data Form and the actual data source document for entering data?

*5. What are the two differences between a main document and a normal document?

6. How do you insert a merge field into a document and how does it appear?

*7. How can you view data in the document in place of the merge fields?

8. How does Word associate merge fields in a main document with the right piece
   of information in the data source?

*9. What is the difference between using File/Print and using Tools/Mail Merge
    when printing a main document?

10. What are two ways to merge documents?

*11. What two ways can you use to select only certain lines of data from the data
     source to merge, rather than every line?

12. Why would you merge documents to a file rather than to the printer?

*13. What is an IF merge field used for?

14. What information does the Mail Merge Helper give once the main document and data source are set up?

*15. What is the difference between how dot-matrix and laser printers handle mailing labels?

Key Terms

Data record	Header row	Merge field
Data source	IF field	Query
Filter	Main document	

Documentation Research

1. What is a header source and when might it be useful?

2. How do you remove an attached data source, and what happens when you do?

3. What are the functions of the other selections under Insert Word Field?

Using Mail Merge to Apply for Jobs

The most popular use for the mail merge facility is the creation of form letters. Many people searching for jobs are sending out many letters and résumés. In this application, you will create a form letter using the Mail Merge feature in Word.

Create a data source with the following merge fields:

```
Title, FirstName, LastName, JobTitle, Company, Address1,
City, State, PostalCode, Position, Contact
```

Save the data source as A:DATA, then enter five names in the data source. Use either real or fictitious names. For the `Position` merge field, enter the position at the company for which you are applying. For the `Contact`, enter a name only if you know someone inside the company. Some data records should have a blank entry in this field.

Create an application letter based on the data source above, using standard business letter format. The first paragraph in the body of the letter should, in your own words, state that you are applying for a specific job, the `Position` merge field. Put up front your best qualifications for that job.

Include an IF statement that causes a sentence to print only if the data in the `Contact` merge field is not blank. The sentence should mention the name of someone you already know in the organization who has encouraged you to apply. To place the `Contact` merge field in the Insert this Text box, use the following steps. Position the cursor where you wish the merge field to appear, then press `Ctrl` `F9`. This inserts a pair of bold braces with the cursor in between. Type between the braces the word `MERGEFIELD` followed by a space and the name of the merge field, `Contact`.

In the second and third paragraphs, target the job you want. Use items highlighted from your résumé about your education, work experience, and activities that give evidence of how you can benefit that company in that position. Somewhere in the second or third paragraph mention the enclosed résumé.

In the last paragraph mention the name of the organization and ask specifically for an interview. If you find that you use certain words repetitively, use the thesaurus to search for suitable synonyms. Proofread carefully, as absolutely no errors are tolerated when you are applying for a job. Save the main document as A:FORM. Print the merged letters.

Working with Long Documents 14

Into the life of every student comes the dreaded assignment of a term paper or report. Word not only is useful for giving a professional appearance to such a document, but also includes several features that provide real help in preparing a long document.

Most authors use an outline of some sort when creating a document that requires any kind of organization. An outline helps you keep a document moving in the right direction as you write it and ensures that no topics are repeated or left out. A long document requires an outline to facilitate covering ideas in an order that will make their presentation effective. Word's outline feature not only provides an easy way to organize and plan your document, but is actually another, structural view of the same document.

Two items in a long document that generally take a great deal of time and work to create are the table of contents and the index. Each requires the author to go through a document, find headings and subheadings and topics or terms that need to be indexed, write down their page numbers, and compile a list of them all. As a document changes, the order and contents of the table of contents will change. The pages where items in the index will appear also change as text is added to and deleted from a document. Word includes features to create these with a minimal amount of effort by the author. This allows you more time to be creative with your writing rather than slavishly spending time alphabetizing and numbering.

Footnotes offer documentation for references made to text from another source. Generally, when you refer to another author's material you are required to give that author credit for the material you used. A footnote reference mark is used in the document body next to the material being referenced that leads to the footnote. The footnote can appear immediately below the text, at the end of the page, or at the end of the chapter or document (called endnotes).

The power of these features is that they are dynamic. Changes to the document are reflected in the outline, and vice versa. Whenever text is moved, any footnotes affected are automatically rearranged and renumbered. Changes in page numbering within the document are updated in the table of contents and index with one keystroke. This unit covers Word's procedures for creating an outline, a table of contents and index, and footnotes.

Learning Objectives

At the completion of this unit you should know

1. how to create an outline,

2. how to promote and demote headings in an outline,

3. how to use Outline view to manipulate sections of text,

4. how to create the table of contents from an outline,

5. how to mark items for the index and how to create the index,

6. how to create, delete, edit, and move footnotes.

Important Commands

Format/Style

View/Outline

Insert/Break

Insert/Footnote

View/Footnotes

Insert/Index and Tables

Outlines

Outlines are created to help you organize documents. Word allows you to take the concept of an outline one step further. The outline that you create to organize your ideas is in fact another view of the same document.

To create an outline, you separate the material to be outlined into major topics. The major topics are then divided into subtopics, and these are divided into yet smaller sections. The level of detail depends on you. Each section of a document has a *heading* as its title. The most general headings might include the chapter names, while the least specific would be subheadings that are titles of a section of one or two paragraphs. The outline is a list of these sections in the order they will appear in your document.

Besides keeping the sequential order of the topics in outline form, Word allows you to actually create the document within the outline. Once the outline is completed, you enter the text for each section under the heading for that topic. A single file contains both outline and document. When you need to view the entire document, select Page Layout view or Normal view to make additions or modifications. To view only the outline, select Outline view to see just the headings in the document. Depending on the detail desired, you may display only major topic headings or any level of subheadings, up to eight levels deep.

Headings, and the material under them, can easily be rearranged, promoted, or demoted to another level by clicking on buttons in a special *Outline toolbar*. In the Outline view, you may choose what *level number* of headings you wish to see, from an exclusive presentation of first-level headings to a comprehensive look at all headings and the text under them.

Another important feature of the outline in Word is that it also helps you maintain consistent heading format attributes. All headings on the same level will be formatted the same way through the use of styles. Modifying the style changes the format for each heading at that level.

To create an outline, type in the headings for each section of your document on separate lines. When the headings are all entered, select View/Outline or click on the Outline View button at the bottom of the screen

The Outline toolbar replaces the ruler at the top of the work area, as shown in Figure 14.1. It contains buttons that allow you to promote or demote headings to different levels.

FIGURE 14.1
The Outline toolbar

FIGURE 14.2
Text in Outline view

- Heading One
- Heading Two
- Heading Three

FIGURE 14.3
Heading One promoted to a higher level

✧ **Heading One**
- Heading Two
- Heading Three

Word assumes that all the headings you entered are normal text. This is indicated by the small open square to the left of each line of text, as shown in Figure 14.2. Text can be changed to a heading by *promoting* it (moving the text to the left in the outline). Headings can be promoted to higher-level headings, or *demoted* to text or lower-level headings (to the right in the outline).

To promote a line from text to a heading, click in or highlight the line and click on the left arrow button in the Outline toolbar.

The open cross next to Heading One, as illustrated in Figure 14.3, indicates that this line is now a heading rather than a line of text. It also tells you that the heading has information under it: either subheadings or text. To demote a heading or make it a lower level, click on the *right* arrow button on the Outline toolbar. The symbols next to the lines do not change, but the heading moves to the right to indicate that it is now at a lower level in the outline. The lines under that heading also move to the right because Word assumes that they are subtopics under that heading. A heading can be demoted to text rather than to another heading level by clicking on the double right arrow on the Outline toolbar.

When all headings in the outline are at the correct level, you may choose how much detail to display in the Outline view. The first-level headings are the titles of the major sections in the document. They are the ones on the left margin in the outline. To display only the first-level headings, click on the 1 button in the Outline toolbar. Any lower-level headings and text in the document will no longer show in the Outline view. Clicking on the 2 button displays first-level and second-level headings, while all others are hidden. Each number button displays headings with that number or lower. The All button displays all headings and text. Selecting a low number on the Outline toolbar to hide text is known as *collapsing* the outline. To *expand* the outline, click on a high number or the click on the All button in the Outline toolbar.

You may also expand or collapse a single heading in the outline. Click in the heading to be affected and click on the minus-sign button in the Outline toolbar to hide its subheadings one level at a time. Clicking on the plus-sign button expands the selected portion of the outline by displaying hidden subheadings under the selected line.

Creating an Outline

An outline is usually created in an empty document; therefore, the first step in creating an outline is to select File/New. Enter the heading for each topic in the document on separate lines. It is not necessary to apply any formatting to the text at this point. Once the headings have been entered, select View/Outline to invoke the Outline view. The square symbol next to each line denotes normal text. When you promote a line by clicking on the *left* arrow, it becomes a first-level heading, and the symbol beside the heading changes. An open plus sign beside a heading denotes text or subheadings below it. An open minus sign beside a heading indicates that there is no subheading or text below it. To demote a line one heading level, click on the *right* arrow. Collapse the outline to view only headings above a certain level, or expand to view all headings and text.

GUIDED ACTIVITY 14.1

Creating an Outline

1. Start Word. Create a new document.

2. Enter the following text.

```
Section One
Introduction
Purpose
Goals
Section Two
Short-Term Goals
Weeks One Through Five
Weeks Five Through Ten
Long-Term Goals
Year One
Year Two
```

3. Select View/Outline or click on the Outline View button.

Word assumes that each line in the document is a line of text rather than a heading, as shown in Figure 14.4. Promote the first line in the document, Section One, to a first-level heading.

FIGURE 14.4
*Lines of text in
Outline view*

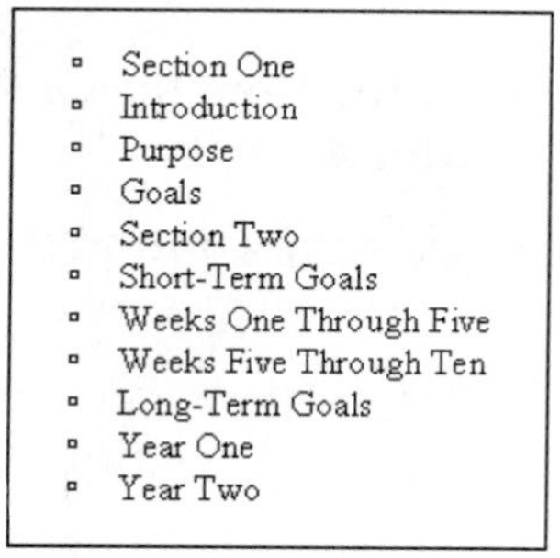

- Section One
- Introduction
- Purpose
- Goals
- Section Two
- Short-Term Goals
- Weeks One Through Five
- Weeks Five Through Ten
- Long-Term Goals
- Year One
- Year Two

4. Position the mouse pointer to the left of Section One and click once. Click on the left arrow in the Outline toolbar to promote the line to a heading.

Section One is now a heading rather than text, as in Figure 14.5. The rest of the lines in the document are still just text. Make the next three lines in the document subheadings under Section One.

FIGURE 14.5
*Section One
promoted to a
heading*

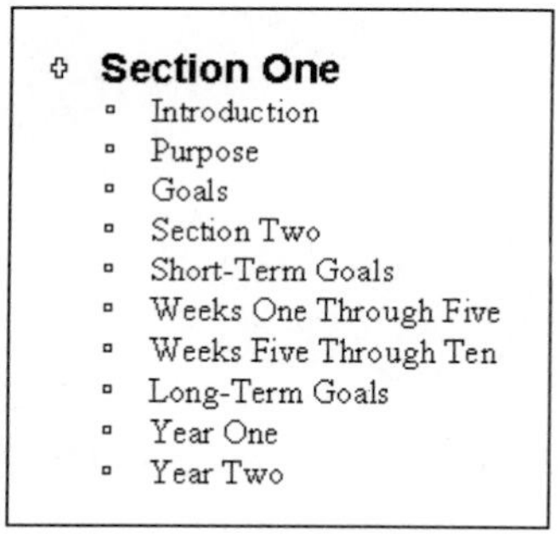

Section One
- Introduction
- Purpose
- Goals
- Section Two
- Short-Term Goals
- Weeks One Through Five
- Weeks Five Through Ten
- Long-Term Goals
- Year One
- Year Two

5. Highlight the Introduction, Purpose, and Goals lines in the document. Click on the *right* arrow button in the Outline toolbar.

As shown in Figure 14.6, Section One is a first-level heading. Introduction, Purpose, and Goals are second-level headings under Section One. The

FIGURE 14.6
*Second-level
headings under
Section One*

Section One
- *Introduction*
- *Purpose*
- *Goals*
  - Section Two
  - Short-Term Goals
  - Weeks One Through Five
  - Weeks Five Through Ten
  - Long-Term Goals
  - Year One
  - Year Two

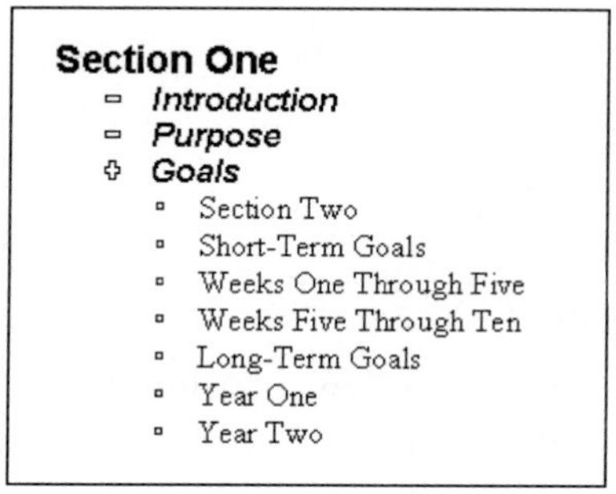

oblong boxes next to `Introduction` and `Purpose` indicate that there are no subheadings or text under these titles.

`Section Two` should also be a first-level heading. `Short-Term Goals` and `Long-Term Goals` will be second-level headings, while the other lines will be third-level headings.

6. Highlight `Section Two`. Select the left arrow button from the Outline toolbar twice to promote Section Two to a first-level heading.

7. Highlight `Short-Term Goals`. Click on the *right* arrow button to make it a second-level heading.

8. Highlight `Weeks One Through Five` and `Weeks Five Through Ten`. Click on the *right* arrow button to make them third-level headings.

9. Make `Long-Term Goals` a second-level heading by clicking twice on the left arrow button, and the two lines under it third-level headings by highlighting them and clicking on the *right* arrow button.

The headings should line up like those in Figure 14.7.

FIGURE 14.7
First-, second-, and third-level headings

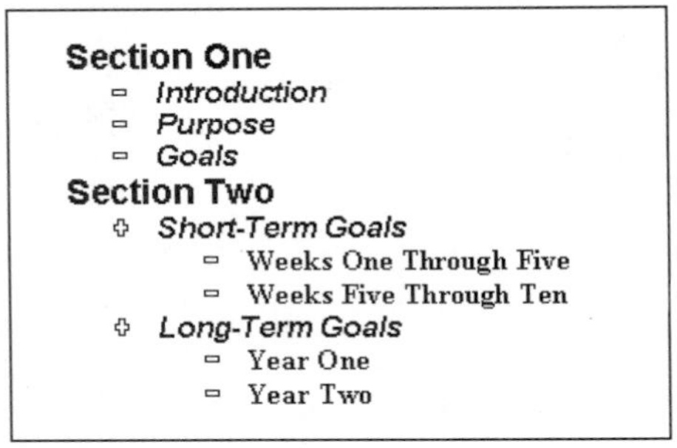

Section One
  ▫ *Introduction*
  ▫ *Purpose*
  ▫ *Goals*
Section Two
  ⬦ *Short-Term Goals*
       ▫ Weeks One Through Five
       ▫ Weeks Five Through Ten
  ⬦ *Long-Term Goals*
       ▫ Year One
       ▫ Year Two

Now that your outline is created, you may choose the level of detail displayed in the Outline view.

10. Click on the 1 button on the Outline toolbar.

The outline has been collapsed to display only first-level headings, and therefore shows faint underlines, as in Figure 14.8. Both headings have subheadings under them, as indicated by the symbols to their left.

FIGURE 14.8
Outline collapsed to show only first-level headings

  ⬦ **Section One**
  ⬦ **Section Two**

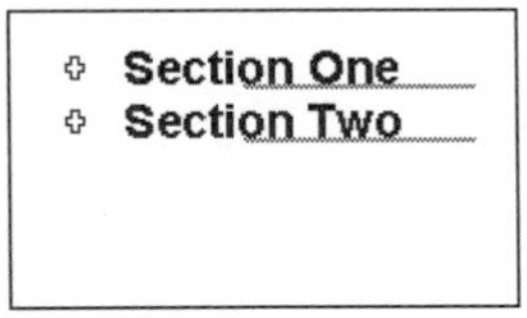

11. Click on the 2 button in the Outline toolbar.

The outline expands to include the first-level and second-level headings, as shown in Figure 14.9. You may also expand a portion of the outline.

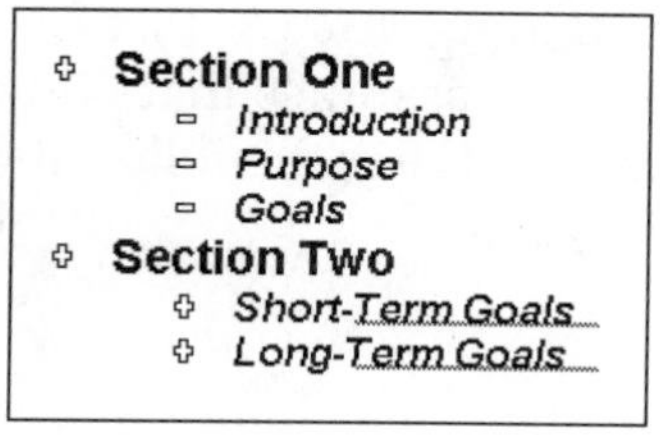

FIGURE 14.9
Outline expanded to include first- and second-level headings

> ⊕ **Section One**
>   □ *Introduction*
>   □ *Purpose*
>   □ *Goals*
> ⊕ **Section Two**
>   ⊕ *Short-Term Goals*
>   ⊕ *Long-Term Goals*

12. Highlight the line containing `Long-Term Goals`. Click on the Expand button that resembles a plus sign on the Outline toolbar.

    The third-level headings under `Long-Term Goals` appear, but the ones under `Short-Term Goals` are still hidden, as shown in Figure 14.10. Only the area highlighted is affected when you click on the Expand or Collapse button (the plus or minus sign).

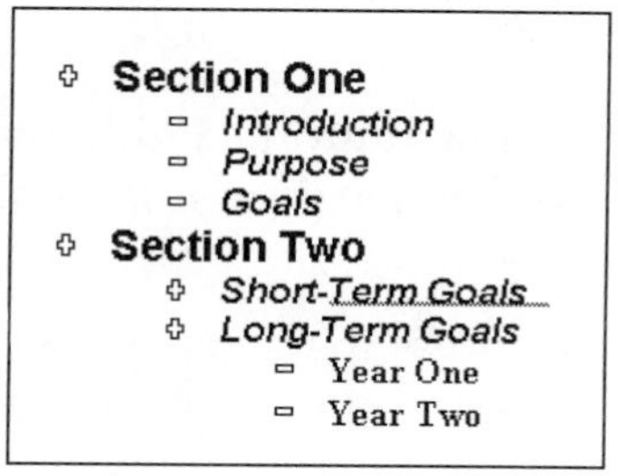

FIGURE 14.10
Long-Term Goals expanded to include third-level heading

> ⊕ **Section One**
>   □ *Introduction*
>   □ *Purpose*
>   □ *Goals*
> ⊕ **Section Two**
>   ⊕ *Short-Term Goals*
>   ⊕ *Long-Term Goals*
>   □ Year One
>   □ Year Two

Modifying and Adding Text to an Outline

Once the outline is created, you may add text under each topic heading. This is done by returning to Normal view or Page Layout view, positioning the cursor at the end of the heading after which you wish to add text, pressing ⏎ Enter to start a new paragraph, and typing the text. When the text is complete, you may move sections of the outline around by collapsing or expanding heading levels or selecting the portion to be moved and clicking on the up arrow and down arrow on the Outline toolbar. All of the subheadings and text under the highlighted heading will be moved along with it. This is an easy way to reorganize a document. By simply moving the title of a section, you also move all of the text under that heading to the new location. After you review the text for continuity and perhaps touch it up a bit, your document is complete.

GUIDED ACTIVITY 14.2

Adding Text and Moving Headings

1. Exit the Outline view by clicking on the Normal View button or the Page Layout View button.

   All the headings should return to the left margin but will retain the format attributes of their respective levels.

2. Position the cursor at the end of the line containing `Weeks One Through Five`. Press `Enter` to start a new paragraph. Word assumes that you want the next paragraph after this heading to be Normal style. Enter the following text:

    `Our first priority is to determine the demand for the product in its current state.`

3. Move the cursor to the end of the line containing `Weeks Five Through Ten`. Press `Enter` and type the following text:

    `The second step is to find ways to modify the product to increase its marketability.`

    Any amount of text can be added under outline headings. Using an outline is an excellent way to write a document because it helps organize your thoughts and can evolve as you think more about your project. When the text has been entered, you can change back to the Outline view and rearrange the document by moving the headings.

4. Select View/Outline or click on the Outline View button. Highlight `Short-Term Goals` and click on the Expand button, which resembles a plus sign. The new text you entered is included in the outline.

5. Click the Show First Line Only button to compress the text somewhat, as shown in Figure 14.11. Only the outline headings have an open minus sign or an open plus sign next to each of them.

FIGURE 14.11
Outline showing the added text

> ⊕ **Section One**
>   ▫ *Introduction*
>   ▫ *Purpose*
>   ▫ *Goals*
> ⊕ **Section Two**
>   ⊕ *Short-Term Goals*
>   ⊕ **Weeks One Through Five**
>   ▫ Our first prioritiy is to determine the demand for the product in its ...
>   ⊕ **Weeks Five Through Ten**
>   ▫ The second step is to find ways to modify the product to increase ...
>   ⊕ *Long-Term Goals*
>   ▫ Year One
>   ▫ Year Two

6. Click on the 3 button on the Outline toolbar.

    Since you chose to see only third-level headings and higher, the text is no longer displayed. When you move a heading to a different location in a document, all subheadings and text under it also move.

7. Position the pointer over the open cross next to `Weeks Five Through Ten`.

    When positioned correctly, the pointer should change shape from a normal pointer to a four-headed arrow.

8. Drag the open cross up. When the horizontal line is between `Short-Term Goals` and `Weeks One Through Five`, release the mouse button.

A horizontal line with an arrowhead will appear as you drag the mark up, as shown in Figure 14.12.

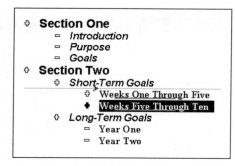

Weeks Five Through Ten has now moved above Weeks One Through Five in the outline.

9. Click on the All button on the Outline toolbar.

   Moving the collapsed heading in the outline also moves anything under the heading, as shown in Figure 14.13. Here, the text under Weeks Five Through Ten moved with it. Using this method, you can move a large portion of a document by simply dragging its title in the Outline view. You may drag the headings directly with the mouse or use the up and down arrow buttons on the Outline toolbar to move a heading up and down. You may move any level heading by using this method.

- ⬥ **Section One**
  - ▫ *Introduction*
  - ▫ *Purpose*
  - ▫ *Goals*
- ⬥ **Section Two**
  - ⬦ *Short-Term Goals*
    - ⬦ Weeks Five Through Ten
      - ▫ The second step is to find ways to modify the product to increase ...
    - ⬦ Weeks One Through Five
      - ▫ Our first prioritiy is to determine the demand for the product in its ...
  - ⬦ *Long-Term Goals*
    - ▫ Year One
    - ▫ Year Two

Formatting Outline Headings

It is important that all of the headings on the same level be formatted the same way. The reader keeps track of major topics in a document by the format of its headings. Word maintains a set of format attributes for each level. Every heading in a level will automatically have these attributes applied to it. The set of attributes for each level is stored in a style. As you learned in an earlier unit, a style is a set of format attributes that are collected under a single name on the toolbar or in the Format/Style dialog box. The name of the style for each heading is the word Heading followed by the number of the level. For example, all first-level headings are formatted to the style Heading 1. You may view and modify the attributes for Heading 1 by selecting Format/Style, as shown in Figure 14.14.

FIGURE 14.14
*The Format/
Style dialog box*

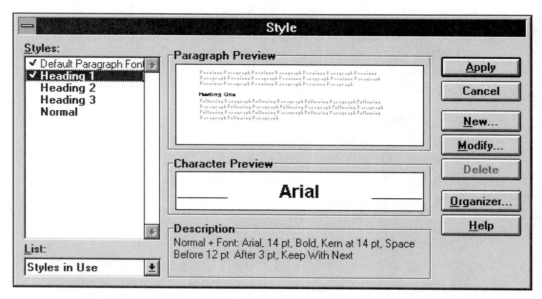

All the attributes for the style are given in the Description box. Highlight the style to be modified, and click on the Modify button.

From the Modify Style dialog box, shown in Figure 14.15, by clicking on the Format button you may change the format of the font; the paragraph; the tabs, frame, or border; or any other attribute. The dialog boxes that appear are the same ones that appear if you select Format/Font, Format/Paragraph, Format/ Tabs, Format/Frame, and Format/Borders and Shading. The difference, though, is that changing the format of the style (rather than formatting the individual paragraphs) changes all the headings at that level throughout the document at one time.

FIGURE 14.15
*The Modify Style
dialog box*

Every title of the level whose style is being modified will reflect the format attributes you select here. This will ensure that all headings of the same level will be formatted the same way. The reader will be able to follow the organization of the document more easily and with greater comprehension because of the consistent headings.

Creating a Table of Contents

The *table of contents* is a listing, in order of appearance, of the major sections of the book. It usually includes chapter titles, headings, and subheadings, along with the page numbers where each appears. The index is an alphabetical listing of subjects and key words in a document, again with page numbers.

Besides helping you create documents in a logical order, the Outline view also allows you to create tables of contents. Each heading in an outline, along with its corresponding page number, can automatically be included in a table of contents. To create a table of contents from outline headings, select Insert/Index and Tables, and select the Table of Contents tab, as shown in Figure 14.16.

FIGURE 14.16
The Table of Contents tab

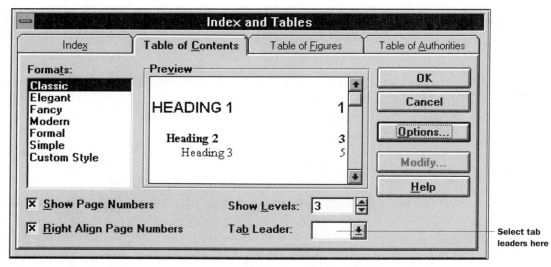

Specify which format you wish the table of contents to have, and preview the effect in the Preview box. When you click OK, every heading in the document above the given level will be included in the table of contents.

GUIDED ACTIVITY 14.3

Creating a Table of Contents

1. Return to Normal view. Move the cursor to the top of the document.

2. Press [Enter] to leave a blank line above Section One. Press [Ctrl][Enter] to insert a page break.

3. Repeat step 2 after positioning the cursor at the beginning of the line containing `Section Two`.

   The cursor should now be on page 3.

4. Move the cursor to page 1. Select Insert/Index and Tables, then preview several formats. Select the one you like best. If the one you choose does not include dot leaders extending from the heading to the page number, select a leader from the Tab Leader drop-down list. Click OK. The result should resemble the table of contents shown in Figure 14.17. Note that the page number for each heading is in the same style and size as the heading.

FIGURE 14.17
The table of contents

SECTION ONE	2
Introduction	2
Purpose	2
Goals	2
SECTION TWO	3
Short-Term Goals	3
Weeks Five Through Ten	3
Weeks One Through Five	3
Long-Term Goals	3
Year One	3
Year Two	3

A table of contents is inserted on the first page of the document. Level-one or first-level headings are against the left margin. Headings of other levels are indented for each level number. The page number where each topic appears is automatically inserted at the right margin.

The entire table is the result of a single field code. When you click in the table of contents, the entire table becomes shaded. To view the field code for the table of contents, select Toggle Field Codes from the shortcut menu, or press Alt F9.

The table of contents or its field code may be highlighted and moved or deleted, but it cannot be deleted with the Backspace or Del keys if the field code is not highlighted. To delete a table of contents (and its field code), highlight the entire table so that it turns an even darker shade of gray and press Del.

Adding an Index

Both a table of contents and an index are helpful to the reader when attempting to find a particular subject or term in a large document. The process of adding an ***index*** is usually quite tedious, but in Word is quite simple. Although the author still has to decide which entries will be placed in the index, Word does the tedious work of gathering the entries and compiling them into alphabetical lists. If the document body has text added, deleted, or moved, the index may be easily updated to reflect the changes.

For each entry to be made in the index, you must place an *index entry field code* in the document. First, highlight the text that should appear in the index, then press the shortcut key combination [Alt][Shift][X]. (The menu selection in this case— Insert/ Index and Tables, select Index, then click Mark Entry—is too tedious to use.) The highlighted text appears in the dialog box, shown in Figure 14.18, and you can fix capitalization, if necessary. Click Mark to insert the index entry field code into the document. You can continue to display the dialog box on screen as you highlight and mark repeatedly throughout your document. Each time you click Mark, a field code is inserted into the document, as shown in Figure 14.19. Word automatically displays these field codes. To hide them, click on the Show/Hide ¶ button.

FIGURE 14.18
The Mark Index Entry dialog box

Mark formats here

Once the index entry field codes are placed in the document, position the cursor at the desired location of the index. Select Insert/Index and Tables and click on the Index tab, shown in Figure 14.20, then click OK. Word searches through the document, collecting each index entry field code. The field codes are compiled into an index and listed alphabetically at the location of the cursor along with the page numbers where each appears. If you selected bold or italic in the Mark Index Entry dialog box as you marked, that attribute is applied to those entries in the index. (Remedy this by selecting the entire index and clicking on the font button you wish.)

FIGURE 14.19
The text and its index entry field code

Purpose·{·XE·"Purpose"·}·¶

FIGURE 14.20
The Index tab

Like the table of contents, the entire index is a single field code. This means that you may not edit or format individual words or characters in the index. It may only be modified as a whole. If index entry field codes are added, deleted, or moved in the document, the index must be updated. To update the index, highlight it entirely and press `F9`. Any modifications made to the entries in the document will be reflected in the index.

GUIDED ACTIVITY 14.4

Creating an Index

1. Highlight Purpose on the second page. Press `Alt` `Shift` `X`. Click in the box next to Bold in the dialog box since this is a heading, and click on the Mark button. Click Close.

   The highlighted text appears in the index entry field code.

2. With the cursor at the end of that line, press `Enter` twice. Type This is the first index entry field code that is not a heading.

3. Highlight first index entry and press `Alt` `Shift` `X`. Click on the Mark button. Do not click Close; leave the dialog box on the screen.

4. Highlight Introduction. Check next to bold, then click Mark to create a bold index entry for the highlighted text. Click Close, so that you can add more text.

5. Press `Enter` twice. Type This is the second index entry field code that is not a heading.

6. Create an index entry by highlighting second index entry and pressing `Alt` `Shift` `X`. Click Mark, but do not close the dialog box.

7. On the Short-Term Goals line, highlight Goals. In the Subentry box, type Short term and click Mark. Repeat for Long-Term Goals, entering Long term next to Subentry and clicking Mark. Click Close to exit the dialog box.

8. Position the cursor at the end of the document and press `Enter` twice. Type Index and apply the Heading 1 style, by clicking on the down arrow next to the style box showing Normal, and selecting Heading 1. Move the cursor to the end of the line, and press `Enter` again.

9. Select Insert/Index and Tables. Preview several of the formats. The run-in choice places the subentries in a single paragraph with the main entry. Choose Classic and Indented. Click OK.

   The index is created from each of the index entry field codes you inserted into the document, with a result similar to Figure 14.21. Notice that the page numbers for the heading entries are bold.

   If any other entries are marked after you compile the index, you must update the index before it will reflect the changes.

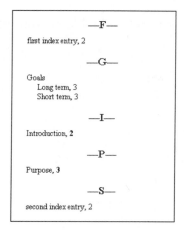

10. Position the cursor at the end of the line containing Year One. Press `Enter` twice. Type This is the third index entry field code that is not a heading. Create an index entry for third index entry.

11. Highlight the index and press `F9`.

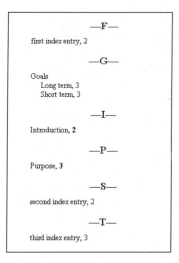

The updated index now includes the latest index entry field code you added to the document, as shown in Figure 14.22.

If you move an index entry to another page, the index will reflect the change when it is updated. When moving text that may be in the index, it is important to make sure that you move the index entry field code along with the text. Click on the Show/Hide ¶ button on the toolbar to view the field codes before attempting to move text; this ensures that the field codes are moved with the text.

Most field codes, such as those for the table of contents or index, are not shown until you select Toggle Field Codes from the shortcut menu or press `Alt``F9`. Index entry field codes are an exception, since they are formatted as hidden text and do not appear with the gray shading within the document.

12. Highlight the entire line containing Purpose, including the index entry field code. Drag-and-drop to move it to the top of the third page.

13. Click in the index to highlight it and press `F9`.

Purpose has changed to page 3 in the index.

14. Since the index heading was added, the table of contents is no longer complete. To update the table of contents, scroll up in the document and click on the table of contents so that it is highlighted and appears shaded in gray. Press `F9`.

15. A dialog box appears, asking whether you wish to update the entire table of contents, or merely update the page numbers. Since you wish to add a heading,

select Update Entire Table and click OK. The updated table of contents appears in Figure 14.23. Save the document.

FIGURE 14.23
The updated table of contents, including the index

Footnotes

Although this unit describes table of contents and index first, in reality, they are the very last items created in a document. *Footnotes* must be created as you type in the text. Whenever an author refers to an outside source in a document, the reference must ordinarily be documented. This is done by inserting a single-character *footnote reference mark* immediately after the text being cited. The footnote reference mark leads the reader to the footnote, which explains in detail the publication from which the text or idea was taken.

Many word processors used to force the writer to take care of footnotes and footnote reference marks manually. This is difficult for several reasons. Because the footnote appears at the bottom of the page, if any text on the page is added or deleted, the footnote must be moved to make sure that it does not move from the end of the page. Additionally, if the text from the outside source is moved, the footnote must be repositioned on the new page. Finally, if the footnote itself is edited so that it fits on a different number of lines, the entire page must be changed so that the footnote still fits at the bottom.

Instead of forcing you to manually create footnotes, Word allows you to insert a footnote reference mark anywhere in the body of your document. After the mark is inserted, you type the footnote into the *Footnote pane* at the bottom of the work area. The footnote is associated with the mark and will automatically appear at the bottom of the page wherever the mark appears. Other than when you edit the footnote, this is the last time you need to see it until the document is printed.

If any text on the page is added or deleted, or if the size of the footnote is changed by editing, Word will adjust the document body to leave enough room for the footnote at the bottom of the page. Additionally, if you move the text containing the footnote reference mark to another page, the word processor will automatically move the footnote to the bottom of the page where the reference occurs. The footnote feature alleviates many problems that writers usually have with footnotes.

Creating Footnotes

Footnote reference marks are inserted immediately after the text that is being referenced from another source. The footnote reference mark is usually a number, but you may choose to replace it with any character.

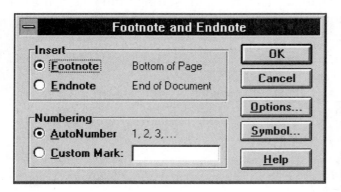

To insert a footnote reference mark, select Insert/Footnote to reveal the dialog box shown in Figure 14.24. This dialog box allows you to specify whether the reference will be a footnote shown at the bottom of the page or an endnote printed at the end of the document (acceptable form in many scholarly and professional publications). In addition, you can specify the numbering scheme you would like to use in the footnotes. Normally, footnotes are numbered consecutively with arabic numerals. Some documents may use ABCs or symbols (such as * † ‡ or §). If you use one of these automatic numbering schemes, Word will keep track of the numbering without your having to type a specific footnote number. You may enter a symbol in the Custom Mark box to use to refer your readers to a footnote; however, Word does not automatically renumber custom marks.

When you have made your selection of footnote or endnote and specified the footnote reference mark, click on the OK button. In Normal view the Footnote pane appears at the bottom of the screen, as in Figure 14.25. In Page Layout view, the footnote appears at the bottom of the page just above the bottom margin, separated from the text with a 2" line. Type in the text of the footnote. Word places a superscript number at the location of the footnote reference mark and the same number at the beginning of the footnote at the bottom of the page. You do not need to keep up with these numbers, because the word processor will increment them for you with each footnote you add. Additionally, if you move a footnote from one location to another, all of the footnotes affected by the move will be automatically renumbered.

> **All Footnotes**   ▾   Close
>
> [1]It's a Wonderful Life, dir. Frank Capra, with James Stewart, Donna Reed, Lionel Barrymore and Thomas Mitchell, RKO, 1946.

Notice that the scroll bar at the right-hand edge of the screen has been split into two scroll bars. The Footnote pane has its own scroll bar, as does the work area. Between the two scroll bars is a black mark called the *split mark*. This mark appears on the vertical scroll bar whenever the work area is divided into two or more areas.

To change the size of the Footnote pane, drag on the split mark. To close the Footnote pane, click on the Close button in the pane. The footnote will not be displayed again unless you choose to edit it or the document is previewed.

Rather than issuing the Insert/Footnote command and specifying the information for subsequent footnotes or endnotes, it is often easier for you to use the shortcut key. Using the shortcut key uses the same settings and inserts the next higher number for the footnote. The shortcut keys are found in Table 14.1.

TABLE 14.1
*Footnote/
Endnote
shortcut keys*

Shortcut Key	Function
Ctrl Alt F	Insert a footnote
Ctrl Alt E	Insert an endnote

GUIDED ACTIVITY 14.5

Inserting Footnote Reference Marks

1. Create a new document. If Page Layout view is selected, change to Normal view.

2. Press Enter. Type `This is text from another author's document.`

3. Select Insert/Footnote. By default, Footnote and AutoNumber are selected. Click on the OK button in the dialog box.

   The Footnote pane appears at the bottom of the screen. It contains a super-scripted 1 (^{1}) followed by the cursor. Another superscripted 1 appears in the body of the document at the location of the cursor before executing the command.

4. Type `This is the first footnote.`

   While this is not an acceptable footnote style, it will be helpful for learning how footnote reference marks work.

5. Close the Footnote pane.

6. Select File/Print Preview. The footnote appears at the bottom of the page where the footnote reference mark is located. Click Close.

7. Type `This is another idea from one of my sources.`

8. Use the shortcut key to insert a second footnote. Hold down the Ctrl and Alt keys and press F. A superscripted 2 (^{2}) appears at the end of the sentence you just typed, and also in the Footnote pane. Type `This is the second footnote.` The result should resemble Figure 14.26. Click Close to close the Footnote pane.

FIGURE 14.26
*The document
and two
footnotes*

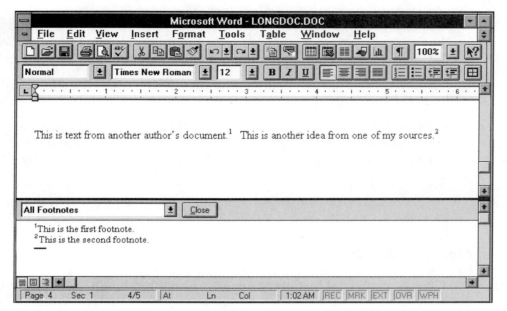

Editing Footnotes

To modify the contents of footnotes or endnotes in Normal view, you need to open the Footnote pane. To do this, either double-click on the footnote reference mark within the document or use the View/Footnotes command. This command acts just like Insert/Footnote by opening the Footnote pane, except that it does not insert a new footnote reference mark in the document body. You may edit or format the text in the Footnote pane and close the pane in the same way you did above.

Footnotes are deleted by highlighting the footnote reference mark in the document body and pressing [Del]. This removes both the footnote reference mark and the footnote text from the document. Deleting the text from the Footnote pane does not delete the footnote reference mark or the space left for it at the bottom of the page or end of the section. Of course, if you delete by mistake, you can recover by clicking the Undo button.

GUIDED ACTIVITY 14.6

Editing and Deleting Footnotes

1. Select View/Footnotes.

    The cursor appears in the Footnote pane at the bottom of the work area.

2. Change the first footnote text to read `This is the modification to the first footnote.`

3. Close the Footnote pane. Select Page Layout view to see the footnote in place.

The footnote has changed to reflect the modification you made. You now decide the footnote is unnecessary and wish to remove it. If you just delete the text of the footnote, the reference mark would still appear within the text.

4. Position the cursor to the right of the superscripted 1 in the document body. Press [Backspace].

The computer beeps to indicate an error. While they may appear as single characters, footnote reference marks are actually hidden markers in the text. Footnote reference marks must be highlighted before pressing [Backspace] or [Del].

5. Highlight the superscripted 1 and press [Del]. Scroll down to the bottom of the page to see that the footnote reference mark and footnote text have been removed from the document.

Moving Footnotes

When a segment of text that contains a footnote reference mark is moved, Word does two things. First, if the footnote reference mark is moved to another page, its associated footnote moves to the bottom of that page. Second, if the order of the footnotes in the document is changed, the word processor automatically rearranges and renumbers the footnotes.

To move a footnote reference mark, highlight it and use cut and paste or the drag-and-drop technique, just as you would move any other text. Usually, however, the footnote reference mark is moved along with a block of text, not by itself. (Some instructors may ask you to move all marks to the end of a sentence.)

GUIDED ACTIVITY 14.7

Moving Footnotes

1. Click on the Undo button to restore the deleted footnote.

2. Position the cursor at the end of the document. Press [Enter] twice. Type This is another reference to an outside source.

3. Press [Ctrl][Alt][F], or select Insert/Footnote and click OK.

In Page Layout view, the cursor jumps to the bottom of the page, rather than to the Footnote pane. The other footnotes are just above. The new footnote will be added next to the superscripted 3.

4. Type This is the footnote number three.

5. Highlight the first sentence in the document, including the first footnote reference mark. An easy way to select an entire sentence is to hold down the [Ctrl] key and click on the sentence. Select Edit/Cut or click on the Cut button.

Scroll down in the document to see that the remaining footnote reference marks change from superscripted 2 and 3 to 1 and 2.

6. Move the cursor to the end of the second sentence. Press ⌷Enter⌷ twice. Select Edit/Paste or click the Paste button.

   The original first line is now the third line in the document. Its footnote reference mark changes to 3.

7. Use the mouse or the cursor to view the bottom of the page, shown in Figure 14.27.

FIGURE 14.27
The rearranged footnotes in Page Layout view

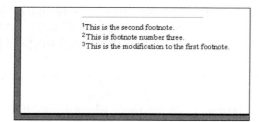

¹This is the second footnote.
²This is footnote number three.
³This is the modification to the first footnote.

   The footnotes have changed places to reflect the new locations of their associated footnote reference marks.

8. Highlight the present first line of text and remove it with Edit/Cut.

   The second footnote reference mark changes to 1 because it is now the first one in the document.

9. Position the cursor at the end of the document and press ⌷Ctrl⌷⌷Enter⌷.

   This inserts a page break. The cursor appears at the top of the second page, as evidenced by the status bar.

10. Select Edit/Paste.

    The cut line of text appears at the top of the second page. Its footnote reference mark has changed to a superscripted 3 to reflect its location in the document with respect to the other footnote reference marks.

11. Page through the document. Each footnote appears on the same page as its associated footnote reference mark.

Summary

Word allows you to create an outline of the headings for each topic in a document. The Outline view provides up to eight levels of subtopic headings. By clicking buttons in the Outline toolbar, headings can be moved, promoted, or demoted to higher or lower levels.

After creating an outline you may enter text under each heading in the outline. This is a useful feature because it provides a guide to maintain the organization of the document. After text has been entered, it may be moved to another location in the document by moving its heading in the Outline view.

It is important for all headings of the same level to be formatted the same way. Word maintains a style for each heading level. The format attributes of styles are changed, using the command Format/Style. When a style is changed, all of the headings of that level reflect the change.

Word allows you to quickly create a table of contents and index for any document. The table of contents is created with the command Insert/Index and Tables. Once the table of contents is created, it must be updated by using [F9] if there are any additions, deletions, or text movements in the document that affect the order of entries in the table. Word searches the document for outline headings and places each one in the table of contents along with the page number where it appears. Any changes to the document can be reflected in the table by highlighting the table of contents and pressing [F9].

Creating an index is also simple. Entries for the index are added to the document with the shortcut key [Alt][Shift][X]. Once the entries have been entered, the index is created by selecting Insert/Index and Tables. Like the table of contents, the index is updated to reflect changes in the document by pressing [F9] with the index highlighted.

Footnotes are added as documentation for references to outside sources. Word handles footnotes by allowing you to insert footnote reference marks into the text. Footnotes are added by using the Insert/Footnote command. This inserts a footnote reference mark at the location of the cursor and opens the Footnote pane. The footnote text is typed into the pane. To edit footnotes, select View/Footnotes, or double-click the footnote reference. This also opens the Footnote pane but does not insert a footnote reference mark into the text. To delete a footnote, highlight its associated mark in the document body and press [Del]. The word processor prints the associated footnote at the bottom of the page containing the mark, or at the end of the document.

Exercises

1. Type in the following text. Save the document as A:EX14_1.

    Microcomputer Development

    Microcomputers have evolved since their creation and proliferation in the late 1970's. Current microcomputers are more powerful than the gigantic mainframe computers of the sixties and seventies.

    HARDWARE

    The most significant change has been the increased *speed* and decreased *cost* of the new microcomputers. New generations of monitors, processors, and printers quickly make "old" technology obsolete.

Monitors

In the span of five years, *computer screens* evolved from single-color, text-only monitors to *high-resolution* color displays. Today's monitors are capable of displaying graphics that look better than *television* images.

Processors

In a single decade, we have seen the creation, maturity, and demise of the 8086, 8088, 80286, and 80386. The 80486 and the more powerful Pentium chip are the most popular processors available today.

Printers

Printers have evolved from single-font, slow, noisy *daisy-wheel* printers to *dot-matrix* printers capable of printing graphics, and finally to quiet, fast *laser* printers. Color printers are now available at a reasonable price that are capable of printing images comparable to photographs.

SOFTWARE

Software is divided into two categories: system and application. System software is used by the processor to communicate with the hardware, and manages files and disks. The programs that you use are called application software.

System

System software includes operating systems and their associated programs. All of the DOS program files are system software. Other operating systems include UNIX, OS/2, and Apple's System 7. These programs are required to make the computer work and to manage files.

Application

Application software is the reason you sit in front of a computer. It includes word processors, spreadsheets, graphics packages, and many others.

In the Outline view, make Microcomputer Development a first-level heading, HARDWARE and SOFTWARE second-level headings, and the other bold words third-level headings. Print the result.

2. Display only level-one and level-two headings. Print the result.

3. Expand the SOFTWARE section. Expand System. Print the result.

4. Move the Application section above System and below SOFTWARE. Print the result.

5. Move the SOFTWARE section above the HARDWARE section and below Microcom-puter Development. Print the result.

6. Insert Page breaks before each heading, including the first heading below Microcomputer Development, so that the text begins at the top of page 2 . Position the cursor at the top of the document. Create a table of contents on the first page from the outline headings in the document. Save the document. Print the first page only.

7. Move the Processors section to the end of the page containing the Printers section. Delete the blank page where Processors used to be. Update and print the table of contents.

8. Continue with the document from Exercise 2. Change the name of the HARDWARE section to MICROCOMPUTER HARDWARE. Update and print the table of contents.

9. Create index entries for the words and phrases in italics. Compile the entries in an index on a page by itself at the end of the document. Print the index page only.

10. Create index entries for the words and phrases that are bold. Make the page numbers for these entries bold. Update and print the index.

11. Move the page containing the Printers and Processors section to a new page immediately after Microcomputer Development. Delete the blank page that used to contain Printers and Processors. Update and print the table of contents and index.

12. Insert a footnote reference mark on page 2 at the end of the sentence referring to the late 1970's. Create a footnote in proper form. Print page 2 with the footnote.

13. Insert a second footnote on page 2, and another on page 3. Print pages 2 and 3.

14. Move the footnote and its associated text from page 3 to page 2. Print the second page only.

15. Move the paragraph containing the second footnote reference mark and the heading to page 3. Print both pages.

16. Delete the second footnote and footnote reference mark on page 2. Print the page.

Review Questions

*1. What is the purpose of using the Outline view in Word?

2. What is different on the Word screen when the Outline view is selected?

*3. How many different heading levels can be created?

4. How are headings moved to higher or lower levels in the Outline view?

*5. How is a heading changed to a line of text in an outline?

6. What buttons can expand or collapse a single heading?

*7. How are headings moved from one location to another in the Outline view?

8. In the Outline view, how can you tell if a heading has other headings or text under it if they are not displayed?

*9. What is the name of the style for second-level headings?

10. How are the format attributes for a style changed?

*11. What headings will be affected if a heading style is changed?

12. How is the table of contents created from an outline?

*13. What does the table of contents actually consist of?

14. How can a table of contents be updated when entries are added to or deleted from the document?

*15. How is an index entry field code created? What is the shortcut key?

16. How is an index created from the index entry field codes? In what order do the index entries appear?

*17. What determines the text that appears in each index entry?

18. How is the index updated when index entries are added, deleted, or moved in the document?

*19. How is an entire table of contents or index deleted?

20. What care must be taken when moving text that may appear in an index? Why must this be done?

*21. Since the index entry field codes may not be displayed, how can they be viewed? Why would you want to view them?

22. What are footnotes used for? Why is it so easy to create and use footnotes in Word? How do footnotes differ from footers?

*23. How are footnotes inserted in a document? What associated items are inserted into the document body when a footnote is created?

24. How are footnotes edited? How is this different from the command used to insert a footnote?

*25. What is a footnote reference mark? How can it be deleted? What else is deleted when a footnote reference mark is deleted?

26. What happens when a footnote reference mark is moved to a different page? What if the order of the footnotes in the document is affected by the move?

Key Terms

Collapse	Footnote reference mark	Outline
Demote	Heading	Outline toolbar
Expand	Index	Promote
Footnote	Index entry field code	Split mark
Footnote pane	Level number	Table of contents

Documentation Research

1. How do you view and print the outline without the headings being in the bold, large fonts of their heading styles?

2. How are numbers added to outline headings?

3. How can you create a table of contents and index for very long documents consisting of multiple files?

4. How may footnotes be printed at the end of a short page of text rather than at the bottom of the page where the footnote reference mark appears?

5. How is a footnote copied (not moved) from one location to another?

Macros and Customizing 15

Many tasks in word processing are repetitive, requiring the user to press the same sequence of keys or make identical menu choices over and over again. As computers become increasingly powerful, more of the repetitive tasks are performed by equally powerful software.

Word allows you to record sequences of keystrokes that you perform often into a structure called a *macro*. These macros can then be executed by pressing a shortcut key, by selecting a command that you place on the Word menus, or by clicking on a toolbar button. These macros are written in an extremely powerful programming language, but you do not need to know programming to create them. To build the macro, you simply execute the key sequence as you normally do while the word processor records your actions to create the program. This unit covers the procedures in Word to create and manipulate macros, as well as those that customize the menus, keyboard, and toolbars.

Learning Objectives

At the completion of this unit you should know

1. how to record a macro,

2. how to run a macro,

3. how to customize the toolbars, menus, and keyboard.

Important Commands

File/Save All

Tools/Macro

Tools/Customize

View/Toolbars

Recording a Macro

Many tasks that you perform in a word processor happen over and over again. You can let Word do most of the work in these repetitive tasks by recording the series of actions required to perform the command.

As an example, consider the actions required to insert a date field code at a location in a document. First, you must select Insert/Date and Time, then select the desired format, check the box for Insert as Field, and finally click OK. Then, to have it updated each time the document is printed, you would need to select Tools/Options, select the Print tab, and check the box Update Fields. If this were a procedure you used often, it could become tedious. Instead of performing this set of keystrokes every time yourself, make Word do the work by storing the commands in a macro.

Before you record the macro, it is a good idea to practice the steps to be recorded to avoid making mistakes and having to record the macro again. If the sequence of actions is quite long, you may wish to write them down before beginning. You may begin the task of recording a macro by selecting the command Tools/Macro and clicking the Record button or by double-clicking REC (for Record) on the status bar at the bottom of the screen.

The dialog box that appears, shown in Figure 15.1, asks you to enter a name and a description for the macro. You may also assign the macro to the menus, the toolbars (or any one individually), or the keyboard. After you click on OK, any key that you press or mouse movement you record will be added to the macro. The mouse has a pointer with a cassette tape attached, to remind you that you are recording, and the Macro toolbar appears on screen, allowing you to pause or stop recording at the touch of a button. Execute the sequence of keystrokes or movements with the mouse as you normally would. The only actions you are not able to perform are highlighting text or moving the insertion point with the mouse. When the sequence is complete, click on the Stop button on the Macro Record toolbar, or double-click again on REC on the status bar. The macro is now stored with the name you entered before starting to record.

In the following Guided Activity, you will automate several tasks

FIGURE 15.1
The Record Macro dialog box

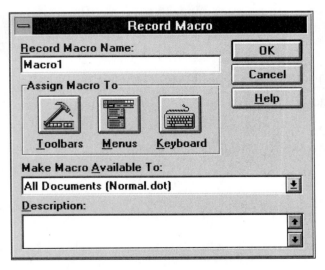

you usually perform before you print a letter on letterhead stationery. Of course, if you planned ahead, you could open a template that had all the settings stored as the default, but too often you find yourself typing a letter first and thinking about formatting procedures later. Rather than execute these commands repeatedly, the Guided Activity will help you create a macro to perform these functions.

GUIDED ACTIVITY 15.1

Recording a Macro

1. Start Word. Create a new document.

2. Enter the following text:

   ```
   Macros make the computer do the boring work, leaving me to
   be creative.
   ```

   Now practice the keystrokes or mouse movements you will be using before recording the macro.

3. Select File/Page Setup. Select the Margins tab, and change the top margin to 2.25". Select the Paper Source tab, and change the paper tray to Manual Feed for both the first and subsequent pages, then click OK. (If you are using a printer that does not have manual feed as a choice, skip that step.) Because you often need to examine the finished letter before you print to make sure it is neither too high nor too low on the page, select File/Print Preview. Click Close.

4. Click Undo to change the settings back. Now record the steps in the macro.

5. Select Tools/Macro and click Record or double-click on REC on the status bar. Enter the name of the macro—Letterhead. In the Description box, enter a phrase that describes what the macro does. For now, don't assign the macro to the toolbars, menus, or keyboard. Click on the OK button.

   If you later assign this macro to a menu or toolbar, the name you give the macro will appear on the menu or next to the mouse when you point to the button on the toolbar. Whatever you type as a description will appear in the status bar when you select it from the toolbar or menu.

6. Select File/Page Setup. Select the Margins tab, and change the top margin to 2.25". Select the Paper Source tab, and change the paper tray to Manual Feed for both the first and other pages, then click OK.

7. Select File/Print Preview.

8. These are all the steps you needed to record, so stop the macro recorder by clicking on the Stop button on the Macro toolbar, or by double-clicking REC on the status bar.

   Your macro is saved under the name Letterhead. Exit the preview screen by selecting Close.

Executing and Editing a Macro

The recorded macro may be executed, edited, or deleted by using the command Tools/Macro, as shown in Figure 15.2.

FIGURE 15.2
The Tools/Macro dialog box

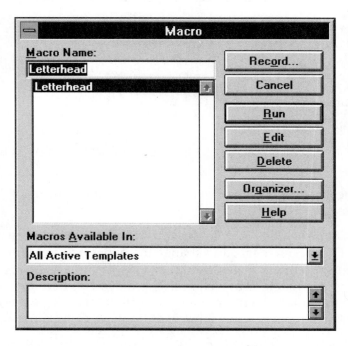

To run the macro, select the macro name and click Run, or double-click its name. The macro will execute exactly as you recorded it. If there are any problems executing the macro, a dialog box will appear with the number of the line containing the error. (Make note of it.)

Clicking the edit button will open a screen displaying the actual programming lines in your macro and the settings in dialog boxes. Macros are recorded in a powerful programming language called *Word-Basic*. Programming in Word-Basic requires a certain amount of knowledge of that language. If you want to (and know how), you can change the macro by adding or deleting program lines at this point. Even if you are unable to write a macro using WordBasic, you should be able to see if there are obvious mistakes in the macro. Choose File/Close to exit the macro editing screen and return to the document.

GUIDED ACTIVITY 15.2

Executing a Macro

1. Click on Undo to change the settings back to normal. Click on the Preview button to verify that the top margin is set at 1". Close preview.

2. Select Tools/Macro.

    The dialog box appears. The list of macros may not be exactly like the one shown in Figure 15.2, since different macros may have been recorded in your copy of Word.

3. Double-click on `Letterhead`, or highlight `Letterhead` and click Run. Word should automatically change the page setup and display the preview screen. Click Close to return to the document.

You can also use the Tools/Macro command to view the programming of the macro.

4. Select Tools/Macro. From the dialog box, highlight the macro name `Letter-head`, then click Edit. The screen will begin with the following information:

```
Sub MAIN
FilePageSetup .Tab = "2", .PaperSize = "1", .TopMargin =
"2.25"
```

and will end with this:

```
FilePrintPreview
End Sub
```

Although the language is confusing, you can see that `FilePageSetup` and `FilePrintPreview` echo the selections you made in recording the macro.

5. Select File/Close to exit the macro program and return to the document.

Customizing the Toolbars

The toolbars in Word for Windows 6.0 are completely customizable. You can display any of eight toolbars on screen at a time. These toolbars may be displayed at their default position on the screen, or dragged onto the screen, or *docked* on (moved to) any side of the screen. You can further customize each toolbar by arranging the buttons in any order, or even drag buttons from one toolbar to another. Word allows you to create a brand new toolbar customized with your favorite buttons. For instant access, macros that you create and other commands may be assigned to a button on a toolbar, and you can even design your own button face.

Rearranging Toolbars

You know how to turn on and off the toolbars with the View/Toolbars command. By checking the selections in the Toolbars dialog box, shown in Figure 15.3, you display one or more of the toolbars on screen in their default position on the screen. The toolbar shortcut menu with the same commands is available by clicking on the *right* mouse button whenever your mouse is pointing at a toolbar.

The Standard toolbar and Formatting toolbar are normally shown below the menu bar and above the ruler. If you wish to move a toolbar, place the mouse pointer over the shaded area behind the buttons and drag it. If you drag a toolbar on top of the work area, it appears as a window floating on screen, with a tiny title bar and Control-menu box, as shown in Figure 15.4. Just as with any window, dragging the border will change its size, dragging the title bar moves it, and clicking on the tiny Control-menu box removes it from the screen. If you drag it to the left or right side of the screen, the toolbar is docked in place with the buttons arranged vertically, often allowing more lines of text to fit in the work area. You may also dock a toolbar at the top or bottom of the screen.

FIGURE 15.3
*The
View/Toolbars
dialog box*

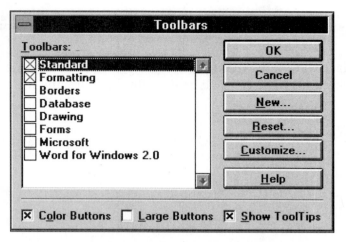

FIGURE 15.4
*The Standard
toolbar as a
floating toolbar*

Control-menu box

Title bar

Point here to drag a docked
toolbar into a floating position.

Just as the location of the toolbars is not fixed, neither are the locations of buttons on the toolbars. You can move buttons around on one toolbar, or drag them between toolbars. The trick to moving buttons is that you must hold down the [Alt] key while dragging. That is because if you attempted to click on a button in order to drag it without holding down [Alt], you would cause the button to perform its function. To copy (not move) a button, hold down *both* [Ctrl] and [Alt] and drag the button to the new location, either on the same toolbar or a different one. Alternatively, you could create a new toolbar and drag all your favorite buttons to one location. That would allow you to display only one toolbar at a time, saving space on the screen for your document.

The changes to the toolbars are automatically saved to the template when you exit Word or choose the command File/Save All. Anytime you wish to reset the toolbars to their default appearance, click the Reset button on the View/Toolbars dialog box.

GUIDED ACTIVITY 15.3

Rearranging Toolbars

1. Select View/Toolbars, and check in every square to display all the toolbars on screen at one time. Press OK.

   The screen is cluttered with toolbars. Toolbars appear above the ruler, floating, and at the bottom of the screen below the horizontal scroll bar, depending on where they were last displayed.

2. Click once on each tiny Control-menu box on every floating toolbar to remove them from the screen.

3. Point the mouse at the shaded area behind the buttons of any toolbar and click the *right* mouse button. The shortcut menu reveals a list of the toolbars with a check next to the ones displayed. Click Borders to remove the Borders toolbar from the screen.

    As you know, you could also remove it from the screen by clicking the Borders button on the right side of the Formatting toolbar.

4. You may also see near the top of the screen the Database toolbar you used in creating the data document in mail merge. Point the mouse at the shaded area between the buttons and drag the toolbar down onto the screen.

    The buttons are arranged in two columns of five buttons each.

5. Resize the floating Database toolbar by dragging on the side border. As you drag, the outline of the box jumps to appropriate sizes to accommodate the buttons.

6. Drag the Drawing toolbar over to the right or left border. When you release the mouse button, the toolbar is docked in its new location.

7. Drag the tiny title bar on the Database toolbar down until the toolbar is docked on the bottom of the screen. When it is correctly docked, the scroll bar will move above the toolbar, and the tiny title bar will disappear.

8. Select View/Toolbar and click to remove the checks next to all the toolbars except three, those for Standard, Formatting, and Word for Windows 2.0. Click OK, and one or more toolbars disappear while three remain on screen.

    The Word for Windows 2.0 toolbar is for people who have used the older version of Word and want to see the buttons in their familiar location. Many of the buttons on this toolbar are found in other places on the Word for Windows 6.0 screen. One button, however, is not—the Envelope button. This button automatically accesses the command Tools/Envelopes and Labels and selects the Envelopes tab, a very handy button to have.

9. Hold down the [Alt] key and drag the Envelope button to the Standard toolbar between the Save and the Print buttons. As you drag, the mouse pointer shows a gray silhouette of a button.

    The button is moved from one toolbar to another. To make room on the toolbar, you may wish to delete a button. The Insert Chart button is less useful if you can get charts from Excel.

10. Remove the Insert Chart button by holding down the [Alt] key and dragging it off the toolbar.

11. Remove the Word for Windows 2.0 toolbar from the screen with the View/Toolbars command.

12. Either save the changes by selecting File/Save All, or reset the toolbars back to their default by selecting View/Toolbars and clicking on the Reset button and clicking OK.

Assigning Macros and Other Commands to a Toolbar

When a macro is very short, it may be more trouble to run a macro from the Macro/Run dialog box than to actually perform the steps the macro covers. A macro may be placed on the toolbars as a customized button to let you execute it with the click of the mouse. You may create a toolbar button for every Word command, and for fonts, styles, and AutoText entries as well.

The Tools/Customize dialog box, Toolbars tab, brings up the same dialog box as the View/Toolbars, Customize button, as shown in Figure 15.5. This dialog box shows every button listed for each menu selection—File, Edit, View, and so on. For instance, when you click on File, you see a display of the buttons for File/New, File/Open, File/Save, File/Print, and many more. To examine the function for each button, click on it and read the description.

FIGURE 15.5
The Customize Toolbars dialog box

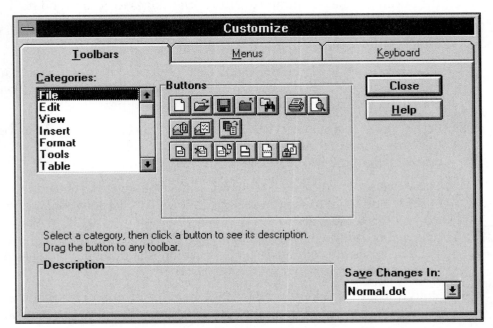

As you scroll through the list of categories, you will see at the bottom the selection Macros. When you highlight Macros, a list of the macros created appears in a box. Click on the Letterhead macro, and the description you gave it appears in the dialog box. When you drag the macro name to the toolbar, a new dialog box appears, giving you several choices for a button face, as in Figure 15.6. You may select one and click the Assign button, or click Edit to create your own button face.

FIGURE 15.6
*The Custom
Button dialog
box*

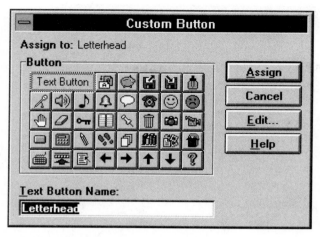

GUIDED ACTIVITY 15.4

Creating a Toolbar and Buttons

1. Select View/Toolbars, and click on the New button. In the dialog box that appears, type the name of the toolbar—say, your first name—and click OK.

   As soon as you click OK, a square toolbar appears on the Word screen. This toolbar has no buttons yet.

2. Scroll down the list under Categories and select Macros. You will see the Letterhead macro that you created in Guided Activity 15.1.

3. Drag the macro name `Letterhead` over to the new, empty toolbar. As soon as you do so, the Custom Button dialog box appears.

   None of these buttons represents a sheet of letterhead graphically, so we'll design one that does. Rather than start from scratch, however, we'll edit a button that is close in design to a letter.

4. Highlight the button that resembles two pages and click Edit. Immediately, the Button Editor appears, as shown in Figure 15.7.

5. Select White and drag over the middle two dark lines. Click on the Erase selection and erase the outer two lines on both the left and right sides. Click on the dark blue button and drag on the third line from the left and right sides to make the outline of the letter and fill in the gaps in the middle of the top and bottom blue lines. Use the light gray to fill in the lines across the letter, and use white to erase the top right gray line. With a dark bright color, trace the letter L in the middle, two lines thick. Your screen should look something like Figure 15.8. When the preview looks the way you want it, click OK.

6. To add a button with text on its face rather than a picture involves a similar process. Select Tools/Customize. Scroll through the categories and select Macros. Click on `Letterhead` and drag to the new toolbar. Select Text Button, and click Assign. The macro name appears on the face of the button. Click Close.

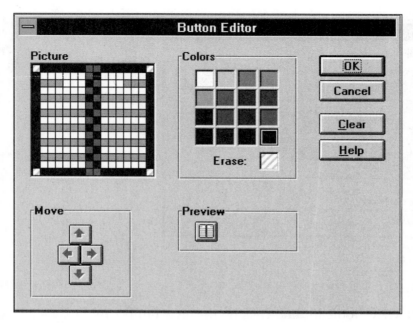

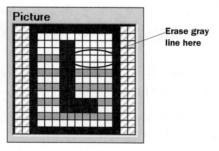

Erase gray
line here

7.   Test the buttons on the toolbar by clicking on the Letterhead buttons you added. Word automatically runs the macro, changing the page setup and displaying the preview screen.

Add a button on your new toolbar that will automatically change highlighted text from all capitals (uppercase) to lowercase, and so on, as you learned with the command Format/Change Case.

8.   Issue the command Tools/Customize. Scroll through the categories and select All Commands. In the list of commands that appears, scroll down until you see FormatChangeCase. Drag the command to the new toolbar. From the Custom Button dialog box, select the button of your choice and click Assign.

You now have three buttons on your custom toolbar.

9.   Test the new button by highlighting a few words of text and clicking on them several times to see the effect.

Customizing Menus

A third way to run a macro is to place it on a menu to access it, rather than cluttering your screen with buttons you only occasionally use. The Menus tab in the Tools/Customize dialog box, shown in Figure 15.9, allows you to assign your macro to a menu, and to customize the menus displayed by adding or deleting commands.

FIGURE 15.9
The Customize Menus dialog box

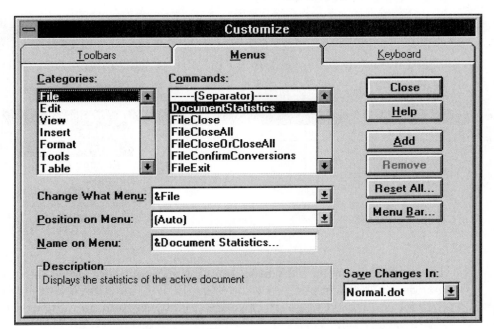

First, pick Macros from Categories, just as you did when customizing the toolbars, and select the macro to be assigned from the Macros list. Highlight the menu to which the macro is to be added in the Change What Menu list. Word suggests Tools. You may select the specific location on the menu, at the top, or the bottom, or may select Auto to have Word place it. If you wish, scroll through the list of commands on the menu and place it in a specific location.

Enter the text for the menu command in the Name on Menu box. This is the actual text that will appear on the menu, so check your spelling and capitalization. Include an ampersand (&) before the letter you wish to type to access the menu selection with the keyboard. Click on the Add button, then click Close to exit the dialog box.

GUIDED ACTIVITY 15.5

Customizing a Menu

1. Select Tools/Customize and select the Menu tab. Scroll through the list of categories and click on Macros to display the list of macros.

2. Select Letterhead from the Macros list box.

You'll add this to the Window menu, since it is relatively short.

3. Select Window from the Change What Menu list. Leave the Position on Menu setting Auto. Under Name on Menu, you will see &Letterhead.

    Word assumes that you want to name the menu command the same thing as your macro. An ampersand (&) is placed before the key that will execute the macro from the keyboard.

4. Click on the Add button to assign the macro to the Window menu. Click Close to exit the dialog box.

5. Click on the Window menu, to see the results, which should resemble Figure 15.10.

FIGURE 15.10
The modified Window menu

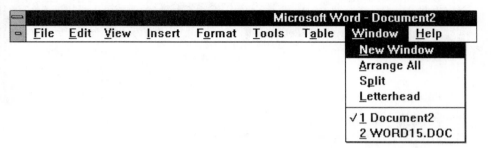

The macro has been assigned to the Window menu, at the end of the current commands, under the name Letterhead. The L is underlined to indicate that L is the key you would press to access this menu selection with the keyboard.

6. Select Window/Letterhead to execute your macro.

Customizing the Keyboard

The fourth way to execute a macro is to use a shortcut key. You may assign the macro to a shortcut key through the use of the Keyboard category under Tools/Customize, shown in Figure 15.11. This option also displays the shortcut keys for commands that are defined by Word. These may also be customized through the settings in this dialog box.

Just as when customizing the toolbars and menus, you must first select the category Macros, then highlight the macro name. After you click in the Press New Shortcut Key list box, you may press a key or a combination of keys to perform this function. If your selection is already assigned to another command, the description will appear under Currently Assigned To (not shown in the figure). If you wish to reassign it, click Assign, or try another to find one not currently assigned to another command. Click Close to register the change and exit the dialog box.

FIGURE 15.11
The Customize Keyboard dialog box

Customize

| Toolbars | Menus | Keyboard |

Categories:
File
Edit
View
Insert
Format
Tools
Table

Commands:
DocumentStatistics
FileClose
FileCloseAll
FileCloseOrCloseAll
FileConfirmConversions
FileExit
FileFind

Close
Help
Assign
Remove
Reset All...

Press New Shortcut Key:

Current Keys:

Description
Displays the statistics of the active document

Save Changes In:
Normal.dot

GUIDED ACTIVITY 15.6

Customizing the Keyboard

1. Select Tools/Customize, and click on the Keyboard tab.

2. Select Macros from the Category list, and highlight Letterhead.

3. Click in the list box labeled Press New Shortcut Key.

4. Hold down the Ctrl and Shift keys and press L for Letterhead.

   This key combination is already assigned. Press Backspace to clear the box.

5. Hold down the Alt and Ctrl keys and press L.

   This key combination is unassigned currently, so it is a good choice.

6. Click on the Assign button, and then click Close.

7. Test your new shortcut key by holding down the Alt and Ctrl keys and pressing L. You might want to keep a handwritten list of your shortcuts by your monitor, for ready reference.

   Since macros and customizing are automatically saved as the Normal template when you exit Word, you may wish to reset them to the default before you finish your work. If you are working in a computer lab, you will need to remove these effects. If you wish to retain the macro and customizing on your own machine, skip the following steps. These commands cannot be undone, so you will be prompted to see if you are sure you wish to delete.

8. To remove the custom buttons from the toolbars, hold down the Alt key and drag the buttons off the toolbar.

9. To remove the custom toolbar from the list of toolbars, select View/Toolbar, highlight the custom toolbar's name, and click Delete. At the prompt, click Yes to delete the toolbar, then click Close.

10. To put the menus and shortcut key assignments back to the default settings, select Tools/Customize. Click on the Menus tab and click Reset All. Click on the Keyboard tab and click Reset All, then click Close.

11. To delete the macros, select Tools/Macros. Highlight the macro names one at a time and click Delete, then answer yes to the prompt asking whether you want to delete the macro. Click Close.

Summary

Word allows you to store sequences of keystrokes and mouse movements in structures called macros. Macros allow you to automate the many repetitive tasks that are encountered in word processing. More of the tedious work can be delegated to the word processor, freeing you for more creative tasks.

Macros are recorded by using the Tools/Macro command and clicking Record; all keystrokes and commands from that point forward will be recorded until you click on the Stop button on the Macro toolbar. You may also start and stop recording by double-clicking REC on the status bar.

You may execute a macro in four ways:

- Select Tools/Macro, highlight the macro name, and click Run.

- Click on a macro button you created.

- Select your macro from a customized menu.

- Use the assigned shortcut key for the macro.

A macro is assigned to a toolbar, a menu, and a shortcut key by selecting Tools/Customize. After selecting which of the three you wish to assign it to, you must then specify the name of the macro, and to which toolbar, menu, or key combination you wish to assign it. If you assign a macro to a button, you may design your own button face or select from several different designs.

Toolbars may be rearranged to suit the user's needs. You may move toolbars to any edge of the screen (called docking), or leave them floating on the work area. Buttons may be moved from one place to another by holding down the [Alt] key and dragging them, or copied by holding down [Ctrl] and [Alt] while dragging. Turn the toolbars on and off by selecting View/Toolbar, or by using the shortcut menu.

The customizing changes you make to Word, such as recording macros and changing the toolbars, menus, and shortcut key assignments, are automatically saved to the Normal template when you exit Word, but can be deleted or reset to the default.

Exercises

1. Create a macro called HEADER that adds your name and your course to a header that will print on the top-right side of every page. The Layout tab of File/Page Setup may have different odd and even pages selected, so remember to clear that setting in your macro.

   Macros are printed by selecting Tools/Macro, highlighting the name of the macro, clicking on the Edit button, and selecting File/Print. When printing is complete, select File/Close to exit the macro edit screen.

   Print the HEADER macro.

2. If you create many letters, you could use a macro that inserts your preferred form of closing with a single keystroke. Assign it to the keyboard before you actually record it. To do this, after naming the macro and typing a description, click on the Keyboard button. Record the following steps: Press [Enter] twice to create a blank line after the text, type Sincerely, press [Enter] 4 times, then type your name. Print the macro, using the directions in Exercise 1.

3. Assign the macros you created in Exercises 1 and 2 to the Window menu. Select the Window menu to make it drop down and display its contents, and press [PrtSc] to copy a picture of your screen to the Clipboard. Open a new document, and select Edit/Paste to copy the screen shown to the work area. Print the document.

4. Place a button on the toolbar to apply double-space formatting. Press [PrtSc]. Open a new document, and select Edit/Paste to copy the screen shown to the work area. Print the document.

5. Create a new toolbar named with your name. Copy (don't move) five of your favorite buttons to it. Dock the new toolbar on one side of the screen. Press [PrtSc]. Open a new document, and select Edit/Paste to copy the screen shown to the work area. Print the new document.

6. Assign one of the macros from Exercise 1 or 2 to a button on your custom toolbar. Create a new, unique button face for it. With the new toolbar appearing on screen, press [PrtSc]. Open a new document, and select Edit/Paste to copy the screen shown to the work area. Print the document.

Review Questions

*1. What is the basic purpose of macros?

2. How are macros created? What preparations should you make before recording a macro?

*3. Give four ways to run a macro.

4. How are toolbars moved around on screen?

*5. How are toolbars turned on to be displayed? How are docked toolbars removed from display? How are floating toolbars removed from display?

6. How are buttons moved from one location to another? How are buttons copied?

*7. What happens when you exit Word after creating a macro or customizing the menu or toolbar?

8. What should you do if you want to remove the changes you made to the menus, toolbars, or keyboard?

Key Terms

Docked   Macro   WordBasic

Documentation Research

1. What macros are supplied with Word, and how are they accessed?

2. How can you adjust the space between buttons on a toolbar?

3. How can you place a clip art picture on a button?

Command List

File Menu

File/New creates a new document. This command allows the user to select a template or a Wizard for a new document. The default template is NORMAL.

File/Open opens a document previously stored on disk. This command allows the user to select from all drives and directories on the computer. The Read Only check box opens a file but does not allow the user to make changes to it. Documents created with other word processors may also be opened. Word for Windows converts file formats of most popular word processors. If the word processor used to create the document is unrecognized, Word for Windows will attempt to open the file as a text-only document.

File/Close closes the active document and removes it from memory. If the document has not been saved, a dialog box prompts you to do so.

File/Save saves the active document under the name located on the title bar. If the file has not yet been saved, the File/Save As command is executed instead.

File/Save As saves the active document under a file name supplied by the user. It also allows the user to select a drive and directory in which to store the document. The document may be stored in any of several popular file formats, including those of most popular word processors, by selecting the desired format from the Save File As Type list box. The Options button gives the user more control over the backup process. The Allow Fast Saves option only saves the changes made since the last time the user saved the document. The Always Create Backup Copy option creates a copy of the original file before you save a modified version by using the same name. Automatic Save is set to a certain interval from this dialog box.

File/Save All saves all currently open files under the names on their title bars, and saves any changes to the template. If a document has not yet been saved, Word for Windows prompts the user for file names for these documents.

File/Find File allows you to preview documents before opening them. You may pick which drives and subdirectories you want to display documents from.

File/Summary Info attaches information to the file to allow for easy identification at a later date. The information includes title, subject, author, keywords, and comments. The Statistics button allows you to see the total editing time on a document, the file size, the number of words, and the dates created and last saved.

File/Templates allows the user to select the template desired for the current document. The organizer allows styles and macros from one template to be copied to another template.

File/Page Setup changes the margins, paper size, paper source, and layout of the pages of a document.

File/Print Preview changes the word processor to the preview screen.

File/Print prints the active document. The user may select the pages of the document and the number of copies to print. The user also determines whether to print the document, summary information, or annotations by selecting options from the Include with Document section. By clicking on Options, the user has access to many selections, including the ability to reverse the print order of the pages (if the printer ejects paper page-up), change the printer to draft mode, or update field codes on printing. The Options button also gives the user the ability to include annotations, summary information, hidden text, and field codes. The Printer button allows the user to select which printer will be used in printing.

Quick Open This portion of the File menu displays the names of the last four documents opened. Often, a user wishes to continue working on a document that was being modified in the last Word for Windows session. Clicking on file names in this list causes Word for Windows to immediately open the document.

File/Exit exits Word for Windows.

Edit Menu

Edit/Undo reverses the effect of the last command executed or key pressed. This command will change, depending on the last action performed. It will undo up to 100 actions.

Edit/Repeat repeats the last action by the user.

Edit/Cut moves the highlighted items to the Clipboard.

Edit/Copy copies the highlighted items to the Clipboard.

Edit/Paste copies the contents of the Clipboard to the location of the cursor in the document.

Edit/Paste Special pastes information from other documents or other applications to the location of the cursor in the document. If you select the Paste Link button (when it is available), when the information in the originating document is changed, it will also change in the document containing the copy of the information.

Edit/Clear removes the highlighted items from the screen without placing them on the Clipboard.

Edit/Select All highlights the entire document.

Edit/Find searches for a segment of text or formatting entered by the user.

Edit/Replace searches for a segment of text or formatting entered by the user and replaces occurrences found with an alternate segment of text or formatting.

Edit/Go To goes immediately to a page, footnote, annotation, or bookmark and other items entered by the user.

Edit/AutoText allows the user to create, edit, and delete AutoText.

Edit/Bookmark marks a place in a document, such as text, pictures, or tables.

Edit/Links allows the user to view and maintain the links established with the Edit/Paste Special command.

Edit/Object allows the user to modify drawings, spreadsheets, or other nontext items in a document.

View Menu

View/Normal changes the work area to the Normal view.

View/Outline changes the work area to the Outline view.

View/Page Layout changes the work area to the Page Layout view.

View/Master Document displays a Master Document as an outline and allows you to view subdocuments.

View/Full Screen hides the title bar, toolbars, and status bar to give you more room to see your document.

View/Toolbars hides or displays the toolbars, hides or displays ToolTips, and creates new toolbars.

View/Ruler hides or displays the ruler.

View/Header and Footer allows the user to enter a header or footer for the document, and displays the Header and Footer toolbar.

View/Footnotes *and* **View/Annotations** open the panes displaying footnotes or annotations.

View/Zoom   allows the user to select the perspective from which to view the document. From the Zoom dialog box, you may choose to see more or less of the document at once in the work area.

Insert Menu

Insert/Break   inserts page, column, or section breaks. Section breaks may be continuous or may go to the next page, next even page, or next odd page.

Insert/Page Numbers   allows the user to select page number formats and locations for the current document.

Insert/Annotation   inserts an annotation marker at the location of the cursor and opens the Annotation pane.

Insert/Date and Time   inserts the current date and time in various formats at the location of the cursor.

Insert/Field   inserts a field code at the location of the cursor. It prompts the user for the type of field code and for any information required by the field code.

Insert/Symbol   allows the user to insert into the document characters that are not available from the keyboard.

Insert/Form Field   inserts fields to create forms that can be filled in on screen or printed and filled in on paper.

Insert/Footnote   inserts a footnote mark at the location of the cursor. It also opens the Footnote pane or moves the cursor to the footnote area of the page, depending on the view currently selected.

Insert/Caption   Inserts captions for tables and illustrations in a document.

Insert/Cross-reference   Inserts a cross-reference to an item in the same document.

Insert/Index and Tables   inserts an index created from index entries in the document at the location of the cursor, or inserts a table of contents from headings formatted with heading styles. May also be used to create a table of figures or a table of authorities.

Insert/File   inserts another document at the location of the cursor. It prompts the user for the file name to be inserted.

Insert/Frame   allows the user to draw a blank frame or places the highlighted text or object in a frame.

Insert/Picture   inserts a file containing a picture at the location of the cursor. It prompts the user for the name and location of the file.

Insert/Object   inserts an object from another software package (such as a spreadsheet or sound object, or item from a miniapplication such as WordArt or Equation Editor) at the location of the cursor.

Insert/Database inserts information from an external data source.

Format Menu

Format/Font allows the user to select character-format attributes from a dialog box.

Format/Paragraph allows the user to select paragraph-format attributes.

Format/Tabs allows the user to set tabs for the current paragraph. This dialog box can also be reached with a button from the Format/Paragraph dialog box or by double-clicking the bottom half of the ruler.

Format/Borders and Shading allows the user to select the border style and shading for the current paragraph.

Format/Columns allows the user to set attributes for columns, including number and width of columns, space between columns, and lines between columns.

Format/Change Case changes the case of the highlighted text—for example, all capitals, to upper- and lowercase letters, then to all lowercase letters.

Format/Drop Cap formats the first letter of the highlighted paragraph in a larger font and places it into a frame within the paragraph or out in the margin.

Format/Bullets and Numbering adds numeric field codes or bullets to the beginning of each highlighted paragraph.

Format/Heading Numbering creates a numbered list out of items that are formatted with heading styles.

Format/AutoFormat examines an unformatted document and formats it with appropriate heading and list styles.

Format/Style Gallery copies styles from a selected template and allows the user to preview the effects of each style.

Format/Styles allows the user to select from predefined styles or to modify the styles.

Format/Frame allows the user to set the size and position of a frame around a picture or object.

Format/Picture allows the user to set the cropping and sizing attributes for a picture in the work area.

Format/Drawing Object modifies the size, line, color, and position of drawing objects in a document.

Tools Menu

Tools/Spelling checks the spelling of a single word, a highlighted segment of text, or the entire document.

Tools/Grammar checks the grammar of a segment of text or the entire document.

Tools/Thesaurus offers synonyms for a highlighted word, and offers antonyms for some words.

Tools/Hyphenation hyphenates a highlighted word or all words affecting line endings in the active document.

Tools/Language allows the user to mark the selected text as a specific language. The spell checker uses the appropriate dictionary for that language when checking the document.

Tools/Word Count gives the number of pages, words, paragraphs, characters, and lines in the current document.

Tools/AutoCorrect allows the user to specify certain errors and how Word should automatically correct them.

Tools/Mail Merge sets up a mail merge. It allows the user to create a main document, set up or open a data source, and merge the data with the main document.

Tools/Envelope and Labels creates an envelope by using the highlighted text as the addressee or by allowing the user to type text into the dialog box. The envelope may be printed or added to the document. Also creates a sheet of mailing labels.

Tools/Protect Document protects a document from changes except for annotations and marked revisions.

Tools/Revision marks revisions instead of actually making them in the document. It allows several authors to suggest changes without affecting the original document. The changes may be removed or accepted with buttons from the dialog box. Also compares the active document with a document stored on disk.

Tools/Macro allows the user to record a new macro or run, edit, and delete previously recorded macros.

Tools/Customize allows the user to add, delete, or change buttons on toolbars and selections on menus, as well as to create or change shortcut keys.

Tools/Options allows the user to customize many different aspects of Word for Windows. Each tab in the dialog box controls a separate set of customizable functions.

Table Menu

Table/Insert Table inserts a table at the location of the cursor after prompting the user for the number of rows and columns in the table. If the document already contains a table, this changes to Insert/Cells, Row, or Column, depending on what is highlighted.

Table/Delete Cells (Columns, Rows) allows the user to delete single cells or entire rows and columns from an existing table.

Table/Merge Cells allows the user to join two or more cells in a table into a single cell.

Table/Split Cells allows the user to split a cell in a table into two or more cells.

Table/Select Row, Table/Select Column, and Table/Select Table highlight the current rows, the current columns, or the entire table, respectively.

Table/Table AutoFormat applies predefined formats to a table, including fonts, column widths, borders, and shading.

Table/Cell Height and Width allows the user to specify the height of the current rows or the width of the selected columns, as well as to set alignment and indentation of the entire table.

Table/Headings causes the headings on the first row of a table to be printed at the top of each page of the table.

Table/Convert Text to Table allows the user to insert highlighted text into a table. Table/Convert Table to Text allows the user to remove the table from around a highlighted segment of text.

Table/Sort sorts highlighted text in ascending or descending order, as selected by the user, either by paragraphs or by column in a table.

Table/Formula performs mathematical calculations and stores the result in fields.

Table/Split Table allows the user to split an existing table in two parts to insert text or graphics between the parts.

Table/Gridlines hides or displays nonprinting table gridlines in the work area.

Window Menu

Window/New Window opens a second copy of the active document so that the user may view two parts of the same document.

Window/Arrange All arranges all open documents so that a portion of each is displayed in the work area.

Window/Split splits the window into two panes so that the user can view two parts of the same document.

Window/Quick Select displays in the bottom portion of the Window menu a list of all open documents. To switch quickly to another open document, click on the document's file name to make it active.

Help/Contents gives the general table of contents for Word for Windows 6.0's Help facility.

Help/Search for Help on allows the user to specify a key word to find related Help topics.

Help/Index presents an alphabetical index of all the topics in Help.

Help/Quick Preview gives information on the new features of Word for Windows 6.0. Also gives Quick Start and help for WordPerfect users.

Help/Examples and Demos gives on-screen examples and demonstrations of many word processing procedures.

Help/Tip of the Day Displays a one-sentence tip on nifty features in Word.

Help/WordPerfect Help gives information and demonstrations for WordPerfect users to learn Word.

Help/Technical Support gives information and telephone numbers for Microsoft technical support.

Help/About Microsoft Word gives registration and copyright information, plus system information about the computer's hardware and software.

Answers to
Review Questions

0-1. A window is a box on the screen that can contain applications, documents, spreadsheets, graphics, and many other items. Windows can be distinguished by their title bars and borders.

0-3. In a text environment, the computer only needs to keep up with about 2,000 characters on the screen at once. In a graphical environment, the computer must control about 800,000 pixels at once on the screen. Graphical environments cause computers to work more slowly because of this additional overhead.

0-5. A window is maximized by clicking on the button in its top-right corner containing an up arrow. To minimize a window, click the button in the top-right corner of the window containing a down arrow.

0-7. The menu bar allows you to access commands that are used to cut, copy, and paste information between applications.

1-1. All Windows applications have a title bar, a Control-menu box, minimize and maximize buttons, and scroll bars. Word 6.0 also provides a menu bar, toolbars, a ruler, and a status bar.

1-3. The [Alt] key is the most important to remember when using the keyboard to execute commands. This key allows you to access menus in the menu bar and commands in dialog boxes without using the mouse.

2-1. The three procedures in word processing are entering and editing text, formatting, and using advanced procedures.

2-3. The [↑] and [↓] arrow keys move the cursor up or down one line. The [←] and [→] arrow keys move the cursor left or right one character. The [PgUp] and [PgDn] keys move the cursor up or down one screen in a document. The [Home] key moves the cursor to the beginning of the current line, whereas the [End] key moves it to the end of the line. Any of these keys may be used in conjunction with the [Ctrl] key to increase the distance the cursor moves.

2-5. The [Shift] key is used to highlight text.

2-7. The insert mode adds typed text at the position of the cursor; the text to the right of the cursor is shifted further to the right to make room for the new text. The overtype mode replaces the character to the right of the cursor with the next character typed.

2-9. Edit/Cut is used to remove highlighted text and place it in the Clipboard. Edit/Copy places a copy of the highlighted text in the Clipboard, leaving the original in place. Edit/Paste places a copy of the contents of the Clipboard at the location of the cursor in a document. The Clipboard is a temporary storage location for items being moved or copied from one location to another.

2-11. The four methods for executing many commands are these:

- Select from the menu.
- Click a button.
- Select from the shortcut menu.
- Press the shortcut key.

3-1. Documents are stored on disks so that they can be retrieved, edited, and printed at a later time. Documents that are not stored on disk are erased when Word for Windows is exited or when the computer is turned off.

3-3. There are two sizes of removable disks: 3.5-inch and 5.25-inch. The 5.25-inch disks can be found on most computers, but the 3.5-inch disks hold more information. Most new computers have at least one 3.5-inch disk drive. The capacity of a 5.25-inch disk is 360KB or 1.2MB, depending on how it is formatted. The capacity of a 3.5-inch disk is 720KB or 1.44MB.

3-5. On 5.25-inch disks, cover the write-protect notch with a special gummed tab designed for that purpose. For 3.5-inch disks, slide the plastic tab from the write-protect hole, uncovering the hole.

3-7. File names must be eight characters or fewer and may contain no special characters.

3-9. The File/New command presents a dialog box allowing you to choose a template or wizard. The New button on the toolbar bypasses the dialog box, creating a new document based on the Normal template.

3-11. The File/Save As command is executed in this case. Since the document has not been saved, it is still called Document1. Word for Windows will request a file name for the document before saving it.

3-13. If a user creates many documents based on the same form, this form can be saved as a template document. Templates can contain text and special formatting common to many documents. When a new document is created based on the template, the text and formatting will already be in place, saving the user time. Some templates come with Wizards that automate the process of creating certain types of documents.

3-15. The Drives sections of the File/Save As and File/Open dialog boxes display the drives available on the computer.

4-1. Highlight the word and select Tools/Spelling or click the Spell Check button.

4-3. Select Tools/Spelling. Word for Windows will check spelling from the position of the cursor to the end of the document. When the end of the document is reached, Word continues to check from the beginning of the document to the original position of the cursor. Because of this, the position of the cursor is not a limitation when checking the spelling of a document.

4-5. It may take several seconds for Word for Windows to display a list of suggestions for misspelled words. If you wish to make corrections yourself without looking at suggestions, click Options in the Spelling dialog box, turn off the Always Suggest option, and click OK.

4-7. The grammar checker not only flags grammatical errors and questionable writing style, it also checks the spelling of a document.

4-9. The thesaurus may be used to find a synonym of a word to get the exact shade of meaning you need. If a word has several meanings, it provides synonyms for each meaning. It also provides antonyms (words of opposite meaning) for some words.

5-1. There are many printers that can be connected to a computer. Three popular types are dot-matrix, laser, and inkjet printers.

5-3. Windows controls printers from the Printers icon in the Control Panel, located in the Main program group.

5-5. The Print button on the standard toolbar bypasses the Print dialog box and prints one copy of the entire document. The Print button on the Preview toolbar goes to the Print dialog box, allowing you to specify the number of copies and which pages to print.

6-1. Character (or font), paragraph, and document are the three levels of formatting.

6-3. Text that already exists is formatted by highlighting it and selecting the desired format attribute. To format text as it is being typed, position the cursor at the desired location of the new text. Select the format attribute to be applied. As you enter text, it will appear with the format attribute selected. When you finish typing the text, turn off the format attribute.

6-5. Word includes often-used commands on the toolbars, while those that are used seldom are only available from dialog boxes.

6-7. The default font for Word is Times New Roman in a 10-point size. To change the default font, issue the command Format/Font, specify the desired font, and click on the Default button.

6-9. Words may be expanded or condensed by highlighting the words and selecting the command Format/Font. Select the tab for Character Spacing, and in the dialog box change the spacing to Expanded or Condensed. You may customize how spread-out the letters will be.

6-11. Word contains special characters, such as typesetters' quotation marks ("curly quotes"), em and en dashes, copyright and trademark symbols. They are accessed from the Insert/Symbols dialog box.

7-1. Paragraph format commands will affect the paragraph where the cursor is located and any other paragraphs that are completely or partially highlighted.

7-3. Left alignment aligns text against the left margin. As the default setting, left alignment is used most often for regular text. Right alignment aligns text against the right margin. It is generally used for short lines of text. Justification aligns text against both margins. It is used in letters or newspapers that have a very formal appearance. Center alignment centers text between the left and right margins. It is most often used for titles and headings.

7-5. A tab is a mark on the ruler used to quickly align text in columns. The four types of tabs work much like the four types of paragraph alignments: text typed after a left tab will have the left edge of the text directly under the tab. Text typed after a right tab will have its right edge directly under the tab. Text typed after a center tab will be centered directly under the tab. Decimal tabs are used to align columns of numbers with their decimal places directly under the tab. Tab leaders are repeated characters that appear between the position of the cursor before the Tab key was pressed and the location of the next tab on the ruler. Tab leaders may be dots, dashes, or underlines.

7-7. These commands are used to keep page breaks from occurring at incorrect places in the document. Keep Lines Together will avoid having a page break in a specific paragraph; the paragraph will always appear complete on one page. Keep with Next will avoid having two paragraphs split by a page break; the two paragraphs will always appear together on the same page.

7-9. When you click the Borders button on the Formatting toolbar, the Borders toolbar appears on screen. From this toolbar you may set borders on the top, bottom, left, or right sides of a paragraph. You may also specify the line style of the border. In addition, you may specify the intensity of the shading behind a segment of text.

7-11. Styles are Word's method for saving a certain format for characters or paragraphs. Once defined, they save time by applying complex formatting with only one step. To define a style, format an existing paragraph to the desired style, then give the style a name in the Style box on the Formatting toolbar and press Enter.

8-1. The Format/Page Setup commands affect the entire document or sections of the document, not just highlighted text or the paragraph where the cursor is located.

8-3. When setting the paper size in the Format/Page Setup dialog box, you must select a paper size supported by the printer selected. The default paper size for most printers is 8½"×11".

8-5.   Margins are the space between the edges of a page and the text printed on it. Indents are the amount of space between the margin and the text. Indents are added to the margins. For example, if the margins are increased, the indentation will still be added to the larger margin size.

8-7.   A gutter is additional space at the edge of a page for document binding. In a document printed on only one side of the page, the gutter appears on the left. In a document printed on both sides of the page, which is the case when Mirror Margins is selected, the gutter always appears on the inside margin of the page.

8-9.   Page Layout view shows the vertical ruler on the left side of the screen. New buttons appear at the bottom of the scroll bar that allow you to jump to the previous page or next page. The document appears as pages on a shaded desktop, with the margins and page numbers visible. Under Zoom Control, there is an option to view Two Pages that is not available in Normal view.

9-1.   Tables are best suited for information that can be displayed two-dimensionally, in rows and columns.

9-3.   Tables are created from scratch with the command Table/Insert Table or by clicking the Table button on the toolbar. You must supply the number of rows and columns for the new table. All the new columns are the same width, so the entire table fits exactly between the left and right margins if you use the button, or you may specify column width exactly if you use Table/Insert Table.

9-5.   Text that is too wide to fit in a table cell will wrap to new lines in the same cell. All the cells on that row of the table will change in height to accommodate the extra lines.

9-7.   To insert a new row at the bottom of a table, position the cursor in the last cell of the table and press Tab.

9-9.   A table is created from text by highlighting the text and clicking the Table button or selecting the command Table/Insert Table or Table/Convert Text to Table.

9-11.   The contents of a table are converted back to text with the command Table/Convert Table to Text. This command is available only when all or part of a table is highlighted.

9-13.   Before a single row or column is inserted, the cursor must be positioned where the new row or column will be inserted. To insert more than one row or column, all of the area where the new rows or columns will be inserted must be highlighted.

9-15.   Cells in a table are merged by highlighting them and selecting Table/Merge Cells. Cells are merged when they contain information that is valid for two or more columns. Before cells are merged, they must be highlighted and must not be previously merged.

9-17.   Cell borders are printed lines used to make cells stand out in a printed table. Cell borders are turned on with the Format/Borders and Shading command or by using the buttons on the Borders toolbar. Gridlines are nonprinting lines that appear on a table by default. Gridlines are turned off and on with the Table/Gridlines command. AutoFormat formats fonts, column widths, borders, shading, and color.

9-19. Tabs may be used to align text in columns within the cells of a table. The decimal tab is most often used to align numbers within the column of a table. To use a tab setting within a table cell, press Ctrl Tab.

10-1. Word for Windows allows you to see pictures and graphics on the screen the way they will appear on paper.

10-3. Displaying pictures in a document slows the speed at which the document will scroll. This may be avoided by selecting Tools/Options/View and checking the box next to Picture Placeholders.

10-5. Cropping trims off a portion of a picture or adds white space to the sides of a picture. Cropping changes the overall size of the picture in terms of what you can see, but the part of the graphic image that remains in view does not change. To crop, hold down the Shift key while dragging the sizing handles.

Scaling enlarges or reduces the graphic image itself. By dragging the corner handles, you will keep the size proportional as you change the overall size. By dragging the handles on the edges, by contrast, you will distort proportions and stretch or compress the graphic.

10-7. To edit a picture, simply double-click it. The screen changes to Page Layout view, the Drawing toolbar appears, and the picture is displayed within a square boundary.

10-9. Pictures may be positioned in any location on the page by placing them within a frame. You may specify the exact position with the Format/Frame command, or, if you change to Page Layout view, you may use the mouse to drag pictures into position on the page.

10-11. Frames allow you to position the picture anywhere on the page but do not appear when you print. Borders print a box around the picture.

11-1. Columns of text allow the reader to scan information more quickly. It is also easier to lay out a page with pictures and advertisements in a multiple-column format.

11-3. Section breaks must be inserted before and after the portion of the document that will be in column format. Section breaks are inserted automatically if text is first highlighted and then the number of columns is chosen.

11-5. Column widths are changed either by dragging the column markers on the ruler, or by setting column widths and the space between the columns with Format/Columns. Column widths are also affected by changing the margins with Format/Page Setup.

11-7. Unbalanced columns appear at the end of a document where the text does not fill the page. To balance columns, insert a continuous section break at the end of the document, and if necessary add or delete a few words to even up the columns.

12-1. Headers and footers are used to place information at the top and bottom of all pages in a document.

12-3. Headers and footers can be created for the first page, odd pages, and even pages. Usually, the first page of a document does not have a header or footer. If a document is printed on both sides of the page, odd and even pages will need different headers and footers to avoid having information close to the binding.

12-5. The buttons on the Header and Footer toolbar allow you to insert the date, time, or page number in the header or footer. To view field codes, press [Alt][F9] or point the mouse at the shaded field code and select Toggle Field Codes from the shortcut menu.

13-1. Mail merge allows you to merge information from a data document into variables in a form document.

13-3. The first line of a data source, called the header row, contains the name of the merge fields. The subsequent lines in the data source document, called data records, contain information to be placed in the form document during merging.

13-5. A main document contains the Mail Merge toolbar between the Formatting toolbar and ruler. It also contains merge fields surrounded by chevrons throughout the document; during the merge, these will be replaced by information from the data document. Normal documents do not contain these.

13-7. To see the actual data from the data source in place of the merge fields in chevrons, click the View Merged Data button.

13-9. File/Print will print one copy of the main document, including merge field codes. Tools/Mail Merge will print one copy of the form document for each line of information in the data document.

13-11. In the Mail Merge dialog box, enter values in the From and To boxes under Records To Be Merged to print one copy of the form document for selected records of information from the data document. You may also set Query Options to filter out only records that meet specified criteria.

13-13. An IF merge field is used to include a segment of text only when certain criteria are true for a record, and to include a different segment of text when the criteria are false.

13-15. Dot-matrix printers handle long, continuously fed strips of labels with tractor feed guides on each margin. Laser printers require individual sheets of labels, usually two or three columns to a page.

14-1. The Outline view allows you to integrate your outline into the document that you are creating. This helps you keep the ideas in the document organized and in order.

14-3. Word for Windows allows up to eight levels of headings in a document.

14-5. A heading is changed to text by positioning the cursor on the heading and clicking the double *right* arrow on the Outline toolbar.

14-7. Headings are moved with the mouse by grabbing the plus or minus to the left of the heading and dragging it to the desired location, or by highlighting and clicking the up or down arrows on the Outline toolbar.

14-9. The second-level heading style is heading 2.

14-11. If a heading style is changed, all headings at that level will be changed. If the Heading 3 style is changed, all level-three headings will change to reflect the modified style.

14-13. The table of contents is actually a field code in the document.

14-15. An index entry field code is created by highlighting the material, pressing the shortcut key [Alt][Shift][X], and clicking Mark.

14-17. The text for the entry is entered into the Mark Index Entry dialog box. Whatever is highlighted before pressing [Alt][Shift][X] will automatically become the entry.

14-19. The entire table of contents or index must be highlighted before pressing the [Del] key.

14-21. Press the Show/Hide ¶ button. You need to see the field codes before you can edit or delete them. You may also want to view them if you are moving text around.

14-23. Footnotes are inserted by selecting Insert/Footnotes or by pressing [Ctrl][Alt][F]. The superscripted footnote reference marks are inserted at the location of the cursor.

14-25. A footnote reference mark is a superscripted number, letter, or symbol that is dynamically linked to the footnote text. You must first highlight the reference mark before you can delete it. Whenever a footnote reference mark is deleted, the accompanying footnote is also deleted from the document.

15-1. Macros store sequences of keystrokes or mouse movements that are used repeatedly in a document. These sequences may be reproduced with a single keystroke or click of the mouse, saving the user time.

15-3. **a.** Select Tools/Macro, pick the name of the macro from the list, and click on Run.

   b. Press the shortcut keys that you assigned to the macro.

   c. Press the customized button on the toolbar.

   d. Select the macro name from a customized menu.

15-5. Turn on toolbars to display them by selecting View/Toolbars and checking the boxes next to the toolbar names. You may also use the shortcut menu to select a toolbar name and display it. Docked toolbars are removed by using the same methods as displaying them. Floating toolbars are also removed from screen by clicking on the tiny Control-menu box in their upper-left corner.

15-7. When you exit, Word for Windows automatically saves any changes you have made to the Normal template.

Using Word with Other Applications

One of the main advantages to using Windows-based software is the ability to exchange information with other applications with very little trouble. You learned some of these techniques in the "Introduction to Windows" unit, where you copied information from the Calculator to a document. When copied, information is stored on the Clipboard. From the Clipboard it may then be pasted into any other Windows application.

Microsoft Word for Windows 6.0 comes with several miniapplications that may be used within a document. The miniapplications include Equation Editor, Chart, and WordArt, which you used in Unit 10, "Pictures and Graphics." All of these miniapplications are accessed in Word through the command Insert/Object.

Inserting objects from the miniapplications or from any other application is called *object linking and embedding*, sometimes called OLE (pronounced *olé*). Both linking and embedding allow you to include information created in other applications. Linking and embedding differ, however, in the way the information is handled.

Embedding causes the actual information, or *object,* to be inserted in the document. This object is simply a snapshot of the original information and does not change if the source information is later altered. Because the object is placed directly into the document, the size of the document increases greatly, and uses up much more space on the disk. When you double-click on an embedded object in a document, the original application opens to allow you to edit, but does not open the original source file.

Linking, on the other hand, sets up a connection between the source and what is displayed in the document. This link causes the information to be dynamic, so that whenever the source changes, the information in the document reflects the change automatically. Since the object is stored in another file, and only the link (the location of the source file) and a picture are stored in the Word document, the size of the document does not increase very much. When you double-click to edit a linked object, both the original application and source file open automatically.

Word allows for the easy exchange of linked and embedded data between many applications. Because Microsoft Office has combined Word with Excel, Access, and PowerPoint, these three applications will be discussed in this appendix.

NOTE   *Working with more than one of these applications running at a time requires a rather powerful computer with plenty of memory, such as a 486 with 8MB of RAM.*

Using Word with Excel

Although you may place numeric or financial information into a Word table and do simple calculations in Word, Excel or another spreadsheet program is generally the better application to use for complex calculations. If Excel is already running, you may use Edit/Copy and Edit/Paste to bring numbers into Word as a table. Using Copy and Paste in this way is neither linking nor embedding, since any formulas in the spreadsheet are converted into values, and the table becomes just part of the text in a document. In contrast, the command Edit/Paste Special allows you to select the option to Paste (and embed) or Paste Link. If Excel is not running, both linking and embedding are accomplished through the Insert/Object command.

Embedding an Excel Worksheet and Chart

Embedding an Excel worksheet may be accomplished in either of two ways: by creating a new worksheet or by opening an existing one. Both are accomplished with the command Insert/Object. The dialog box contains two tabs: Create New and Create from File. The Insert Microsoft Excel Worksheet button on the Standard toolbar, as shown in Figure C.1, may be used in place of the Insert/Object command to create a new worksheet.

After you specify the desired size of the spreadsheet by dragging on the grid, the computer opens Excel. A sample spreadsheet surrounded by a crosshatched border appears, and the Word menus and toolbars are replaced with those from Excel, as in Figure C.2, although your document is still on the screen.

At this point, you have access to all of Excel's functions, formulas, and tools to build a spreadsheet. You cannot save the spreadsheet as a separate file, but that would be unnecessary, since this spreadsheet will be saved entirely within the Word document. To restore Word's menus and toolbars, simply click anywhere in the document outside the spreadsheet area.

FIGURE C.1
The Insert Microsoft Excel Worksheet button

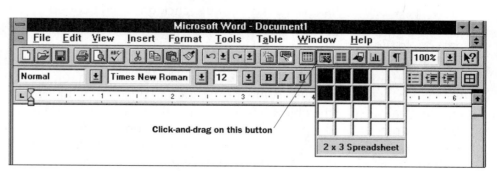

Click-and-drag on this button

2 x 3 Spreadsheet

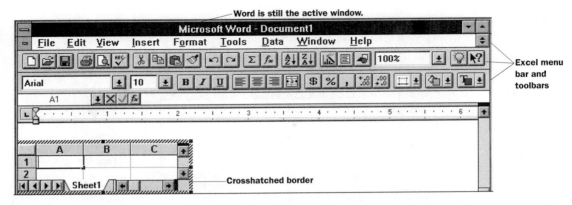

FIGURE C.2
Word's menu bar and toolbars replaced with Excel's

Within the document, the spreadsheet appears with gray gridlines. When you click on the spreadsheet, sizing handles appear, just as on a picture, and the status bar prompts you to double-click to edit the spreadsheet. Double-clicking on the spreadsheet reopens Excel, replaces the menu bar and toolbars again, and allows you to edit without closing the document or Word. This exciting feature is termed *in-place activation*.

You may view the field code that is riding behind this spreadsheet by selecting Tools/ Options, selecting the View tab, and clicking Field Codes (the shortcut key to toggle View Field Codes is [Alt][F9]). The field code for the spreadsheet is { EMBED Excel.Sheet.5 }. Deleting, sizing, moving, and framing are performed by using the same processes you use for pictures.

If you have a spreadsheet or a chart already created and wish to copy all or a portion of it into Word, you may use the command Edit/Paste Special (if Excel is already running), as shown in Figures C.3 and C.4. The contents of the dialog box

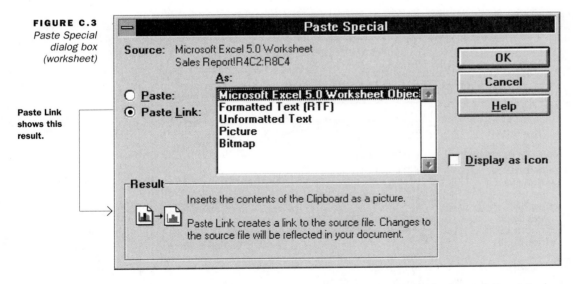

FIGURE C.3
Paste Special dialog box (worksheet)

change, depending on what is contained on the Clipboard. In either case, what is inserted into the document will not change, regardless of changes made to the Excel worksheet or chart. Both may be edited in place, using the Excel menus and toolbars, without flipping into another window.

FIGURE C.4
*Paste Special
dialog box
(chart)*

Paste shows
this result.

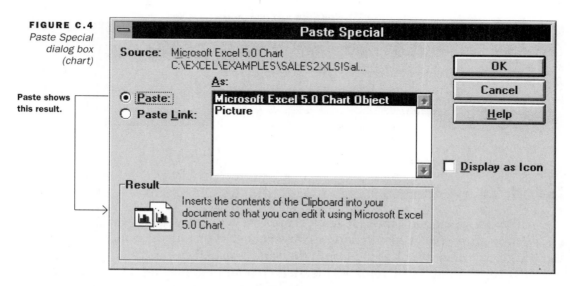

Even if Excel is not currently running, you may use the command Insert/Object to insert an existing Excel worksheet or chart without switching to the Excel window. The Insert/Object dialog box Create from File tab, shown in Figure C.5, resembles the File/Open dialog box. It allows you to specify the name and location of the file. The main difference is that you will only be able to access an entire worksheet, not a highlighted portion. Of course, since the embedded spreadsheet is an object, you may crop and scale to display only the desired portion of the spreadsheet.

Two check boxes at the bottom-right corner of the dialog box give two handy options. By clicking the check box you may establish a link to the source file, rather

FIGURE C.5
*The Insert/
Object dialog
box, Create
from File tab*

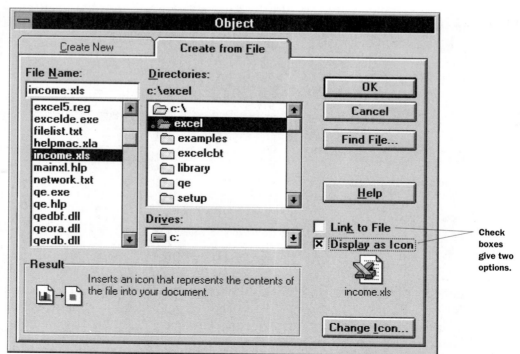

Check
boxes
give two
options.

than embedding the entire file. Clicking the check box next to Display as Icon allows you to include information that may only be used as reference. Including an icon in the file conserves space on screen, but when the reader double-clicks it, the linked or embedded spreadsheet or chart is displayed. When you check this box, you have the option of changing the icon that will represent the object.

Linking Word to Excel

Linking may be a better choice than embedding if the amount of data is very large, since the data is stored in the source file rather than within the Word document. Linking is also better than embedding if you want the numbers to be dynamic rather than simply a snapshot of the spreadsheet at a certain time. Like embedded spreadsheets and charts, double-clicking linked ones opens Excel and allows for editing. The difference in editing linked charts and spreadsheets is that Excel opens the original source spreadsheet, allowing you to make changes that affect the document.

You cannot tell the difference between a linked chart and an embedded chart merely by their appearance. When you press [Alt][F9], however, the field code shown for a linked chart contains within dark braces the key word `link`, as well as the name and location of the source file, for example, `{ LINK Excel.Sheet.5 "C:\\EXCEL\\SALES.XLS" "Sales Report![SALES.XLS]Sales Report Chart 1" \a \p }`. **Because the linked chart in the document is connected to the source in Excel, any changes that occur in the original spreadsheet are reflected automatically in the document. The embedded chart remains unchanged.**

Embedding may be a better choice than linking in some circumstances. For example, if the source document is located where it may not always be accessible, such as on a network server, a linked chart or spreadsheet will appear only if the source is available. Embedded charts or spreadsheets are always available. If a source file is moved or renamed after a portion of the file has been linked to a document, an error message appears in place of the chart or spreadsheet: `Error! Not a valid link`. The links must be managed or updated manually with the Edit/Links command, shown in Figure C.6.

FIGURE C.6
The Edit/Links dialog box

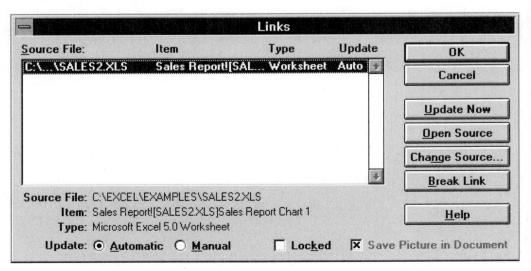

Word may also shift information into Excel. Portions of a document may be copied to, embedded in, or linked with a worksheet. The document may be inserted as text in a cell, inserted as a document object, or placed into a text box.

Using Word with Access

A database is often used to contain information that can be categorized. Word tables may be used as a small database, as we saw in Unit 13, "Mail Merge." For very large amounts of data, however, Microsoft Access or another database application is more appropriate.

You may use an Access query or table as the basis for a mail merge data document. To do this, use the Mail Merge Helper to connect the main document to the data source. Clicking the Get Data button allows you to specify a file. When you select an Access file, you may either insert the database into a Word table if it is not too large, or insert only field codes rather than the actual data. In either case, you can run a query to limit the data to those fields and records that meet specified criteria, rather than using the entire database.

Using Word with PowerPoint

PowerPoint and Word work together seamlessly to create presentations from a document outline, or to create an outline from a presentation without repetitive typing. Any Level 1 headings in a Word outline are turned into titles on PowerPoint slides, with subheadings becoming the text on the slides. You may use the simple copy and paste technique to move text between Word and PowerPoint. Additionally, you may use the Report It button in PowerPoint 4 to automatically convert the presentation to a Word outline. The Present It button in Word reverses the operation, exporting the outline information in the current document into PowerPoint. To access the Present It button, select the command File/Templates. Click to select the CONVERT.DOT template and click Add. This brings up a dialog box similar to File/Open in which you need to specify the location of the template. The template is found in the \MACROS subdirectory under \WINWORD. Highlight the file name and click OK. Because this Present It is a macro, it has been customized to its own toolbar and button, and you can view them by clicking View/Toolbar and selecting Present It.

Not only can you share text between Word and PowerPoint, you can also share clip art. PowerPoint comes with beautiful, fully-colored graphic images that are a wonderful addition to the images that come with Word. Microsoft has made it possible to access the clip art through the Clip Art Manager without opening Power-Point.

For users who only have access to older versions of PowerPoint, you can select the clip art images in PowerPoint and use Copy and Paste to move them into Word documents. In this case, the clip art is considered a graphic, not as embedded or linked. Double-clicking any of these images allows you to use the Drawing toolbar for editing.

Index